Family Life and Youth Offending

D1742823

Family Life and Youth Offending examines the relationship between the causes of youth offending and the legal duty of the state to address those causes. In his globally relevant new study Arthur provides the evidence that improving the family environment could be the most effective and enduring strategy for combating juvenile delinquency and associated behavioural, social and emotional problems. In so doing the author argues that youth crime prevention policy should therefore focus on the family context in which offenders find themselves and resources should be diverted from more traditional criminal justice measures and practices.

The book addresses several topical issues:

- how current child welfare legislation, in particular the Children Act 1989, could be employed to prevent children who are at risk of engaging in antisocial and delinquent behaviour from offending
- why greater use is not made of the present legislative framework in preventing youth crime
- how existing legal powers could be used in order to discourage and divert young people from engaging in offending behaviour
- how international efforts to prevent youth offending have developed in recent years, focusing on countries such as the United States, Canada, Japan, Scotland, France and Scandinavian countries.

Arthur abandons the traditional 'welfare versus justice' dichotomy and instead outlines a new approach that focuses on the rights and needs of young people in troubled circumstances and their families. This approach recognises the right of young people in trouble to the development and delivery of preventive services.

This timely new book will be essential reading for students and researchers in criminology, law, social policy and youth studies, as well as professionals and policy-makers working in the area of youth delinquency.

Raymond Arthur is a Senior Lecturer in Law at the School of Social Sciences and Law, University of Teesside. He regularly publishes articles on preventing juvenile offending, the impact of family life on youth offending and the youth justice system in leading refereed journals including: (2005) 'Punishing Parents for the Crimes of their Children', *Howard Journal of Criminal Justice* 44 (3), 233–253 and (2005) 'The Youth Justice System in England and Wales: complying with international human rights law', *International Family Law*, September, 157–160.

Routledge advances in criminology

Family Life and Youth Offending

Home is where the hurt is

Raymond Arthur

 Routledge
Taylor & Francis Group

LONDON AND NEW YORK

First published 2007
by Routledge
2 Park Square, Milton Park, Abingdon, Oxon OX14 4RN

Simultaneously published in the USA and Canada
by Routledge
711 Third Avenue, New York, NY 10017

Routledge is an imprint of the Taylor & Francis Group, an informa business

First issued in paperback 2012

© 2007 Raymond Arthur

Typeset in Sabon by Wearset Ltd, Boldon, Tyne and Wear

British Library Cataloguing in Publication Data
A catalogue record for this book is available from the British Library

Library of Congress Cataloging in Publication Data
A catalog record for this book has been requested

ISBN13: 978-0-415-40844-8 (hbk)
ISBN13: 978-0-415-51454-5 (pbk)

For Siobhán

Contents

1 Introduction

Overview

Over 150 years have passed since a little-remembered Victorian social worker named Ellice Hopkins first coined the phrase 'were it not a thousand times better instead of sending our ambulances to the foot of the cliff we should build a fence at the top' (quoted in Watson 1973: 44). Although this phrase has become very well worn in countless contexts, as far as tackling youth crime is concerned the point she made is still very relevant. This book is concerned with building 'a fence at the top of the cliff' which will prevent children from becoming involved in antisocial and offending behaviour in the first place. The book will argue that ways need to be developed to target young people who are in danger of becoming offenders long before they fall into this category. If we can identify these vulnerable young people at an early age, work can be undertaken with them and their parents to help them lead more productive and law-abiding lives and prevent them engaging in antisocial and offending behaviour. Even a modest reduction in youth crime offers potentially significant gains: fewer victims suffering injury or loss, fewer lives blighted by the fear of crime, reduced public expenditure on the youth justice system and an end to overcrowding in young offenders' institutions. Additionally, the prevention of youth crime offers the prospect of fewer young offenders leading adult lives damaged by their early involvement in crime and the criminal justice system. Thus, the potential human, social and economic benefits of preventing youth crime are considerable.

This book will argue that the well-established empirical link between child maltreatment and subsequent juvenile offending behaviour provides a strong rationale for viewing child welfare interventions as youth crime prevention techniques. The book will examine how existing child welfare legislation could be employed to prevent children who are at risk of engaging in antisocial and delinquent behaviour from offending. It will investigate why greater use is not made of the present legislative framework in preventing youth crime, and consider how existing legal powers could be enforced in order to discourage and divert young people from engaging in offending behaviour.

While youth crime prevention strategies have been proposed in the past, they usually relate solely to preventing 'reoffending' by children. My overarching aim is to examine how we can, in the long term, prevent children from engaging in offending behaviour in the first place and therefore prevent the pre-school children of today from influencing the crime statistics in five to ten years. Thus, the emphasis will be on the early prevention of juvenile offending rather than the treatment or rehabilitation of known offenders by the criminal justice system.

Criminological research spread over half a century has demonstrated with considerable consistency that the root causes of juvenile offending behaviour can be classified into the following key areas: family (in particular, the child-rearing and parenting processes); education (including school attendance and educational performance); and lifestyle choices (for example, substance abuse and the young person's peer group associations).[1] While recognising that there are various causes of juvenile offending behaviour, this book will not seek to provide an analysis of how all these 'root causes' of youth crime could be tackled. Instead, it will focus on delinquency prevention measures directed towards improving the family conditions associated with juvenile offending. Specifically, the book will examine the role that the Children Act 1989 can play in preventing children from becoming involved in youth crime. I focus on the Children Act as the 1989 Act places a duty on local authorities to provide support and services aimed expressly at improving parenting skills, supporting families under stress and discouraging juvenile involvement in crime. The central question this book will address is whether the 1989 Act could alleviate the difficult family circumstances that give rise to juvenile offending and consequently reduce levels of youth crime.

Scope

The starting point for the book is an examination of the extent to which family factors propel young people into lives of crime. Historically, family interactions have been assumed to influence criminal behaviour. For example, Aristotle (1941) asserted that in order to be virtuous, 'we ought to have been brought up in a particular way from our very youth'. Nineteenth- and twentieth-century theorists concur with this view. From the concerns of those in the Child-Saving movement in the nineteenth century (Andry 1957; Bazelon 1976) to the present (Farrington 1996; Shoemaker 1995), the family has been regarded as a major influence in the presence or absence of youth offending behaviour. These explanations of youth crime suggest that the relationship between parent and child is the causal mechanism that determines whether tendencies towards antisocial and offending behaviour are inhibited or allowed to develop. The thrust of these arguments is that early prevention which fosters an ideology that links family problems, social inequality, economic deprivation and juvenile offending should be the basis of any attempt to reduce the risk of children engaging in offending behaviour. On the basis of these views, this book will assert that child welfare agencies, namely the local authorities, and their efforts to reduce child abuse and neglect, have a central role to play in the prevention of juvenile offending.

Chapter 2 will offer an extensive examination of over 50 years of criminological research in order to assess the role of the family in the development of juvenile antisocial and offending behaviour. By shifting the debate from the nature of the juvenile offence to the nature of the juvenile offender, my intention is to shift justifiable intervention from the penal system to the child and family welfare system. Essentially, Chapter 2 will aim to resolve the question of whether preventive family casework, as legislated for in the Children Act 1989, could, in principle, provide the most viable youth crime prevention and control strategy.

The search for causes will be paralleled by a search for methods of controlling and correcting the causal factors. The challenges that confront children who are at risk of engaging in antisocial and offending behaviour and their families are complex, deep-rooted and multifaceted. Programmes and measures that seek to prevent offending require a broad synthesis of agencies and disciplines, including teachers, doctors, psychiatrists, counsellors, police and other professionals. However, this book is only concerned with preventive initiatives designed to reduce risk factors for juvenile offending at the family level. From this point of view there is no need for a wholly new approach or for the introduction of new early intervention instruments that focus specifically on youth crime. The obligations of the state to assist families that need help in bringing up their children are already laid down in the Children Act 1989. The Children Act 1989 and accompanying guidance provide an invaluable framework for action by local authorities to support families and to provide for children considered to be vulnerable or 'in need'. The Children Act 1989 not only requires local authorities to support children in families under stress but also gives them a specific duty to take measures that discourage juvenile involvement in crime (Schedule 2(7) Children Act 1989).

Local authority duties are also informed and influenced by section 17(1) of the Crime and Disorder Act 1998, which provides that it shall be the duty of each authority to do all that it reasonably can to prevent crime and disorder in its area. This principle is also reaffirmed in section 37 of the Crime and Disorder Act 1998, which places all those carrying out functions in relation to the youth justice system under a statutory duty to have regard to the new principal aim of preventing offending by children and young people. It is intended that this aim should be achieved through interventions which tackle the particular factors that put the young person at risk of offending (Home Office *et al.* 1998: 10). The duty of the state to prevent juvenile offending is reaffirmed in various instruments of international law, such as, for example, the United Nations Convention on the

Rights of the Child and the United Nations Guidelines for the Prevention of Juvenile Delinquency (the Riyadh Guidelines).

Chapter 3 analyses the provisions of the Children Act 1989, as well as the Crime and Disorder Act 1998 and all other relevant instruments of domestic and international law, and evaluates the precise duties and powers of local authorities in relation to deterring potential young offenders from becoming involved in crime, thus providing a complete picture of the resources and support services that are available to help families to become competent in dealing with their own problems and in guiding and nurturing their children. While acknowledging that the Children Act is not a panacea for juvenile offending, Chapter 3 endeavours to answer the crucial question of whether steps taken under Parts III, IV and V of the Children Act 1989 to reverse the forces that disrupt and damage families could also have a positive impact on reducing juvenile crime.

A key question for local authorities will be whether they can coordinate their support to the families of children who are at risk of offending with their other duties and responsibilities to children in need, children at risk of suffering significant harm and children in their care. Local authorities have not been given specific guidance on how to link the provision of family support services under Part III of the Children Act 1989, their compulsory powers of intervention under Parts IV and V, and their duties towards children they are looking after under section 22 of the 1989 Act and the Children (Leaving Care) Act 2000[2] with their duty to encourage children not to engage in offending behaviour (Schedule 2(7) Children Act 1989, section 17(1) Crime and Disorder Act 1998). Chapter 4 will comprehensively establish this link by exploring the formal assessment procedures developed to ascertain the dimensions of social care needs of children being assessed within the parameters of the Children Act 1989. It will determine whether children at risk of engaging in offending behaviour ought to be seen and dealt with either as children in need under Part III of the Children Act 1989, or as children at risk of significant harm under Parts IV and V of the 1989 Act; and therefore will establish whether the children identified in Chapter 2 are in fact legally eligible for the services examined in Chapter 3.

While the legislation defines children in need, the legal definition requires operational interpretation, as the concept is critical to ensuring that the required support for children and their families will be provided. The deliberately broad definition of need means, in practice, that the services provided by any local authority to a particular child or to any category of children will depend almost entirely on how the local authority defines and prioritises the concept of need. Therefore, it is essential to examine how local authorities understand their duties under the Children Act 1989 and establish what priority is accorded to children at risk of engaging in offending behaviour. Chapter 5 will scrutinise the approach adopted by local authorities in defining case priorities and considers a number of vital questions, namely: do local authorities consider that the provision of services used to promote and safeguard the welfare of children with family support needs are the same services that could help prevent youth offending? When defining children in need, do local authorities consider those at risk of becoming offenders as children in need? How do local authorities interpret the requirement to prevent children from offending? The evidence that will substantiate this chapter will be drawn from a wide range of research studies across a number of disciplines, as well as from the accumulated experiences of those who are responsible for implementing the policy. The findings from this analysis will determine whether local authorities consider that the children examined in Chapter 2 fall within their ambit of responsibility.

Just as government has not been slow to enlist, or even enforce, the cooperation of parents in the fight against youth crime,[3] so families should now feel entirely justified in demanding the full cooperation of the state. Chapter 6 will concentrate on the extent to which those children at risk of engaging in offending behaviour can enforce their right to local authority services. Chapter 6 will consider the consequences of local authorities' failing to fulfil their duty to discourage children from engaging in offending behaviour. In doing so, this chapter addresses a number of fundamental moral and legal issues: can society justifiably punish children for their crimes if it has failed to fulfil its obligations to those children as members of society? Will the failure of a local authority to provide a reasonable level of care give rise to an action in negligence and/or breach of a statutory duty where a juvenile subsequently engages in offending behaviour? This is important because the prospect of liability for negligence and breach of statutory duty could encourage local authorities to improve their performance in carrying out their duties in relation to preventing youth offending.

The focus of this book is on young people who have not officially offended but have been identified as being at risk of doing so, and the potential for preventing them from engaging in antisocial and offending behaviour in the first place. The experience of local authorities in coordinating arrangements to protect children from abuse and neglect, their extensive responsibilities in the youth justice field, their role in developing children's service plans and the fact that they are accountable to the local community make them most suitable to take a lead in the area of youth crime prevention. Local authorities provide a structure that spans youth justice services, social services, health services, education authorities and child and family welfare services. The Children Act 1989 and related legislation provide local authorities with the legislative framework needed to deter young people from becoming involved in crime. How far the Children Act 1989 will fulfil this preventive aspiration will only be determined by investigating the kind of policies and programmes the local authority develop, the organisation and structure of individual local authorities, and how the services are delivered to families. This analysis will explain why the legislation is not being implemented in its entirety; why not all children at risk of engaging in offending behaviour are receiving services appropriate to their needs; and why such children are not discouraged from involvement in criminal activity. If local authorities are to play a successful role in youth crime prevention, any disparity that exists between the statutory policy and everyday practice of local authorities must be rectified and the preventive provisions of the Children Act 1989, and related legislation, must be enforced.

2 Family life and youth offending

Introduction

All the indications from recent research suggest that the punishment of young offenders, whatever its political or moral acceptability, is ineffective in preventing youth offending (Audit Commission 1996; Hawkins 1996; Howard League 1996). Once a juvenile is apprehended by the police and referred to the youth court, subsequent rehabilitation services, no matter how skilled, have been shown to have far less potential for success than if they had been applied before the youth's overt contact with the law. Preventing young people from ever offending could therefore have a greater impact on the level of youth crime than any changes to the criminal justice system. The aim must be to identify children and young people who are at risk of becoming involved in criminal activity and changing their behaviour before bad habits take root.

The object of this chapter is to investigate what is known about the risk factors that predispose young people to offending behaviour, and thus identify where intervention could potentially be most successful in preventing children being drawn into offending behaviour.

Risk factors for youth offending

Criminological research conducted over 50 years has clearly documented many correlates of juvenile offending behaviour. Significantly, throughout the literature parental contribution has been emphasised in terms of both the positive and the negative contribution it can make to growth and development. For example, one of the most ambitious projects to investigate why some young people commit crime, and to assess how far criminality can be predicted, was the Cambridge study in delinquent development undertaken by D.J. West in 1961 (West 1969, 1973, 1982; West and Farrington 1977). A sample of 411 working-class boys aged 8 were selected from six primary schools in Camberwell, London. They were contacted again when aged 10, 14, 16, 18, 21, 25 and 32 to examine which of them had developed a delinquent way of life and why some had continued a life of crime into adulthood. About 20 per cent of the sample had been convicted of criminal offences as juveniles. However, only 23 young men (this represents less than 6 per cent of the sample) amassed 50 per cent of the total convictions. Most of these 'chronic offenders' shared common characteristics. West outlined five major factors that had a significant association with the likelihood of children becoming offenders. The five key factors were as follows:

1   Coming from a low-income family. Of 93 such boys, 33.3 per cent became juvenile offenders, compared with 16.7 per cent among the rest of the sample. Income was categorised by taking into account a number of circumstances including number of children, housing conditions, family possessions, style of living and whether the family was supported by social agencies. As a rough guide, in 1962–63 a family of two adults and four children was classified as 'low-income' or 'poor' if it had less than £15 weekly; it was classified as 'comfortable' if it received more than £20 per week. Most of the families classified as poor were existing at a level similar to those who qualify for, or were actually receiving, National Assistance at that time, so the degree of material deprivation among them was quite severe.

2   Having parents considered by social workers to have performed their child-rearing duties unsatisfactorily. Of 96 such boys, 32.3 per cent became juvenile offenders. The unfavourable features that contributed to the general rating of 'unsatisfactory' parental behaviour included marital conflict, the dominance of one parent over the other in decision-making relating to children, inconsistency between the parents in their handling of the child, attitudes of indifference, positive rejection or neglect, over-strict or erratically varying discipline and harsh methods of enforcement.

3   Having a parent with a criminal record. Of 103 such boys, 37.9 per cent became juvenile offenders, compared with 14.6 per cent among the rest of the sample.

4   Coming from a large family, defined as four or more other surviving children born to the boy's mother prior to his tenth birthday. Of 99 such boys 32.3 per cent became juvenile offenders.

5   Having below-average intelligence on testing, defined as having an IQ of 90 or less on Raven's Progressive Matrices Test. This test measures non-verbal intelligence. Of 103 such boys, 31.1 per cent became juvenile offenders, compared with 15.9 per cent of the rest of the sample.

The possession of any of these adverse factors effectively doubled the likelihood of becoming a juvenile offender. These risk factors have emerged consistently in the most rigorous empirical research on the aetiology of juvenile crime in projects elsewhere in England (Farrington 1996; Kolvin *et al.* 1990; Utting 1996) and also in the United States (Dembo *et al.* 2000;

Sampson and Laub 1993; Seydlitx and Jenkins 1998), Scandinavian countries (Pulkkinen 1988; Stattin *et al.* 1997), New Zealand (Maxwell and Robertson 1995; Moffitt and Silva 1988), China (Curran and Cook 1993; Zhang and Messner 1994), Taiwan (Simons *et al.* 2000; Deng *et al.* 1994) and Hong Kong (Gray 1997).

Most of West's predictors for juvenile involvement in offending behaviour relate to the family, thus the most logical place to begin preventing juvenile offending behaviour is the family. In order to understand precisely the nature and scope of the effect of family life on juvenile offending behaviour, I have outlined eight primary indicators of juvenile offending behaviour under the heading of family factors that all these studies agree are indicators of susceptibility to youth criminal activity. These are as follows:

- inadequate parenting;
- child abuse/maltreatment;
- family disruption;
- poor parental supervision;
- parent and sibling criminality;
- teenage parents;
- unstable living conditions;
- effects of economic disadvantage.

In this chapter I will examine how each of these factors impacts upon juvenile offending behaviour. This analysis will provide a basis for assessing whether a strategy for tackling family problems, inadequate parenting and unstable family conditions offers a real prospect of preventing young people turning to crime.

Family factors causing youth offending

Inadequate parenting

The description of parenting as being 'inadequate', 'unreasonable', or 'ineffective' refers to pervasive characterisations used in a large body of research. Such expressions are used generically to identify the troubling family patterns that are prevalent in the lives of young offenders, and should not be interpreted as disparaging the efforts of parents. Most contemporary criminological research has shown that the major contributing factors within the family to the development of criminal propensities are to be found in the child-rearing and parenting processes (Brown 1998; Loeber and Farrington 1998; Newburn 1997). Although notions of good parenting practice may vary from time to time and from culture to culture, nevertheless these criminological theories are in agreement regarding the components of effective parenting. Involvement and interaction of parents with their children and strong family bonding have the potential to protect children against the development of antisocial and offending behaviour (Catalano and Hawkins 1996: 149–197). Competent parents show high levels of warmth and support, articulate standards for behaviour, monitor their children's behaviour and engage in inductive reasoning and consistent discipline when infractions occur. Decades of research by criminologists has established that this style of parenting promotes positive child development, and the absence of these parenting behaviours increases the chances that a child will engage in antisocial and offending behaviour (Farrington 1996; Glueck and Glueck 1962; Gottfredson and Hirschi 1989; Loeber and LeBlanc 1991; McCord and McCord 1959; Simons *et al.* 1998; Snyder and Patterson 1987). As the authors of the *Newcastle 1,000 Family* survey stated, 'good parenting protects against the acquisition of a criminal record' (Kolvin *et al.* 1990: 26).

Most of these criminological studies have relied either on a longitudinal research strategy, where child-rearing practices in the family have been analysed and later linked to different outcomes among children in those families; or on retrospective reports, where childhood family histories of aggressive, antisocial, criminal or violent individuals have been examined. For example, in a retrospective survey of over 900 youths aged 12–19, Cernkovich and Giordano (1987: 305) showed that those youths most prone to offending behaviour in the samples were most likely to have conflict with their parents and to have difficulties with parents over friendship choices. Loeber and Stouthamer-Loeber also arrived at similar conclusions. They based their findings on the Pittsburgh Youth Study, which was a prospective longitudinal survey of 1,517 Pittsburgh boys at ages 7, 10 and 13 during 1987–88. Self-report data were compared with records of the Juvenile courts and questionnaires completed by the boy's teacher and main caretaker (Loeber and Stouthamer-Loeber 1986: 97; Loeber *et al.* 1991: 37, 1998).

Children exposed to poor family management practices are at an increased risk of becoming involved in crime (Yoshikawa 1994). Poor family management practices include parents' failure to set clear expectations for children's behaviour, failure to supervise and monitor children, excessive and severe, harsh or inconsistent punishment, including child maltreatment and neglect, weak relationships between parents and children, poor child-rearing skills, family discord and low family income. Hawkins and Catalano identified parenting practices such as lack of supervision, inconsistent or overly punitive disciplinary practices or high levels of family conflict as variables that place young people in the category of being at risk of engaging in crime (Hawkins and Catalano 1992; Hawkins *et al.* 1995). Persistent and serious offenders seem to have experienced particularly problematic childhoods in terms of deprivation and parenting, with inadequate parenting being a crucial factor (Coupet 2000: 1312; Vaughan 2000). The amount of interest a parent expresses in the child's development is also an important factor. In the study of families in Newcastle, Miller *et al.* (1974) analysed the records of 63 children, mostly boys, who were convicted before their fifteenth birthday and found what they called a 'marked deficiency of parentcraft'. By this, Miller *et al.* meant a father or mother who was not rated highly as being kind and effective, or one who showed less than average interest in his, or her, children's development.

Quality of parenting interacts with parental psychological well-being and mental health. Zahn-Waxler *et al.* (1990) found that depressed mothers had a higher risk of having children with persistent aggressive and antisocial behaviour problems than did non-depressed mothers. Parental mental health is a significant contributor to parents' discipline strategies, which in turn represent a chief determinant of child antisocial behaviour (Davenport *et al.* 1989; Patterson 1986). There is also considerable evidence to suggest that parental alcohol and drug abuse affects parenting skills. Parents who abuse illicit drugs and alcohol are disposed to experience difficulty in organising their lives; become unpredictable, inconsistent and ineffective with their children; neglect their own and their child's physical needs; and become insensitive to, unresponsive to, angry with and critical of their children (Coleman and Cassell 1995; Greco-Vigorito *et al.* 1996; Stein *et al.* 2002; Velerman 1996). Furthermore, parental substance abuse is a dominant feature among households implicated in child abuse (Felitti *et al.* 1998; Fleming 1998), and directly predicts drug and alcohol problems for their children (Kilpatrick *et al.* 2000; Sheridan 1995). Thus, parental mental health problems, alcohol abuse and drug use can directly impact upon the child's propensity to offend.

Reviews of the findings from various studies report a familiar pattern regarding children whose mothers have been the victim of domestic violence. Exposure to domestic violence detrimentally impacts upon the child's social competence. Such children have often been reported as having greater behavioural problems than children from non-violent homes, and show signs of anxiety and low self-esteem (Buehler *et al.* 1997; Fergusson and Harwood 1998; Herrera and McCloskey 2001; Humphreys *et al.* 2001). These children also have a tendency towards showing aggressive and offending behaviour. They are much more vulnerable to being directly abused either by becoming caught in the attack upon their mothers (very occasionally their fathers) or by being abused in separate incidents in which the abuser uses physical assault to control not only his partner but also the children in the household (Edleson 1999). There is also some evidence that children are at an increased risk of physical abuse from mothers who are themselves the subject of abuse (O'Keefe 1995). The prevalence of domestic violence in child sexual abuse cases is now also coming to light (Hester and Pearson 1998; McGuigan and Pratt 2001). Clearly, these issues will affect the quality of care available to children living with domestic violence. Research suggests that when domestic violence is present, parents may be emotionally numb and uncommunicative, and thus be less available to their children (Osofsky and Fenichel 1994). Mothers may become disabled during physical attacks and are also increasingly vulnerable to mental health problems through sustained violence and abuse. Stress caused to a mother as a result of domestic violence often reduces her capacity to meet her children's emotional needs. Other studies found that in relationships involving domestic violence, parents may give inordinate attention to one another and therefore ignore their children's needs (McKay 1994).

The contention that young people commit crimes as a result of inadequate parenting and parental difficulties has been an abiding feature of the debates on juvenile offending. Chapter 3 will examine the range of measures and interventions that are available to respond to the poor parenting which gives rise to juvenile offending.

Child abuse/maltreatment

Every study of the personal and social experiences of known juvenile offenders reveals that almost all of them have endured various kinds of abuse, neglect, deprivation and misfortune. They are far more likely than the general population to have experienced child abuse and to have been in local authority care. For the purposes of this study, and for ease of explanation, the term 'child abuse' is classified into four categories based on inter-departmental guidelines (Home Office *et al.* 1991: 49): emotional abuse, physical abuse, sexual abuse and neglect. These categories of abuse are not mutually exclusive and will often overlap; for instance, emotional abuse may often accompany or follow from physical or sexual abuse. Therefore, it is neither realistic nor beneficial to deal with each category individually. It is more useful to consider these categories as generic and thus regard child abuse as an umbrella concept for varieties of specific forms of abuse.

Widom found that adolescents who have been physically and/or sexually abused and neglected as children are 53 per cent more likely to be arrested as a juvenile, and 38 per cent more likely to commit a violent crime than their counterparts who did not suffer such abuse (Widom 1989a, b, 1991; Widom and Maxfield 1996). Widom used a prospective cohort design comprising cases of physical and sexual abuse and neglect involving 908 children. Official criminal histories for a large sample of substantiated and validated cases of physical and sexual abuse and neglect from the years 1967–71 were compared with those of a matched control group of individuals with no official record of abuse or neglect. Additionally, the research found that those who had been abused and/or neglected as children 'were also more likely to average nearly 1 year younger at first arrest ... to commit nearly twice as many offences and to be arrested more frequently' (Ruttenberg 1994). Females generally feature less frequently than males in arrest statistics; however, abused females were more likely than control females to have an arrest as an adult (Widom 1989a). Girls with a history of physical child abuse were arrested for violent offences proportionately more than boys with similar histories (Herrera and McCloskey 2001: 1048).

Smith and Thornberry (1995) concluded that a history of childhood maltreatment, serious enough to warrant official intervention by child protection services, significantly increases the chances of involvement in self-reported and official delinquency. Their data were drawn from the Rochester Youth Development Study, a multi-wave panel study in which 1,000 young Americans and their primary caretakers were interviewed every six months over a five-year period. Additional data were collected from the Rochester public schools, police departments, Department of Social Services and other agencies that had contact with the sample youth. In a follow-up study, Thornberry (1996) established that children who experienced multiple forms of family violence in the home, such as child abuse, spouse abuse and parental conflict, were twice as likely to commit violent acts themselves. Among youths in non-violent families, 38 per cent reported involvement in violent crime. This rate increased to 60 per cent for youths who experienced one form of violence, to 73 per cent for those exposed to two forms of violence and to 78 per cent for adolescents exposed to all three types of family violence. Peacock (1999) also ascertained that the majority of pupils in a secure unit for the most violent offenders in the United Kingdom have suffered physical, emotional and/or sexual abuse for periods of their lives. Curtis (1999: 13) determined it significant that 75 per cent of young people convicted of the most violent and serious offences have themselves been physically, sexually or emotionally abused. Childhood abuse also predicts a wider range of problems for children, including mental health problems, drug and alcohol problems, and homelessness (Bangard 1997; Bensley *et al.* 2000; Ireland *et al.* 2002). As will be seen later in this chapter, these problems are all predictive of juvenile offending behaviour.

Gwyneth Boswell's research in 1994 confirmed the strong relationship between child abuse and violent juvenile offending; she examined the backgrounds of 200 young people sentenced to custody, pursuant to section 53 of the Children and Young Persons Act 1933.[1] Of the total sample, 100 had been sentenced for murder under section 53(1) of the Act and 100 for a range of other serious crimes, including manslaughter, under section 53(2). Her study revealed that 72 per cent of the sample group had experienced some form of emotional, sexual, physical, organised ritual abuse or neglect as a child (Boswell 1995). Boswell also noted that children who witness or experience abuse over a prolonged period emerge severely damaged themselves as adults. By that standard, some 91 per cent of section 53 offenders interviewed could be said to have suffered from that type of stress as a child. Accordingly, there is little doubt that childhood abuse constitutes unresolved trauma, which is likely to manifest itself at a later date. Boswell's findings are confirmed by various international studies. For example, a report for the Department of Correctional Services in South Africa reveals that the 'mostly violent young offenders who took part in the pilot study had experienced very many traumatic experiences in their personal lives' (Wedge *et al.* 2000). The pilot study involved 25 young offenders whose ages ranged from 14 to 22. The authors used similar research methodology and made similar theoretical assumptions as in the English study by Boswell. In New Zealand, Fergusson and Lynskey (1997: 629) found that young people reporting exposure to harsh or abusive treatment during childhood had elevated rates of juvenile offending. Data were gathered over the course of an 18-year longitudinal study of a birth cohort of 1,265 New Zealand children. Regular assessments of family, social and related circumstances, and juvenile offending were made at annual intervals. At age 18, retrospective reports of exposure to physical maltreatment were obtained. Another study by the New South Wales Bureau of Crime Statistics and Research reveals that in urban New South Wales (Sydney, Newcastle and Wollongong) an increase of 1,000 neglected children results in an extra 256 juveniles involved in crime (New South Wales Bureau of Crime Statistics and Research 1997).

Parents who rely heavily on harsh punishment or who are erratic in their discipline are twice as likely to have children who offend (Cohen and Brook 1994; Farrington 1994; Straus *et al.* 1996). In their follow-up of nearly 700 Nottingham children in intact families, the Newsons reported that physical punishment by parents predicted later convictions (Newson and Newson 1989). Harsh punishment is also associated with more violent and more frequent offending (Cohen and Brook 1994; Straus 1991; Straus and Donnelly 1995). The fact that boys are hit harder and more often than girls may help to explain the higher prevalence of violence in young male offenders. Inept parenting practices, such as an uncaring attitude, poor supervision, inconsistent discipline and a failure to explain moral principles, tend to be correlated with the use of corporal punishment (Eamon 2001; Turner and Finklehor 1996). Thus, when researchers report a correlation between parental use of physical punishment and juvenile involvement in antisocial behaviour, it may be that the association is spurious because of the correlation of both of these variables with factors such as parental warmth, monitoring and inductive reasoning. The elevated rates of adjustment problems in this group may be due to the family environment and context in which physical punishment occurs, rather than the traumatic effects of such treatment on longer-term adjustment.

While there may be a tendency to consider physical or sexual abuse to be more severe forms of maltreatment, neglect needs to be considered as an equally significant risk factor for later developmental outcomes such as juvenile offending. Neglect by parents, poor maternal and domestic care before the age of 5 and the absence of a good relationship with either parent have all been shown to increase the risk of behaviour problems and subsequent offending (Utting *et al.* 1993; Yoshikawa 1994). Zingraff *et al.* (1993, 1994) report that neglected and physically and sexually abused children are more likely to appear in official records of child offenders than their non-abused peers. They found that episodes of abuse and neglect can damage healthy emotional and social development. Healthy development establishes a crucial foundation upon which long-term commitment to established societal norms and values can be built. Law-abiding behaviour is one example of this long-term commitment. The central maltreatment sample for Zingraff *et al.*'s study sample was drawn from the North Carolina Registry of Child Abuse and Neglect, which is maintained by the State's Division of Social Services. The sample comprised 655 children with substantiated reports of maltreatment.

In considering the application of these categories of abuse, it has to be acknowledged that some children may be more adversely affected by some of these acts than others, some by a single act of abuse and others by spasmodic or consistent acts of abuse over time. Children of different ages, at different developmental stages, from diverse environments and with differing experiences who are exposed to vastly different forms of maltreatment are likely to manifest vulnerabilities in a wide variety of age-specific ways. Understanding the relative impact of different types of abuse, the extensiveness and variety of abuse, recurrent abuse, the developmental stage of the child at the time of maltreatment, and differences in aetiology according to race and gender are just some of the missing gaps in the existing research. As a result, the research studies may have underestimated the impact of child abuse and maltreatment on juvenile offending behaviour. It is possible that the research findings understate the magnitude of the relationship between child abuse and juvenile offending, since not all instances of maltreatment are known by the agencies that were involved in the studies.

The evidence examined also suggests that the majority of maltreated young people are not arrested and do not report involvement in serious antisocial behaviour. Many who are abused are therefore resilient to offending behaviour. Factors related to resilience to abuse include compensating parental support (Herrenkohl *et al.* 1994; Kendziora and O'Leary 1993), intellectual capacity and school achievement (C.A. Smith *et al.* 1995; Zingraff *et al.* 1994). While maltreatment is certainly no guarantee of later offending, it is nonetheless striking that a history of maltreatment and abuse significantly increases the risk of the child's becoming involved in antisocial and criminal conduct. Interventions with maltreated children that focus on the development of such protective factors may make the difference in youth making a transition past the maltreatment experience into productive adulthood.

There are occasions when the immediate protection of children from harm demands that they be taken away from their natural family.

However, the frequency of delinquent behaviour and social failure among children placed in care, especially those who experience a succession of different placements, is so daunting as to suggest that alternatives deserve consideration whenever possible. The Home Office's National Prison Survey in 1991, for example, found that 26 per cent of those in custody had some previous experience of care before they were 16 years of age, rising to 38 per cent of the 17- to 20-year-olds being held (Home Office 1991). The Howard League Trouble-shooter Project at Feltham Young Offender Institution in 1997 found that over a three-year period about 33 per cent of the young people in the institution had been in public care, usually having been removed compulsorily from their parents because of abuse or neglect (Curtis 1999: 194). The Chief Inspector of Prisons' Report confirmed that a substantial proportion of young prisoners have had contact with social services, or have spent timebeing 'looked after' (Chief Inspector of Prisons 1997). Ball and Connolly (2000: 600) recognised that the fact that 20 per cent of their cohort were either in care or accommodated by local authorities, supports the view that 'looked-after' children[2] are disproportionately represented among youth court defendants. Ball and Connolly collected data on a sample of 522 school-aged defendants sentenced in urban areas throughout England and Wales. Quantitative and qualitative data were collected from court registers, court files, pre-sentence and school reports, questionnaire responses from magistrates and supervising officers, and interviews with the offenders. Haines and Drakeford (1999), Hagell and Newburn (1994) and Bottoms (1995) each underlined that contact with the official 'care system' prevailed among their respective sample of young offenders. Thus young people with a background in state care are more likely to engage in juvenile offending behaviour. This tendency may be attributable to the intensity with which the risk factors cluster together in their lives, rather than an additional factor that needs to be identified. Alternatively, the disproportionate numbers of looked-after children who commit offences may be due to the fact that too many young people experience very little support upon leaving care, in terms both of financial help and of guidance and advice (Utting 1997), and consequently their life chances are unacceptably restricted (Department of Health 1999: 2.6). Care leavers face the challenge of setting up and managing a home, getting a job and developing a support network at a very young age. They tend to move to independent living at a younger age than those who live with their families, and most experience emotional difficulties (Dimigen *et al.* 1999; Minnis *et al.* 2001; Minnis and Del Priore 2001) or develop a drug problem (Ward *et al.* 2003).

An inescapable question which emerges from this analysis is that if children's basic human right to grow up free from all forms of neglect, abuse and exploitation were accorded due respect in all circumstances, could this represent an important step in protecting juveniles from becoming offenders? This question will be addressed in Chapter 3.

Family disruption

The topic of broken homes has been a central part of delinquency theory since the emergence of criminology in the nineteenth century. The term 'broken home' is used in this context to refer to an operational component of a large body of research. Its use is not intended to imply the existence, or advocacy, of any particular standard or ideal family constellation. In fact, the position advocated in this text is that family structure is less important as a determinant of social relationships than is the nature of the relationship among the members of any family context.

One of the clearest differences between delinquents and non-delinquents concerning broken homes is provided by the Gluecks' retrospective comparison of the backgrounds of 500 delinquents and 500 non-delinquents. Over 60 per cent of the delinquents came from broken homes, as compared with slightly more than 33 per cent of the non-delinquents (Glueck and Glueck 1950). In the Cambridge study, West (1982) also found that experience of divorce or parental separation before the age of 10 was associated with future offending behaviour. Separations occasioned by illness or death bore comparatively little relationship to offending, but separations caused by the breakdown of the parent's marriage were very significant precursors to youth offending behaviour (Loeber and Stouthamer-Loeber 1986). Compared with the rest of the sample, the offenders included proportionately more than twice as many from homes broken by circumstances other than death. Haskell and Yablonsky (1982) reported the findings of eight studies from 1929 to 1971 that investigated the relationship between broken homes and youth crime. The range of offenders from broken homes was 23.6 per cent to 61.5 per cent, while the range of non-offenders was 12.9 per cent to 36.1 per cent. Farrington (1983) also found that family disruption, as measured by separation from a parent, nearly doubled the chances of a cohort member becoming an offender by the age of 25. Hagell and Newburn (1994), in their study of persistent young offenders, refer to the chaotic lives of many juvenile offenders, characterised by high levels of stress and family break-up. For Dennis and Erdos (1992) it is 'common sense' that family breakdown and rising crime will go hand in hand. Findings by Wedge *et al.* (2000), further reinforced by other studies in South Africa (Segal *et al.* 1999), indicate that broken homes were one of the main issues mentioned by young people as having influenced their decision to commit crime.

Family disruption was also a factor in discriminating offending girls from non-offending girls in Wadsworth's study. Offending girls, although few in number, were almost twice as likely to come from a home broken by divorce or separation as boys. The age at which the break occurred was also found to be important: family breaks early in a child's life, during the years of greatest dependency, were more likely to result in subsequent criminal behaviour (Wadsworth 1979). Data from the longitudinal Oregon

Youth Study, which relied on criminal records and self-report data, suggest that boys whose parents had divorced by the time they were 10 were observed to exhibit more behavioural problems than children in intact families (Capaldi and Patterson 1991).

Broken homes stand for a cluster of interacting circumstances. Added to the emotional stress occasioned by the loss of a parent is the stress caused by consequential loss of income and the deterioration in standards of child care that may come about through a parent being unexpectedly left to cope alone. The existence of marital separation may influence youth deviance through mechanisms such as weak, or inconsistent, parental support. Parents might withdraw from or neglect the child, or allow aggression to spill over into the parent–child relationship such as in the form of severe physical punishment (Erel and Burman 1995; Harrist and Ainslie 1998). Kiernan (1992) found that the risks of other disadvantageous events occurring, such as teenage pregnancy or leaving home because of ill feeling, were higher in lone-parent families caused by divorce than in intact families. The lower achievement and higher incidence of social problems of children from broken homes may therefore be attributable to poverty and to the reduced capacity of a lone parent to supervise and otherwise participate in the development of the child (McLanahan and Sandefar 1994). Thus, the term 'broken home' can be shorthand for a constellation of social problems such as emotional stress, financial worries, inadequate housing and isolation.

However, the widely held assumption that having two parents is automatically a safeguard against criminal conduct is not supported by evidence. There is, for example, a very obvious contrast to be drawn between children who grow up in a loving one-parent family and children who grow up in families with both their parents but are neglected or abused. Wright and Wright (1994) found that the relationship between juvenile offending behaviour and marital discord is stronger than that of living with a single parent, and there is no difference in offending behaviour between those living in a broken home and those living in an intact home that includes conflict. A study in Massachusetts showed that the prevalence of offending was high for boys reared in broken homes without affectionate mothers, and was almost as high for those children reared in united homes characterised by parental conflict (McCord 1982). Rickel and Becker-Lausen (1995) substantiated the finding that homes that are intact, but unhappy and neglectful, are as likely to produce delinquents as those that are broken, but where the children are consistently loved and nurtured. The quality of care offered to, and experienced by, children is the crucial factor.

The important conclusion is that family discord is the main reason for the link between broken homes and youthful offending behaviour. Familial conflict affects children's socio-emotional functioning by disrupting effective parenting practices. Thus, while it may be informative and helpful to know why disrupted family situations may contribute to youth crime, it should not be forgotten that it is not the legal status of the marriage that matters most in this situation. Of rather greater importance is the socio-emotional status of the patterns of interaction among the members of the family. Given this evidence, Chapter 3 will examine whether policies that strengthen the family and improve the family environment might be effective strategies for preventing young people from becoming involved in juvenile offending.

Poor parental supervision

Parental supervision refers to the degree of monitoring by parents of their child's activities, and their degree of watchfulness or vigilance (Farrington and Loeber 1999). Poor supervision involves a combination of laxity in applying rules of behaviour and lack of vigilance in watching over the child's activities and his or her whereabouts. Poor supervision could be one of the most important ways in which parents fail to protect their children from becoming involved in criminal activity. Many studies show that parents who do not know where their children are when they are out, and parents who let their children roam the streets unsupervised from an early age, tend to have delinquent children. This was certainly the opinion of Glueck and Glueck (1950: 261) based on their protracted studies of cohorts of American delinquents. Similarly, a survey in Liverpool found that 11- to 15-year-old boys who were left free on the streets for three or more hours an evening were markedly more prone to engage in vandalism (Gladstone 1978).

Harriet Wilson has arrived at a similar conclusion from a survey in the West Midlands of families affected by varying degrees of social handicap. Wilson chose two samples of 60 families that reflected a comparable range of deprivation. One group was chosen from high-crime inner-city neighbourhoods and the other lived on run-down suburban estates. Parents who were lenient in their supervision, for instance allowing their children to roam the streets without a set time for return and without knowing where they were, were more likely to produce delinquents, and highly likely to do so if they resided in areas characterised by high rates of delinquency. Wilson (1980) discovered that the rate of delinquency in homes where parental supervision was lenient was more than seven times that for families assessed as being strict. Wilson (1987) carried out a follow-up survey six years later and found no reason to alter her central conclusion that parental supervision was the most important single factor in determining juvenile delinquency. She believed that lax supervision in this setting is not a deliberate choice of a permissive style of parenting; instead it should be described as abandonment.

Among the concurring evidence, Riley and Shaw (1985) also examined the influence of parental supervision. They asked parents of their national sample of 750 14- and 15-year-old boys and girls how often they knew whom their son or daughter was with, where they were going and what they were doing. The results showed that greater supervision resulted in a lower risk of children becoming offenders. Differences in levels of parental supervision could also be one of the most important reasons for differences in levels of offending between male and female juveniles. As Riley and Shaw found, parents had different ideas about the appropriate levels of supervision for their sons and daughters. Daughters received much higher levels of supervision, whereas males are allowed greater latitude of behaviour and thus are freer to deviate.

A Home Office study has also confirmed strong links between poor parental supervision and juvenile convictions (Graham and Bowling 1995). Graham and Bowling used self-report data from a nationally representative random sample of 1,721 young people aged between 14 and 25 years old in England and Wales. Those in the sample were interviewed about their background, family life, school experiences, aspects of their current lifestyle, drug use and criminal offences. This study showed that 42 per cent of juveniles who had low or medium levels of parental supervision had committed offences, whereas only 20 per cent of juveniles who experienced high levels of parental supervision had offended. This study stressed parental supervision as the factor most closely correlated with criminality in young people. In the Second Youth Lifestyle Survey those who were poorly supervised were also found to be more likely to be offenders. This survey was carried out between October 1998 and January 1999. A sample of 4,848 young people living in England and Wales were interviewed at home. Alongside questions about crime, the young people surveyed were also asked about their background and lifestyle. 'Poor parental supervision' was defined as parents rarely or never knowing either where their children were or whom they were with when they were out of the house. The relationship between offending and parental supervision was particularly strong among younger teens: 27 per cent of boys aged 12–17 years who were poorly supervised were offenders, compared to just 9 per cent who were better supervised. Poorly supervised girls were also more likely to be offenders (Flood-Page *et al.* 2000: 33; Campbell and Harrington 2000: 4). The Audit Commission (1996: 6) also concluded that the single most important factor in explaining criminality in a young person is parental supervision. American studies have also shown that lax and ineffective parental monitoring is consistently linked with offending adolescents (Gorman-Smith *et al.* 1996; Kumpfer and Alvarado 2000; Weiss *et al.* 1992).

Parental supervision of children is a key component of positive parenting, both as a predictor of delinquency and as a protective measure. A study of 72 families in high-crime areas of Glasgow suggested that the 'traditional child-rearing pattern of strict, working-class parents' appeared to offer children protection against delinquency (Layborn 1986). Improving parental supervision of poorly supervised children could therefore potentially reduce their offending significantly.

Parent and sibling criminality

Of the five of West's key predictive factors of juvenile offending, which were examined at the beginning of this chapter, parental criminality was considered the most powerful (West 1982: 44). Using the same sample as West, Farrington *et al.* (1996a) confirmed that if children had a convicted parent by the time they were 10 years of age, then that was the 'best predictor' of their becoming criminal themselves. Of 102 men in Akers's study sample who had a convicted father, 51 per cent were offenders, compared with only 23.8 per cent of the 281 men whose fathers had no known conviction record (Akers 1997). At all levels of income the presence of a parental criminal record increased the likelihood of the children engaging in offending behaviour, proving that the parents' criminogenic influence was not merely a reflection of social class (West and Farrington 1977: 177).

If other family members were convicted, this also increased the chances of criminality in sons. This result has been found consistently in a range of studies (Farrington 1983; Hawkins and Catalano 1993; Hawkins *et al.* 1992; Osborn and West 1984; Wiebush *et al.* 1995). For example, the Gluecks found that in a majority of cases where reliable records were available, criminality, if not a family tradition, was certainly a common occurrence: 'It is clear that in all the groups of offenders we have studied over the years . . . the familial picture that emerges is excessively tainted by criminalism among grandparents, parents and siblings' (Glueck and Glueck 1974: 49). Similarly in the Pittsburgh Youth Study, arrest of fathers, mothers, brothers, sisters, uncles, aunts, grandfathers and grandmothers all predicted the boy's own delinquency (Farrington *et al.* 2001). In West's study it emerged that of 21 members of the sample study with a mother, but not a father, with a conviction record, 47.6 per cent became offenders. However, because convicted fathers were more numerous than convicted mothers they influenced more boys. A delinquent brother increased the likelihood of criminality whether or not the father also had a record. Deviant siblings contribute to juvenile offending to the extent that they serve as poor role models for conduct problems (Lauritsen 1993). Farrington, summarising the lessons to be learned from the Cambridge Study of Delinquent Development, found that having convicted parents and offending siblings predicted self-report as well as official offending (Farrington 1992).

The belief that offending is legitimate tends to be built up if children have been exposed to attitudes and behaviour favouring offending, especially by members of their family (Farrington 1997). However, there is no evidence to suggest that criminal parents directly encourage their children to commit crimes or teach them criminal techniques. Hirschi (1983: 8) maintains that criminal parents may not recognise patterns of criminality in their own children. In effect they are not punished for their misdeeds not because parents do not want to punish bad behaviour, but because these parents literally do not see their children's behaviour as wrong. Thus, the sons and daughters of criminal parents are not taught that stealing, for instance, is wrong. Also, youths with criminal parents are less well supervised. In the Cambridge Study, after matching for parental supervision there was only a slight association between parental criminality and subsequent juvenile offending behaviour (West 1973: 42). McCord (1991: 219) compared families in which fathers had been convicted for serious crimes with families in which the fathers were not known to be criminals. Approximately twice a week, counsellors visited the homes of 253 boys from 232 families over a six-year period. McCord concluded that criminal fathers were more likely to be absent from the homes in which their sons were reared and parental conflict was more likely to be present in their families. Sampson and Laub (1993: 69) also deduced that parents who commit crimes are more likely to use harsh discipline in an inconsistent manner. It is possible, therefore, that the link between the parent's criminality and the child's offending is due to a lack of social responsibility among criminal parents which reveals itself in a lax attitude to the social training of their sons. These results are concordant with the core argument of this chapter that antisocial behaviour develops when the normal social learning process based on rewards and punishments from parents is disrupted by erratic discipline, poor supervision, parental disharmony and unsuitable, antisocial or criminal parental models. Furthermore, these results substantiate my hypothesis that child welfare interventions and policies that strengthen the family offer the potential to effectively prevent juveniles from engaging in antisocial and offending behaviour.

Teenage parents

Research has shown that children born of teenage parents have a greater chance of low school attainment, antisocial school behaviour, aggressive behaviour, substance abuse and engaging in early sexual intercourse than children born of older parents (Baker and Mednick 1984; Hagan and Parker 1999; Nagin *et al.* 1997). In addition, children of teenage mothers are also more likely to become offenders (Conseur *et al.* 1997; Gronger 1997). In Newcastle upon Tyne, Kolvin *et al.* (1990: 80) reported that mothers who married as teenagers, a factor strongly related to teenage pregnancy, were twice as likely to have sons who became juvenile offenders.

Studies show that the principal reason for this correlation is that teenage parents tend to use the 'inadequate' parenting practices analysed throughout this chapter (Morash and Rucker 1989). There is evidence, for example, that teenage parents are less proficient than adults in problem-solving and display higher levels of parenting stress (Passino *et al.* 1993). Teenage parents are more likely to experience poor health, poverty and relationship breakdown (Social Exclusion Unit 1999). Their youth, inexperience and poverty suggest that they may experience particular difficulties and stress in raising children (UNICEF 2000). Children growing up in households with young mothers are significantly more likely to be physically neglected, poorly supervised and emotionally deprived, and to have parents who have little interest in their education. Also, periods of at least temporary separation are much more common in households with young mothers (Nagin *et al.* 1997: 154). Adolescent parents are at a stage in life in which they lack the maturity and development necessary to raise a child properly. Early pregnancy may thwart the parents' development and cement in place ineffective parenting practices. These underdeveloped aspects of adolescent life betray a deeper inability to socialise a child appropriately. As a result, the child is more susceptible to criminal behaviour in youth. Thus, maternal childbearing age may not be a causal factor as such; rather, it is a marker for problems in the child's environment that are shaping his or her development. These findings should not be interpreted as implying that teenage parents are solely responsible for the antisocial behaviour of their children. Rather, the account is an attempt to explain why maternal age is a predictive factor for juvenile offending behaviour.

Unstable living conditions

Young people living in unstable conditions are more likely to offend. Wincup *et al.* (2003) studied 160 homeless young people in Cardiff, Brighton, Canterbury and Birmingham over a period of 18 months from January 2001. Those interviewed admitted to very high levels of offending (95 per cent). Many were living in temporary accommodation with little support. From data on a sample of 390 homeless young people in Toronto, it was found that a significantly greater proportion of homeless young people commit offences after rather than before leaving home (McCarthy and Hagan 1991). Those who live at home with parents are less likely to offend and, when they do, are more likely to stop as they get older (Graham and Bowling 1995). Homeless young people who engage in more serious offending are the least likely to be deterred from crime by threat of punishment (McCarthy and Hagan 1991). Most young people who are homeless leave home because of the breakdown of family relationships, often with step-parents. Some are told to leave home, others leave because of family disputes or sometimes abuse (Gallagher 1998; Kiernan 1995). Experiencing abuse within the family is a frequent explanation for homelessness (Carlen 1996; Hutton and Liddiard 1994). A background of being in care was also identified as a potential precursor to homelessness: 39 per cent of Wincup's sample had been looked after by the local authority and 17 per cent had become homeless subsequent to being looked after (Wincup *et al.* 2003: 11). Chapter 3 will use this evidence to assert that a wide range of family-based interventions focused on providing parents with support in bringing up their children may impact positively in reducing the likelihood of juvenile offending.

From the factors outlined it is inescapable that the family is a vital component in any consideration of juvenile offending. The nature of the parent–child interactions and the general atmosphere within the home, whether broken or intact, has been consistently related to youth criminality. In addition to direct assessments of parental performance there are other factors to be considered which may affect the quality of parenting and hence the likelihood of children's becoming offenders. Where parents are in a situation of economic disadvantage, the difficulties associated with the parenting role may well be compounded. To ignore economic conditions in the explanation of delinquency would be myopic and unproductive.

The effects of economic disadvantage

Carved above the main entrance of the Central Criminal Court at the Old Bailey in London are the words 'Defend the children of the poor and punish the wrongdoer'. This apparently straightforward injunction has proved extremely difficult to carry out, because in the youth courts of England and Wales it appears that the wrongdoers are also the children of the poor. The aetiological linkages between economic deprivation and juvenile offending are well established in academic criminology and are vividly evidenced in seminal and defining studies from both the United Kingdom and the United States. For example, the Gluecks found that 57.4 per cent of the families involved in their studies had been dealt with by numerous social welfare agencies, largely economic relief organisations (Glueck and Glueck 1974: 59). Similarly, Miller *et al.* (1974) also highlighted a 'clear excess of delinquent children from families from lower social classes'. Gladstone's findings show that among boys whose father had unskilled or semi-skilled jobs, 42 per cent reported a high involvement in vandalism as against 30 per cent of those whose fathers had higher-status jobs (Gladstone 1978). Wadsworth (1979), in his national sample, discovered that 4 per cent of sons of 'upper-middle' families had become delinquent by age 21 compared with 21.9 per cent of sons from 'lower-manual' families. These results show that delinquency, as indicated by criminal records, is three times more common among the sons of unskilled manual workers than among those of professional and salaried workers. West (1982) also found that family income was a key factor: 33.3 per cent of boys from low-income families became juvenile offenders, compared with 16.7 per cent of boys from higher-income families. West concluded that future offenders were more likely to have been part of a low-income family, lived in run-down housing and shown signs of neglect by their parents. Recidivists with two or more convictions stood out even more starkly: 20 per cent came from a background of low income compared to just 5.5 per cent among the rest. Ousten (1984) also verified a relationship between social class and criminality for both boys and girls, although it was more pronounced for boys. For example, the proportion of boys who received a police caution or were convicted by the age of 18 was 17.3 per cent if the main breadwinner was in the professional, managerial and skilled non-manual group. This figure was 28.6 per cent if the main bread-winner was in the skilled manual group and 35.4 per cent if in the semi-skilled and unskilled manual group. The corresponding figures for girls were 1.6 per cent, 4.1 per cent and 7.5 per cent respectively.

Pursuing the lives of a more recent generation, the Child Health and Education Study of over 13,000 British children born in 1970 has con-firmed that antisocial behaviour in pre-school children is consistently asso-ciated with social and economic disadvantage (Osborn 1984). In the *Newcastle 1,000 Family Study* three generations of families were studied over a 30-year period (Kolvin *et al.* 1990). The survey began by investigat-ing the health of 847 children born in Newcastle upon Tyne during May and June 1947. The study was resumed in 1979 and included a compari-son between the backgrounds of children who later acquired a criminal record and those who did not. The families were classified as 'non-deprived', 'deprived' and 'multiply deprived' using a variety of measures including parental illness, poor housing, poor mothering and marital insta-bility. The more deprived the family, the more likely it was that their chil-dren would offend. By age 33, 18 per cent of the non-deprived children had been convicted of an offence, a much smaller proportion than the 49 per cent of the deprived and 66 per cent of the multiply deprived. The find-ings showed that one in six children living in more affluent districts became offenders compared to one in three in the poorest neighbourhoods. A study by the New South Wales Bureau of Crime Statistics and Research has confirmed the long-held perception that economic and social stress arising from unemployment, poverty and lack of family support strongly correlates with juvenile crime (New South Wales Bureau of Crime Stat-istics and Research 1997).

What emerges from the official crime figures and the longitudinal research examined above is that children from low-income, working-class families are more likely to become juvenile offenders than those from com-fortable middle-class homes. Economic hardship has a growing and devas-tating effect on families. Poverty influences children through its impact upon parents' behaviour towards children. For example, the stress caused by poverty is believed to diminish parents' capacity for supportive and consistent parenting. Families living in poverty are unable to provide the necessary emotional support and stimulation critical to healthy child development. Family incomes and poor housing can lead to weaker parental supervision and control (Tarling 1993; Utting *et al.* 1993). Economic hardship, even among parents living together and in rural areas, can contribute to parental conflict and poor parenting, and consequently to delinquency and other behavioural problems among the children in these families (Conger 1992). Low income and lack of full-time employment have also been shown to increase the likelihood of abuse by parents (James 1995). Also, living in disadvantaged settings can lead to the belief that economic survival through conventional channels is not possible (Guerra *et al.* 1995; Hammond and Yung 1994). Thus, economic and environmental factors collaborate to make it more difficult to be an effective parent.

Yet economic deprivation does not appear sufficient on its own for delinquency to develop. Factors within the care-giving environment, and possibly within the children themselves, are seen to modify the influence of poverty and disadvantage (Tracy *et al.* 1990; Werner and Smith 1992). As the authors of the *Newcastle 1,000 Families* study observed, those children from deprived backgrounds who avoided a criminal record had tended to enjoy good parental care and supervision in a less crowded home. Approaching puberty, they showed relatively good intellectual development and a positive temperament. The statistics showed that 70 per cent of deprived children receiving poor maternal and domestic care before the age of 5 became involved in criminal activity, whereas only 40 per cent of children from deprived backgrounds whose parental care was judged to be good became offenders (Kolvin *et al.* 1990). Rutter and Giller (1985) made a comparable point in their exhaustive review of the literature on juvenile crime. They noted that any statistical relationship between economic status and juvenile crime in the Cambridge study disappeared once the influence of poor parental supervision was taken into account. From another longitudinal research project, the Oregon Youth Study, which focused on 10-year-old boys using criminal records and self-report data, it emerged that the statistical connection between socio-economic status and the children's early offending behaviour was entirely mediated by family management practices. In other words, economic pressures were affecting the way that parents behaved, and that in turn affected the behaviour of their children.

Living on a low income in a run-down neighbourhood does not make it impossible to be the 'affectionate, authoritative parent of healthy, sociable children. But it does undeniably make it more difficult' (Utting 1995: 40). Although poverty, deprivation and social exclusion can never justify crime, it is a fact that these feature all too frequently in the backgrounds of young offenders, and any attempts to control offending behaviour that ignore the established facts of economic disadvantage will inevitably fail.

Limitations and implications of findings

Virtually all the theories discussed thus far have focused on male participation in juvenile offending behaviour. This inattention to females is attributed to their limited involvement in crime and antisocial behaviour. The results of official figures and self-report surveys indicate that, overall, males are more likely to engage in offending behaviour than females (Chesney-Lind and Shelden 1992; Hartless *et al.* 1995; Hindelang 1971). In 1999 in England and Wales there were 145,700 known male offenders between the ages of 10 and 17 years and 35,900 female offenders. Thus, male offenders outnumbered female offenders by a ratio of 4:1 (Crime and Criminal Justice Unit 2000). In 2000, 2.2 per cent of all offenders were 10- to 17-year-old females, whereas this figure was 9.2 per cent for 10- to 17-year-old males (Crime and Criminal Justice Unit 2001). In 2001 the ratio of known male juvenile offenders to known female juvenile offenders was just over 4:1 (Crime and Criminal Justice Unit 2002), and in 2003–04 this ratio was 5:1 (Youth Justice Board 2005a). This overwhelming preponderance of male offending over females seems to be a universal feature of the criminal justice records of all modern countries, enduring over time and confirmed by self-report data (Maguire 1997: 177). Males are also more likely than females to engage in serious juvenile offending (Farrington 1996). Females are not involved in violent offences to the same extent as males, and female offending is not considered as threatening as male offending (Chesney-Lind and Shelden 1998). Although family process variables facilitate the understanding and predicting of offending behaviour among both male and female juveniles, there are gender differences in the way these processes are played out. For Moffitt, the causal process does not necessarily differ between males and females. Moffitt (1994) claims that girls are less likely than boys to encounter the full range of the predictive factors for the development of offending behaviour. For example, females are supervised more closely than males, making females more averse to engaging in offending behaviour.

It is equally important to recognise that the statistically significant 'predictors' which I have employed rarely, if ever, approach the realms of certainty. For example, 71 per cent of the boys in the Cambridge study whose upbringing combined three of the most important risk factors – low income, a parent with a criminal record and poor parenting skills – later acquired a criminal record. Nonetheless, that triad of predictors identified only a minority of all the boys who were eventually convicted or cautioned (West and Farrington 1977). Similarly, although a computer analysis in New Zealand taking the ratings of children's pre-school behaviour correctly classified 66 per cent of those who were offenders at age 15, it also picked out a much larger number of children who did not later find themselves in trouble with the police (White 1990).

Although proper attention must be paid to the pitfalls involved in targeting initiatives, considerable scope exists for interventions whose aim is to prevent crime by reducing criminality. None of these limitations invalidates an understanding that family and social factors are of special importance in the context of youth crime, and that this is even more the case with recidivists, whose persistent offending accounts for such a high proportion of known crime. Crude theories of causation and reductionist aetiology are problematic, but the connection between the difficult family and material circumstances that beset increasing numbers of children and their offending behaviour cannot reasonably be ignored or denied. What appears important in decision-making is the degree to which we discount the culpability of youth in the light of the influence of familial forces. If juveniles are considered to be autonomous beings who are as capable of making rational choices as adults are, thus granting less weight to the influence of negative family factors as direct causes of their behaviour, then a retributive response is warranted. However, if juvenile offending behaviour is understood as a phenomenon caused by negative family factors working upon the innocent individual, then a parentalistic rehabilitation approach might be favoured to correct the problem. The evidence provided in this chapter proves that youth crime is a by-product of a low standard of living coupled with child neglect. These findings emphasise the need for prevention policies and interventions to avoid a narrow focus on the crime and to take into account the family, social and contextual factors that are frequently associated with juvenile offending.

Young offenders: children in trouble or troubled children?

It is apparent from what I have outlined thus far that there is a trend emerging which involves an increasing convergence in the explanations offered for offending behaviour by the young and for childhood problems such as drug abuse, poor educational attainment and poor mental health. Reviews of risk factors for problem behaviour such as substance abuse, mental health problems and school drop-out suggest that most of the risk factors for youth offending behaviour also predict these problems. Thus, delinquency, school problems, psychological problems and drug use cluster around the same individuals (Stattin and Magnusson 1995, 1996).

For instance, Graham and Bowling (1995: 42) found that for both males and females the odds of offending for those who truanted were more than three times greater than for those who had not. Of those males temporarily excluded from school, 75 per cent were offenders, and 50 per cent of females temporarily excluded from school were offenders. Those who persistently truanted from school were even more likely to admit offending. Although permanent exclusion from school was less common, the effect was even more pronounced than for temporary exclusions. In Graham and Bowling's study, five out of the eight females who had been permanently excluded from school admitted offending, and all 11 of the permanently excluded boys admitted offending. The small number of permanent exclusions means that these findings are tentative. However, Ball and Connolly (2000: 603) found that 80 per cent of 10- to 15-year-olds sentenced to supervision in England and Wales were not attending school, owing to truancy or school exclusion. Clearly, there is a reciprocal relationship between delinquency and truancy and school exclusion. Truancy and school exclusion may be both a cause and a consequence of juvenile offending behaviour. Schools may use exclusion to respond to problematic behaviour, including persistent non-attendance and offending behaviour; therefore, it is difficult to determine which causes which. Nonetheless, the probability of committing offences rises considerably for those who are truanting or excluded from school, especially permanently excluded.

Low intelligence, however measured, and poor school performance or achievement have also been identified as important factors in discriminating delinquents from non-delinquents (Glueck and Glueck 1974; Tarling 1993). In the Cambridge Study 33 per cent of the boys scoring 90 or less on a non-verbal intelligence test (Raven's Progressive Matrices) at age 8 were convicted as juveniles, twice as high a proportion as for the remainder (West 1982). Furthermore, this relationship was found when delinquency was measured by self-report as well as convictions. In a prospective longitudinal survey of 120 Stockholm males, low intelligence measured at age 3 significantly predicted officially recorded delinquency (Stattin and Klackenberg-Larsson 1993). Frequent offenders (those with four or more offences) had an average IQ of 88 at age 3, whereas non-offenders had an average IQ of 101. Also, in the Perry Preschool Program in Michigan, low intelligence at age 4 significantly predicted the number of arrests up to age 27 (Farrington and West 1993; Schweinhart *et al.* 1993). Wadsworth (1979) found that boys classified by primary school teachers as 'poor or lazy workers' when they were 10 years old were more likely to become delinquents than those regarded as 'very hard' or 'hard' workers. A similar classification made by secondary school teachers when the boys were aged 15 was also found to be related to delinquency.

The family has an important role to play in children's school adjustment, attendance and performance. Parents' involvement in school and monitoring of school performance lessens the likelihood of school failure and associated outcomes such as delinquency (Smith and Stern 1997: 403). In Wadsworth's study, comprising just over 5,000 persons born in 1946, it was found that the more interest parents took in their son's schooling, as measured by teachers, the less likely it was that the son would become a juvenile offender (Wadsworth 1979). Wadsworth's study was an investigation into the health, growth, development and criminal records of the children in the survey. At primary school, 25 per cent of boys whose parents were rated lowest became juvenile offenders compared with 7.5 per cent of those rated highest. Even greater differences were found at the secondary school stage, 34.2 per cent and 8 per cent respectively. Graham and Bowling (1995) found that school truants usually had a poor relationship with one or both parents, family members in trouble with the law, and low attachment to family, and were poorly supervised in that their parents frequently did not know where their child was, whom they were with or what they were doing. Research indicates that child sexual abuse has a significant impact on children's education, including social development, school behaviour, learning, bullying and truancy (Nugent *et al.* 1998). Such children are more likely to truant from school and to engage in offending behaviour.

Strong links have also been established between mental health problems in children and young people and juvenile offending. The term 'mental health problems' is used generically to cover a range of types and severity of psychological and psychiatric difficulties and disorders that are experienced by children and young people, including emotional disorders, conduct disorders, hyperkinetic disorder, development disorders and psychotic disorders. Rutter found that the rate of mental health problems is high in young offenders, particularly in persistent young offenders (Rutter 1990; Rutter and Smith 1995; Rutter *et al.* 1998). A diagnosis of a primary mental health disorder was found in 33 per cent of young men aged 16–18 sentenced by a youth court (Gunn *et al.* 1991), and screening of 10- to 17-years-olds attending a city centre youth court revealed disturbingly high levels of both psychiatric and physical morbidity, including learning difficulties, mood disorders, mental illness and frequent use of alcohol and illicit drugs (Farrington *et al.* 1996b).

Certain groups of children are at greater risk of developing mental health problems than others. Children who do not do well at school, whether because of low IQ or because of a specific learning disorder, are at an increased risk of mental health problems, whose incidence may be as high as 40 per cent (Graham 1986). The Audit Commission (1999a) found that 9 per cent of children with mental health problems were looked after by the local authority, compared with 0.5 per cent in the general population. Poor and inconsistent parenting is linked with mental health problems in young children and adolescents. Poor supervision, erratic and/or harsh discipline, parental disharmony, rejection of the child and low involvement in the child's activities have been consistently shown to contribute to mental health problems in children (Cleaver *et al.* 1999; Farrington 1994). The lives of young people with mental health problems are often characterised by chronic residential instability and difficult family relationships. These children are more likely to come from low-income families, to have previously lived outside the home and to come from reconstituted or single-parent families (Frensch and Cameron 2002; Quinn and Epstein 1998; Wells and Whittington 1993). Children of neglectful parents are more likely to suffer impaired psychological development and are also at greatest risk of drug and alcohol abuse and delinquency (Steinberg 1990). In the Office for National Statistics study (2000), 47 per cent of children assessed as having a mental health disorder had a parent who was likely to have a mental health problem, such as anxiety or depression.

Many research studies have found evidence of a strong association between juvenile substance abuse and antisocial behaviour in young people. Indeed, worldwide, almost every survey of these behaviours has found some form of association between them (Howard and Zibert 1990; Huizinga *et al.* 1994; Inciardi and Pottieger 1991; Johnson *et al.* 1991). The results of a Home Office research study on drug testing of arrestees found that 11 per cent of 16- to 20-year-olds tested positive for opiates, as did 5 per cent for cocaine (Bennett 1998). In the Audit Commission study of 103 young offenders on supervision orders (Audit Commission 1996), approximately 65 per cent of the sample had used cannabis, over 20 per cent had used ecstasy, over 10 per cent had used cocaine and approximately 6 per cent had used heroin. By contrast, research on non-offending samples of young people of similar age show the lifetime prevalence of ecstasy use to be around 5 per cent, and that for heroin 1 per cent (Parker *et al.* 1995). A study of 50 young offenders on probation for a range of offences found that almost all reported lifetime experiences of at least one illicit substance, with an extremely large proportion who had used crack cocaine (38 per cent), heroin (24 per cent) or methadone (14 per cent) in the previous month (Williamson *et al.* 1996). Collinson found that drug use figured centrally and excessively in the lives of 59 per cent of a sample of 80 young male offenders in custody (Collinson 1994a, 1996). His sample reported figures of 54 per cent for lifetime prevalence of LSD use, 43 per cent for ecstasy and 20 per cent for heroin and cocaine or crack.

The Youth Lifestyles Survey supports the finding that juvenile drug use and juvenile offending are associated (Flood-Page *et al.* 2000). Of the serious and persistent offenders[3] aged 12–17, 38 per cent of males and 20 per cent of females admitted using drugs in the past 12 months, compared to 7 per cent of males and 4 per cent of females for the rest of the cohort. The Youth Lifestyle Survey found that 75 per cent of persistent offenders reported lifetime use of drugs (Goulden and Sondhi 2001). In addition to finding raised general prevalence rates, the survey also suggests that the rates of use of drugs such as crack cocaine and heroin are significantly higher among young serious and persistent offenders than they are in the general population. Hammersley *et al.* (2003) examined a sample of 293 young people who were clients of 11 youth offending teams in England and Wales between summer 2001 and summer 2002. Each young person completed an extensive structured questionnaire on a one-to-one basis under the guidance of a researcher. The questionnaire included questions on substance use, offending behaviour and family and social background. The group members were highly delinquent; most had committed multiple types of offences repeatedly. Substance use among the sample exceeded the rates of the Youth Lifestyles Survey offender group and the British Crime Survey group. Most of the sample had consumed alcohol (91 per cent), cannabis (86 per cent) and ecstasy (44 per cent). Drug use was highest among the most frequent offenders and lowest in the less frequent offenders. Over half of the sample agreed that alcohol or drugs had been associated with their offending and 44 per cent said that they sometimes committed crimes to get money for drugs or alcohol.

Research indicates that the risk factors for substance abuse and delinquency overlap substantially (Hawkins *et al.* 1995). These include poor parental supervision, a disrupted family background, poor psychological well-being, difficulties in school, school exclusion, truancy, low educational achievement, having been abused, having been in care, parental divorce or separation, or having a family member with a criminal record (Bennett 2000; Collinson 1994b; Lloyd 1998; Newburn 1999). It has been suggested that substance abuse and delinquency develop together in a common 'causal configuration' (Elliott *et al.* 1985. Thus, associations between juvenile offending and drug use may exist because of the shared antecedents of drug abuse and delinquency, rather than because drug use causes offending.

Many youths entering the youth justice system have serious multiple problems in terms of their school achievement, psychological health, alcohol and drug abuse. Most of these problems are preceded by the family problems discussed throughout this chapter. Thus, a key feature of the risk factors investigated in this chapter is their interconnectedness; these family problems are best viewed as a 'web of causation'. They are all specific expressions of a common underlying propensity to problem behaviour that contributes to a syndrome of antisocial behaviour that runs wider than offending. The obvious conclusion from this analysis is that the tangled roots of youth crime lie to a considerable extent inside the family. Delinquency is found in damaged, and damaging, families. The family problems of young people propel them into deviance and so into expanding penal institutions. The connection between the difficult family circumstances that plague increasing numbers of children and their subsequent offending behaviour cannot be ignored or denied. Chapter 3 will consider the measures that can be used to respond to the family conditions considered in this chapter.

Public policy view of young offenders

These explanations for juvenile offending behaviour have been a characteristic feature of the history of youth crime control. The first public body to investigate youth offending behaviour, established in 1815, was the Committee for Investigating the Causes of the Alarming Increase of Juvenile Delinquency in the Metropolis. The committee's evidence was taken from interviews of children already incarcerated in prison. It concluded that among the main causes of juvenile offending in England's developing and industrialising capital city were the improper conduct of parents and the want of education (Committee for Investigating the Causes of the Alarming Increase of Juvenile Delinquency in the Metropolis 1816: 26). The causes of crime were found to be firmly rooted in the low moral condition of parents and in parental neglect.

Such views were not merely an English idiosyncrasy. This view of young offenders was also prevalent in Canada in the late nineteenth and early twentieth centuries. Section 38 of the Canadian Juvenile Delinquents Act 1908 states that 'every juvenile delinquent shall be treated not as a criminal, but as a misdirected and misguided child and one needing aid, encouragement, help and assistance'. During the parliamentary debates surrounding the Act, protection of the child and protection of the interests of society were presented as means of achieving each other: protecting the child means that a good citizen is moulded and a useful member of society is formed.[4] It was believed that no distinction should be drawn between neglected and delinquent children: all should be recognised as being of the same class and should be dealt with in a manner which served the best interests of the child. It was not the first time that a Canadian law had linked children in danger with delinquent children. The Ontario Acts of 1887 and 1893 on child protection had been designed at least partly to address the issue of delinquency. These laws made it possible to place children declared guilty of minor offences in industrial schools until then reserved for children whose parents neglected their upbringing. In 1891 the Canadian Commission on the Prison and Reformatory System of Ontario concluded that the chief causes of crime in the community were the want of proper parental control, the lack of good home training and the 'baneful influence of bad homes, largely due to the culpable neglect and indifference of parents' (Province of Ontario 1891).

In the United States the founders of the juvenile court assumed the role of benevolent parent and social worker rolled into one. The first official juvenile court judge asked, 'why is it not the duty of the state, instead of asking merely whether a boy or a girl has committed a specific offence, to find out what he is physically, mentally, morally...?' (Mack 1909: 107). Using broad discretion, the juvenile court judge was to provide the necessary help and guidance to a young person who might otherwise proceed further down the path of chronic crime (Fox 1996). Until the last quarter of the twentieth century, the juvenile court in the United States was viewed as the 'nexus where psychology and philanthropy were to combine and place a rational and loving hand on wayward youth' (Simon 1995: 1364). In 1974 the United States Congress decided that effective delinquency prevention programmes were needed to reduce the flow of juveniles into the justice system. In the congressional view, today's dependent and neglected children became tomorrow's offenders. It was seen as imperative that the cycle be broken and the labelling of these children as delinquents avoided. Labelling them as delinquents would set into motion a self-fulfilling prophecy that might enhance the likelihood of subsequent delinquency and criminality (Committee on the Judiciary 1974). In making this recommendation, Congress adopted the approach recommended by the Crime Commission of 1967, giving top priority to youth crime prevention by addressing, among other factors, family problems (United States Government 1967).

Today, however, the American youth justice system has undergone a sea change in its perception of juvenile offenders and their parents. The most striking development is the law's reconceptualisation of young offenders as violent predators warranting retribution, rather than as wayward children in need of a guiding hand. A profusion of laws have been enacted to arm communities in their fight against juvenile criminality, a development that has transformed the focus of the juvenile court from an indispensable examination of the best interests of the child to an overarching concern with public safety, child punishment and individualised accountability (Feld 1998: 842). For example, Davidson (1995) observed that the three most common legislative responses to juvenile crime are: (1) increasing penalties, including finite and lengthier periods of incarceration for young offenders; (2) lowering the age and other prerequisites for transferring juveniles accused of serious crimes from juvenile to adults courts; and (3) funding new detention and correctional centres as well as boot camps with rigid, military-like regimens. Youthful malefactors, especially those charged with serious offences, are now widely viewed as essentially incorrigible (DiFonzo 2001; Dolgin 1999; Feld 1991).

In England, throughout most of the twentieth century juvenile offenders were perceived as in need of protection and redirection rather than punishment. For example, in 1927 the Moloney Committee stated its members' belief that neglect leads to youthful offending behaviour. They considered substituting civil proceedings in the Juvenile Court (Home Office 1927). Rather than criminalising neglect, this measure would have recognised crime as a symptom of neglect, through decriminalisation. The committee recognised the importance of the welfare of young offenders, most of whom were victims of social and psychological conditions and in need of individualised treatment. In this respect the committee felt that there was little to distinguish the young offender from the neglected child: 'It is often a mere accident whether he is brought before the court because he was wandering or beyond control or because he committed some offence. Neglect leads to delinquency' (Home Office 1927: 6).

The recommendations of the Moloney Committee formed the basis of the Children and Young Persons Act 1933.[5] In 1946, almost 20 years after the Moloney Committee, the Curtis Committee reported on the existing models of provision for children who were deprived of a 'normal' home life (Home Office 1946). While deprived children were the focus of the Curtis Report, the committee noted that deprived children and young offenders were both victims of family and environmental circumstances that triggered emotional disturbance. Following the report of the Curtis Committee, the Children Act 1948 set up local authority children's departments to provide for the first time a specialised and individualised social work service to meet the needs of young people. The justification for extending the state's right to intervene was the belief that the roots of young people's problems were in 'the malfunctioning of individuals and their faulty upbringing'. The Ingleby Committee also accepted the view that the needs of the neglected child and the young offender were the same, both being a product of 'family failure'. The Ingleby Committee was set up in 1956 to look into the operation of the juvenile court and consider what new powers and duties could be given to local authorities to prevent the neglect of children at home (Home Office 1960). Because few of the recommendations of the Ingleby Committee were incorporated into the Children and Young Persons Act 1963, the 1963 Act was quite a limited measure. Nonetheless, it expanded the category of 'in need of care and protection' to that of being 'in need of care, protection and control'. Local authorities were also given the duty to engage in preventive work with children and families thought to be 'at risk'. Whereas the Children Act 1948 had given social workers the task of rescuing children by taking them into care, the 1963 Act was more ambitious in that it sought to prevent trouble before it developed.

The Children and Young Persons Act 1969 was underpinned by a philosophy of treatment that removed any lingering distinction between children who offended and those who needed care and protection. The causes of offending and deprivation were seen as the same: both types of children suffered from essentially the same problems and had the same treatment needs. Section 1(2) of the 1969 Act provided that one reason justifying a civil care order or a supervision order was that the young person was guilty of any offence, excluding homicide. It also had to be proved that there was a need for care and control which the young offender was unlikely to receive unless a court order were made.[6] The separate power to commit a child to care in criminal proceedings (section 7(7) Children and Young Persons Act 1969) also reflected a fundamental purpose in the legislation, which was to treat all children in trouble as children in need of care and protection. The effect of these provisions was to explicitly acknowledge that committing an offence could be a symptom of social need. The 1969 Act gave primacy to the family and the social circumstances of the deprived and underprivileged; it aimed to reduce the criminalisation of young people and to increase the support and care available to them. The 1969 Act, however, did not have an easy passage through Parliament. Conservative politicians argued that it was unjust, that it gave insufficient recognition to the constructive role of the juvenile court, and that it interfered with police work with juveniles, especially in regard to more serious offences (Bottoms 1974). The Magistrates' Association was also opposed to the Children and Young Persons Act 1969, blaming it for the vast increases in juvenile crime (Berlino and Wansell 1974), thus precipitating a moral panic about the powerlessness of the juvenile court. Following the defeat of the Wilson government in the 1970 general election, the incoming Heath administration was no more inclined to implement the provisions of the 1969 Act when in government than it had been to support them in opposition. Consequently, large sections of the 1969 Act were never implemented and the social welfare ideology underlying the Act never came to fruition. Juvenile courts continued to function largely as they had before, and though care proceedings following commission of an offence were made possible, such powers were used sparingly (Cavadino and Dignan 1992; Newburn 1997; Rutter and Giller 1983).

The Criminal Justice Act 1982 aimed to provide the courts with more flexible and effective powers for dealing with young offenders. The 1982 Act abolished Borstals but replaced them with youth custody sentences which were fixed by the courts and not by social workers. The 1982 Act expanded the use of detention centres and empowered the courts to incarcerate young offenders for periods exceeding three years. However, the 1982 Act also represented a trend towards looking to alternatives to incarceration for young offenders. The Act embraced the idea of 'intermediate treatment' for offenders aged 17–21, effectively raising the age limit of supervision orders made in juvenile courts for young people aged 10–16. The 1982 Act provided that no court should impose any custodial sentence on a person aged under 21 years unless it was satisfied that no other sentence was appropriate because the offender had shown himself to be unable or unwilling to respond to non-custodial methods of treatment; or because a custodial sentence was necessary for the protection of the public; or the offence was so serious that a non-custodial sentence could not be justified (section 1(4) Criminal Justice Act 1982). This trend towards diversion, decriminalisation and decarceration is also reflected in the Criminal Justice Act 1988, which made theft of an automobile a summary offence (therefore making it more difficult to impose custodial sentences on young offenders), and the Criminal Justice Act 1991, which excluded 14-year-olds from youth custody and transferred 17-year-old defendants to the youth court.

From the 1990s onwards, there was a noticeable change in the tenor of official concern about juvenile offending in England. Policy responses became predicated upon a conceptualisation of a demonised, threatening and lawless youth as distinct from a vulnerable, threatened and disadvantaged childhood (Goldson 1999: 274). Thus, as occurred in the United States, the symbolic image of the 'young offender' became ascendant and the lived reality of the 'child in need' was overshadowed. This trend reached fever pitch after the tragic murder by two 10-year-old boys of the 2-year-old James Bulger in February 1993, when the then Prime Minister, John Major, declared that 'society needs to condemn a little more and understand a little less'.[7] The significance of John Major's statement was profound in signalling the shape that subsequent developments in policy and legislation would take. This harsh stance set the tone for refocusing policy and practice in relation to children in trouble upon punishment, retribution and the wholesale incarceration of children. The Children Act

1989 had already removed from the juvenile court the power to order a young person into the care of a local authority (sections 90(1) and (2) Children Act 1989).[8] Care and supervision orders can now only be made in the family proceedings court, leaving the youth court to deal exclusively with criminal matters. The Criminal Justice and Public Order Act 1994 lowered the age at which children could be detained in custody for grave crimes such as manslaughter or other crimes of violence[9] from 14 to 10 years of age. The 1994 Act introduced a range of new measures that extended the court's remand and sentencing powers to younger offenders by introducing secure training orders for 12- to 14-year-old persistent offenders, increasing the maximum length of detention in a young offenders' institute from 12 to 24 months for 15- to 17-year-olds and allowing the court to remand 12- to 14-year-olds.

In his speech to the Labour Party Conference in 1995, Tony Blair promised that he would give a high priority to supporting the family as 'an effective caring and controlling social unit'. Again, in 1997, Tony Blair stated that '[Labour] will uphold family life as the most secure means of bringing up our children.... [Families] should teach right from wrong. They should be the first defence against anti-social behaviour' (Blair 1997). However, legislation introduced since 1997 continues to reflect an ideological conviction in favour of punishment in which more and more people, including children, are brought within the criminal justice system for an ever-growing range of criminal behaviour. The Labour government's response to youth offending ignores the complex patterns and inter-related problems identified throughout this chapter. For example, the presumption of *doli incapax* (being incapable of crime) was abolished by section 34 of the Crime and Disorder Act 1998, a measure that further erodes the special protection historically afforded to children (Bandalli 1998a, b). Section 73(2)(b) of the 1998 Act gives the Secretary of State power to make custody available for children under the age of 12, and courts will be able to use it where necessary for the protection of the public from the child's further offending, whether or not the offences are serious. Section 130 of the Criminal Justice and Police Act 2001 grants the courts new powers to remand into secure accommodation persistent young offenders aged 12–16.

If juvenile offending is to be prevented, then ways need to be developed which target young people who are in danger of becoming offenders long before they fall into this category. Methods of preventing delinquency, should be grounded in knowledge about the causes of delinquency or at least in knowledge about risk and protective factors that predict delinquency. Policy responses to juvenile offending should no longer be based upon a misguided notion of a threatening and lawless youth, but instead should reflect the research which proves that most young offenders have suffered a vulnerable, abusive and disadvantaged childhood. This chapter has demonstrated that juvenile offending behaviour represents a breakdown by the family and child to teach and learn, respectively, proper conformity to lawful social order. The extensive research findings examined in this chapter promote the view that antisocial and offending tendencies can be inhibited by parents who demonstrate empathy and warmth to their children. Explicit recognition of this will preface the analysis of the remainder of this book.

Conclusion

A thought from Tolstoy's *Resurrection*, written in 1899, seems to be as relevant today as it was then:

> 'It is quite obvious this is no extraordinary villain but just an ordinary person ... and that he became what he is simply because he found himself in circumstances which create such people. And so it seems obvious that if we don't want lads like this we must try to wipe out the conditions that produce such unfortunate individuals.'
>
> (Tolstoy 1899: 166–167)

The search for means of preventing antisocial and offending behaviour by children and young people should be based on a coherent philosophy. A salient approach is that the family, even though badly attenuated or disturbed by conflict, morally questionable or broken by divorce or death, continues to be the institution of choice for the socialisation of children. No nursery or scientifically run children's homes have been found to successfully duplicate the socio-psychological environment that nurtures children into stable adults. All efforts that strengthen the family as a viable and constructive agent in the socialisation of children will help to prevent the emergence of deviance. Chapter 3 will examine the efficacy of child care and child welfare legislation in preventing young people engaging in offending behaviour.

Summary

This chapter has examined what is known about the family factors that propel young people into lives of crime and assessed the connection between the difficult family circumstances that beset increasing numbers of children and their offending behaviour. The chapter also considered other influences in the backgrounds of young people, external to their family, that make it comparatively more likely that they will behave antisocially and engage in unlawful conduct. Such influences include the child's mental health, school attendance and academic performance, and drug and alcohol use. The chapter confirmed that the same family factors that contribute to juvenile offending behaviour also contribute to these problems. Thus, it concluded that the family must be regarded as a central feature in the presence or absence of juvenile antisocial and offending behaviour. On the basis of this evidence, Chapter 3 will consider whether existing child welfare legislation, primarily the Children Act 1989, can inhibit these damaging family factors and therefore prevent the onset of juvenile offending.

3 Role of the local authority in preventing youth crime

Introduction

One of the most promising, and therefore the most important, methods of dealing with youth crime is by ameliorating the conditions of life that drive young people to commit crimes and that undermine the restraining rules and institutions erected by society against antisocial conduct (Arnold and Jordan 1998; Thornberry *et al.* 1991). The evidence examined in Chapter 2 suggests that the relationship between parent and child is the mechanism that determines whether tendencies towards aggressive and antisocial behaviour are inhibited or allowed to develop, and that youth offending behaviour must be addressed in the context of the family and not just the child.

No assertion is being made that parents are to blame for behavioural problems such as youth offending behaviour. Rather, given the need to make families function better, the obligation and objective of our society must be to develop and provide the environment, the resources and the opportunities through which families can become competent to deal with their own problems. Where the family is not functioning properly, the parents should be assisted in guiding and nurturing the child, through the provision of various resources and support services that equip them to be good parents, reduce their isolation and promote both their welfare and that of their children. Parents who are bringing up their children in difficult circumstances can be helped to improve their parenting skills and produce better-behaved, more trustworthy children who need less expensive supervision and intervention later on. Public services can guide young people towards responsible behaviour by providing help with parenting, structured nursery education, support in schools and positive leisure opportunities.

However, it is neither desirable nor justifiable for the state to involve itself in every aspect of family life or to dictate to parents how to raise their children. The underlying philosophical premise with regard to any state intervention is that the state might justify its intervention only by showing that the family cannot provide for itself (Goldstein *et al.* 1979: 9).

The Children Act 1989 identifies a unique role for the state in helping families to meet their responsibility, and in providing support to children whose lives include a number of the circumstances that have been identified in Chapter 2 as risk factors for offending. While acknowledging that prime responsibility for children's upbringing lies with parents, the 1989 Act places a duty on local authorities to safeguard and promote the welfare of children within their area who are in need and to provide services specifically aimed at preventing entry into long-term care or court proceedings (section 17 and schedule 2(7) Children Act 1989). Given that the overriding philosophy of the 1989 Act is that children are best brought up by their families (section 17(1) Children Act 1989), this appears to be a general encouragement to local authorities to offer services to families that may be experiencing some of the difficulties examined in Chapter 2, so as to try to avoid the worst effects of family conflict and to prevent children engaging in offending behaviour.

While the Children Act 1989 is not a panacea for youth offending, nonetheless it requires local authorities to provide interventions that improve parenting skills and children's physical and mental health, and reduce risks of child abuse and consequently potentially reduce the risk of children engaging in offending behaviour. Therefore, the focus of this chapter will be on the role that the Children Act can play in preventing juvenile offending. I will examine each of the powers and duties that local authorities possess under the Children Act and other relevant legislation, and assess how these can be used to deter potential young offenders from engaging in offending behaviour. Chapter 4 will then investigate whether the children investigated in Chapter 2 have any legal entitlement to the provision of resources and services examined in Chapter 3.

Local authorities' youth crime prevention duties and powers

Family support services

In order to discharge the general duty to safeguard and promote the welfare of children in their area who are in need and to promote the upbringing of such children by their families, local authorities have been given a number of duties in relation to the provision of what might broadly be described as family support services (section 17 Children Act 1989). Family support has a very broad meaning and can include any activity or facility, provided either by local authorities or by community groups or individuals, aimed at providing advice and support to parents to help them in bringing up their children (Audit Commission 1994: 39). The Children Act *Guidance* stresses that family support services must be multi-faceted to reflect different aspects of children's development (Department of Health 1991b).[1] Such support can include financial assistance, alternative accommodation for children or various services to relieve stress on the family (Thoburn *et al.* 2000: 2). Provision should be made for advice, guidance, counselling, home help and assistance with travelling to use a service provided under the Act. Family support could also include family aids or perhaps therapists who might advise on improving family dynamics. Occupational, social, cultural or recreational activities or assistance with holidays may also be provided (schedule 2(8) Children Act 1989). Services may be provided on a one-off or episodic basis, or over a longer period of time (Department of Health 2000a: 1.31).

Family support is about mobilising support for children's normal development, promoting the child's safety, preventing the child from leaving the family, reducing stressors in the child's and family's life, promoting competence in the child, connecting the child and family members to relevant support and resources, and promoting morale and competence in parents (Gilligan 2000: 13–14). The aim is to help families to maintain or restore their ability to raise their children by themselves and thus relieve stress and promote the welfare of children (Department of Health 1994: 2.2). Indeed, to make it absolutely clear that it is 'family' and not just 'child support' that is required, the Children Act states that any section 17 service may be provided for the family of a particular child in need or for any member of his or her family, if it is provided with a view to safeguarding or promoting the child's welfare (section 17(3) Children Act 1989). The overall value underlying family support services is premised upon the need to pre-empt a more intrusive or disadvantageous outcome.

The value of family support services should not be underestimated, as they keep families together and can be a critical resource for parents and children who are striving to overcome adverse circumstances. Family support provides a positive opportunity to influence the quality of life for children and their families; help parents overcome problems with child care; and prevent the difficult behaviour exhibited by some children from deteriorating to the point of delinquency (Audit Commission 1994: 4.4; Catrano 2000: 121). Hence, family support services are an essential foundation stone of any system designed to protect children from becoming involved in offending behaviour.

Family centres

A keystone in the provision of family support is the family centre. Every local authority must provide such family centres as it considers appropriate in relation to children within its area (schedule 2(9) Children Act 1989). Provision of family centres should be available to a wide range of families and children of all ages, rather than restricted to children defined as being in need. A 'family centre' is described as a centre at which a child, the parents, persons with parental responsibility for the child or any other person looking after the child may attend for (a) occupational, cultural, social or recreational activities; or (b) advice, guidance or counselling, during which time they may also be provided with accommodation. Family centres should include services ranging from intensive casework, parenting skills, family functioning, packages for families with children in need, toy libraries, child health clinics and out-of-school clubs (schedule 2(3) Children Act 1989). Family centres could also include volunteer-based befriending schemes such as those provided by Home Start and Newpin, drop-in centres, parent–toddler groups, play buses, playgroups, day nurseries, supported childminding, holiday schemes and other supervised activities for children and young people. Such schemes have an important preventive function because they supervise children who might otherwise engage in offending behaviour (Department of Health 1991b: 3.11).

The broad philosophy of family centres is their mission to sustain children in families, promote effective parenting and enhance the level of support to families in the community (Pitthouse *et al.* 1998: 190). The family centre aims to strengthen family life, reduce the risk of children suffering deprivation or becoming damaged or delinquent, and help them to reach their full potential (Phelan 1983: 39). Research has shown that family centres are particularly active in five forms of preventive activity: preventing the reception of children into care, preventing the reception of children into custody, preventing neglect and abuse, preventing children from experiencing poor parenting and preventing them from experiencing severe social disadvantages (Holman 1988). Family centres thus represent a particularly flexible framework within which to deliver support services to families where there are child offending concerns. Moreover, the French equivalents of the family centre, *centres socio-culturels*, specifically promote child welfare and working with young people at risk of delinquency. Some *centres socio-culturels* have *animateurs* who work on local socio-cultural activities, including self-help groups in physical and mental health, and youth work especially promoted to prevent delinquency (Blatier 1998, 1999a, b). Accordingly, family centres have the potential to improve the social skills of children and increase the capacity of parents and consequently to arrest the factors, identified in Chapter 2, that influence whether young people become involved in crime.

Day care

Day care is defined as any form of care or supervised activity provided for children during the day, whether or not it is provided on a regular basis (section 18(4) Children Act 1989).[2] Local authorities must provide appropriate day care for children in need in their area who are aged 5 or under and not yet attending school (section 18(1) Children Act 1989).[3] They must also provide appropriate care and supervised activities outside school hours and during school holidays for children in need in their area of any age who are attending school (section 18(5) Children Act 1989). They also have the power to provide either of these services for children in their area who are not in need (sections 18(2) and (6) Children Act 1989).

The day care provisions of the Children Act 1989 enable many imaginative schemes to be devised and supported. Early years centres such as nursery schools, day nurseries and family centres all aim to provide care and education opportunities that promote the development of young children and offer practical support to parents (Hill *et al.* 1995: 157; Pitthouse *et al.* 1998; Pugh 1994). Early years centres provide children with development-enhancing experiences with their peers and other caring adults outside the immediate family (Hawthorne Kirk 1995: 99). Day care services can help parents under stress cope with their children's behaviour by supporting them, giving them respite and providing a range of resources from mutual self-help to parent-craft training and health education (Scottish Office 1993). Day care services may identify children for whom there are concerns about their developmental progress or well-being, or alternatively parents who may have difficulties in responding to their child's needs sufficiently or appropriately. Early childhood behaviour that is aggressive or disruptive can be addressed by intensive and structured nursery education targeted to those at risk (Audit Commission 1996: 96). Day care services may refer families to social services departments; contribute to the assessment of children and their parents or caregivers; provide a specialist assessment of family relationships; or provide services that support the child's development and strengthen the parent's capacity to respond (Department of Health 2000a: 5.59).

The preventive functions of day care and family centres have been convincingly argued. Research demonstrates that children who take part in pre-school programmes receive an educational advantage that decreases the risk of their involvement in delinquency and crime (Bartol and Bartol 1998: 248; Gibbons *et al.* 1990; Holman 1988). Pre-school education has been described as 'life enhancing for mainstream children and life changing for those who are disadvantaged' (Utting *et al.* 1993: 43). From this analysis it is unequivocal that local authority provision of day care has the capacity to effectively impede the deleterious family factors examined in Chapter 2. The cost of not providing adequate levels of day care is an inevitable increase in youth crime.

Accommodation

Services should be designed to enable children to live with their families and to support families in that role, as well as to protect and support children. But occasionally it may be necessary to provide accommodation for children away from home. A local authority must provide accommodation for a child in need in its area who requires accommodation as a result of:

a there being no person who has parental responsibility for him;
b his being lost or having been abandoned; or

c the person who has been caring for him being prevented (whether or not permanently, and for whatever reason) from providing him with suitable accommodation or care.

(section 20(1) Children Act 1989)

If the child is temporarily lost, he or she needs to be looked after and the child's parents will resume care as soon as he or she is found. 'Abandoned' was not defined in the 1989 Act, or in previous legislation, but has been held to mean 'leaving the child to its fate'.[4] Where a person is prevented from providing a child with suitable accommodation or care, it will depend upon the circumstances whether a partnership arrangement or care proceedings are more appropriate. If the child is suffering significant harm, the authority will want to consider carefully whether the welfare of the child requires a care order rather than an agreement for accommodation, because where a child is accommodated, the child is not 'in care' and the authority does not have parental responsibility for the child. In these circumstances the local authority depends for its powers substantially on the agreements reached with parents, although some powers are necessarily implied from the existence of its statutory duties (Bainham 1998: 335).

The child may also be received into voluntary care. Under section 20 of the Children Act 1989 a local authority is empowered to provide accommodation for any child in its area if doing so would safeguard or promote the child's welfare, even if there is a person with parental responsibility who is able to accommodate the child (section 20(4) Children Act 1989). The voluntary accommodation service under section 20 may not be provided if a person who has parental responsibility for the child objects and is able and willing to provide, or arrange for the provision of, accommodation for the child (section 20(7) Children Act 1989). The effect of an admission into voluntary care is that if there is a parent, then that parent retains custody of the child, the local authority having only temporary care and control (Bridge *et al.* 1990: 4.5). *Guidance* states that the voluntary accommodation of a child by a local authority is now to be viewed as a service providing positive support to a child and his or her family (Department of Health 1991b: 2.13). Voluntary care is no longer to be seen as an unfortunate outcome, but instead stands alongside other preventive services such as day care, financial aid, family support services and family centres (Packman and Hall 1998: 3; University of Leicester and Department of Health 1991: 64).

The role that voluntary accommodation may play in the complex picture of preventing youthful offending behaviour is of special interest. The provision of accommodation firmly encapsulates the principle of ameliorating the family factors that compel young people to engage in offending behaviour. For example, the power to provide accommodation could be very effective in alleviating the plight of young homeless people. Children are not automatically deemed to be homeless applicants under the

Housing Act 1985 by virtue of their age. However, in *R* v. *Oldham Metropolitan BC, ex p Garlick*[5] the House of Lords drew attention to the provisions of the Children Act 1989 which require local authorities to provide accommodation for a child who is 'in need'. In *R (on the application of G)* v. *London Borough of Barnet; R (on the application of W)* v. *London Borough of Lambeth; R (on the application of A)* v. *London Borough of Lambeth*[6] Lord Scott held that there is an undoubted duty imposed by section 20 of the 1989 Act on local authorities to provide accommodation for homeless children. Local authorities have also been given new powers to tackle homelessness under the Homelessness Act 2002. The Homelessness Act ensures that people who flee their homes because of any form of violence must be treated as homeless and cannot be referred back to their home if there would be a risk of violence there (section 10 Homelessness Act 2002). Under section 12 of the Homelessness Act 2002, housing authorities are required to refer homeless persons with dependent children who are ineligible for homelessness assistance or are intentionally homeless to social services. In such cases, if social services decide the child's needs would be best met by helping the family to obtain accommodation, they can ask the housing authority for reasonable assistance in this, and the housing authority must respond. Furthermore, section 116 of the Adoption and Children Act 2002 confirms that local authorities have power to provide accommodation for homeless families with children, and accommodation so provided does not make such children 'looked after'. Accordingly, the provision of appropriate accommodation can make an important contribution to meeting the developmental needs of children and consequently inhibit the factors investigated in Chapter 2, which influence young people's involvement in crime.

Assistance in kind and assistance in cash

Section 17(6) affirms that the services provided by a local authority in the exercise of its functions in relation to children in need 'may include giving assistance in kind, or in exceptional circumstances, in cash'. Assistance may be unconditional or subject to conditions as to the repayment of the assistance or its value, in whole or in part. The means of the child and his or her parents must be taken into account before assistance is given or its conditions imposed. Section 17(6) recognises that it is essential to assist families in a practical way if they are properly to care for their children. The power of a local authority to provide this sort of assistance has unquestionable value in the challenge of confronting juvenile crime.

Preventing children from committing crime

Increasing recognition of the potential role of local authorities in preventing delinquency and youth offending is reflected in Schedule 2 of the Children Act 1989, which requires local authorities to take reasonable steps to encourage children in their area not to commit criminal offences.[7] *Guidance* suggests that in addition to intermediate treatment for those at risk of offending, and the supervision of juvenile offenders, this might involve setting up advice and support services for parents, the provision of family support services, family centres, day care and accommodation, and ensuring that children in need gain maximum life benefits from educational opportunities, health care and social care, thereby leading to reduced rates of offending by such children (Department of Health 1991b). Hence, the Children Act recognises that the local authority's duty to assist children in need is directly connected to its responsibility for preventing youthful offending behaviour. Thus, the relevance of family support systems to delinquency and crime prevention is acknowledged.

Local authority duties are also informed and influenced by section 17(1) of the Crime and Disorder Act 1998, which provides that it shall be the duty of each authority to exercise its functions with due regard to the need to do all that it reasonably can to prevent crime and disorder in its area. The Crime and Disorder Act 1998 gives local authorities a number of new powers in relation to their duty to prevent young people from engaging in offending behaviour by enabling them to make targeted early interventions with young children at risk of offending. Such powers include the child safety order, the child curfew scheme and the anti-social behaviour order.

Child safety order

The local authority may apply for a child safety order under section 11 of the Crime and Disorder Act 1998. The child safety order is designed to protect children under 10 who are at risk of becoming involved in crime or who have already started to behave in an antisocial or criminal manner (Home Office 1997: 5.5). If a magistrates' court, upon the application of a local authority, is satisfied that one or more of the conditions, outlined below, are fulfilled with respect to a child under the age of 10, then it may make a child safety order (section 11(1) Crime and Disorder Act 1998). The conditions are that:

a the child has committed an act which, if he had been aged ten or over would constitute an offence;[8]

b a child safety order is necessary for the purpose of preventing the commission by the child of such an act as described in (a);

c the child has contravened a ban imposed by a curfew order;

d the child has acted in a manner that has caused, or was likely to cause harassment, alarm or distress to two or more persons not of the same household as himself.

It would appear from these conditions that the order can be made before any act of criminality has occurred (Hayes 1999; Rodgers and Sparrow 1999; Vaughan 2000).

A child safety order places the child under the supervision of the responsible officer (either a social worker from a local authority social services department or a member of a youth offending team) and requires the child to comply with such requirements as are specified in section 11 of Crime and Disorder Act 1998. Section 11 provides that the court may specify such requirements as are considered desirable in the interest of ensuring that the child receives appropriate care, protection and support, and is subject to proper control for the purpose of preventing any repetition of the kind of behaviour that led to the order being made in the first place. Failure to comply with the order will leave the way open for local authorities to commence care proceedings.[9] The standard of proof applicable to child safety order proceedings is that of civil proceedings (section 11(6) Crime and Disorder Act 1998). Hence, the order appears to act in a similar vein to a supervision order under section 31 of the Children Act 1989. However, the important difference between these two orders is that the maximum duration of the child safety order is three months, unless the circumstances necessitate an extension to a total of 12 months (section 11(3) Crime and Disorder Act 1998). By contrast, a supervision order will last for 12 months, with further extensions possible to a maximum of three years.

The child safety order is founded on the belief that early intervention is more effective than waiting until the child is old enough to be dealt with under the youth justice system (Hayes 1999: 318). Part of the thinking informing child safety orders is protective of children; responsible adults normally take the view that young children should not be out late at night and should not be involved in offending behaviour. Thus, the order supplements the existing welfare provisions available under the Children Act 1989 by providing an opportunity to intervene positively to protect the welfare of a child who appears to be at risk of becoming involved in crime (Home Office 2000). By the emphasis on the parental role within youth crime, whether it be from a point of lack of control or simply lack of interest, responsibility for crime is clearly being placed not just on the individual, but within the family unit. However, a consequence of the child safety order is that children under 10 who have committed, or might commit, offences will be penalised despite the fact that children under the age of 10 are below the age of criminal responsibility and accordingly are not considered to be capable of committing criminal offences. Thus, it appears somewhat anomalous that the child should be held accountable within the civil jurisdiction. It is also questionable whether punitive orders are the best means of controlling children under 10 and preventing them from offending or behaving disruptively. It may well be more productive to increase the resources and funding for family support services for children in need and their families.

Child curfew scheme

To enable the local authority to prevent crime by young people, section 14(1) of the Crime and Disorder Act 1998 allows a local authority to implement a child curfew scheme. Such a scheme creates a ban on all children under the age of 10 being in a public place within a specified area during specified hours otherwise than under the effective control of a responsible person aged 18 or over (section 14(2) Crime and Disorder Act 1998). Sections 48 and 49 of the Criminal Justice and Police Act 2001 raise the age limit of child curfew schemes to cover unsupervised children up to and including the age of 15. The 2001 Act also allows chief police officers, as well as local authorities, to apply for a child curfew scheme. Local child curfew schemes are designed with the dual aim of maintaining order and of protecting the local community from the alarm and distress caused by groups of young people involved in antisocial behaviour at night, and also to protect young children who, because they are on the streets unsupervised, may be at risk of harm or of engaging in offending behaviour (Bright 1998). Local authorities can impose these curfews on the basis that such children are at risk of engaging in offending behaviour. There is no criminal penalty for any child found in breach of the curfew order; it is designed solely to protect children and reduce the risk of their offending and behaving antisocially (Home Office 2001). Where a child is found in breach of a curfew, the local authority must be informed and must, as soon as practicable, investigate the reasons for the breach. This investigation may reveal a need for the support services examined in this chapter, or breach of the curfew may constitute sufficient grounds for the imposition of a child safety order. Because the order can be made even where children in the area concerned have committed no offence, it is arguable that this order penalises the normal behaviour of ordinary children who are hanging about on the streets (Gelsthorpe and Morris 1999: 215). This may be one of the reasons why local authorities have been reluctant to apply for curfew orders (House of Commons Research Paper 2001; Joint Committee on Human Rights 2003; Walsh 2002).

Anti-social behaviour order

Section 1(1) of the Crime and Disorder Act 1998 allows relevant authorities (namely the local authority or the police) to apply to the magistrates court for an anti-social behaviour order (ASBO) if it appears to the authority that the following conditions are fulfilled with respect to any person aged 10 or over, namely:

a that the person has acted in an antisocial manner, that is to say in a manner that caused, or was likely to cause harassment, alarm or distress to one or more persons not of the same household as himself; and b that such an order is necessary to protect persons in the local government area in which the harassment, alarm or distress was caused or was likely to be caused from further antisocial acts by him.

Acting in an antisocial manner is defined as acting in a manner that caused or was likely to cause alarm or distress, and includes behaviour that puts people in fear of crime (section 19(1)(a) Crime and Disorder Act 1998). The Solicitor-General expanded upon this definition by maintaining that the anti-social behaviour order is intended to deal with behaviour that is 'so intrusive as to make a real, unpleasant impact on neighbours and others affected' (quoted in Rutherford 1998: 14). An individual complainant cannot apply to a magistrate court for an anti-social behaviour order. If an individual considers that there is a need for an order, he or she will need to make a representation to the local authority or the police. If neither of these bodies decides to seek an anti-social behaviour order, the individual may seek to challenge the decision not to proceed by an application for judicial review.

An anti-social behaviour order prohibits the defendant from doing anything specified by the order. The order lasts for a period of not less than two years and can only prohibit conduct; it cannot specify positive acts to be done. Breach of the order is a criminal offence punishable by a fine and/or imprisonment for up to five years (section 10 Crime and Disorder Act 1998). In *R* v. *Manchester Crown Court, ex parte McCann & Ors*[10] the Court of Appeal held that proceedings to obtain an anti-social behaviour order were civil and not subject to the stricter criminal rules of evidence. This decision also stated that the standard of proof is flexible, to be applied with greater or lesser strictness according to the seriousness of what has to be proved. The court concluded that the categorisation of an application for an anti-social behaviour order as a civil matter did not create an infringement of the Human Rights Act 1998.

The Police Reform Act 2002 allows local authorities or the police to apply for an interim anti-social behaviour order to stop antisocial and offending behaviour at the earliest stage possible. Alternatively, young people engaging in, or at risk of engaging in, antisocial behaviour may be asked to sign an acceptable behaviour contract (ABC). An ABC is an individually written agreement by a young person with the police and a partner agency, such as the local authority, youth offending team or school, not to carry on with antisocial conduct such as harassment, creating graffiti, criminal damage and verbal abuse. Acceptable behaviour contracts are flexible in terms of content and format, and provide an effective means of encouraging children and parents to take responsibility for unacceptable behaviour. Anti-social behaviour orders and acceptable behaviour contracts are designed both to deter future antisocial behaviour and to prevent worsening of existing behaviour, without having to resort to criminal sanctions (Campbell 2002a, b; Collins 2001). These orders are import- ant tools for local authorities in their attempts to reduce crime and antiso- cial behaviour as they enable local authorities to intervene to prevent antisocial and offending behaviour by children aged 10 and above who are considered at risk of offending. The Criminal Justice Act 2003 introduced an innovative new Individual Support Order (ISO) (section 322 Criminal Justice Act 2003). This new order extends the protection that ASBOs provide to the community by requiring children and young people with ASBOs to undertake individually tailored activities, such as attending treatment for substance abuse. This will improve the effectiveness of an ASBO by engaging the child or young person in addressing the root causes of his or her actions and aiming to solve these problems.

While I have expressed reservations over the elements of compulsion in the Crime and Disorder Act 1998, nevertheless it has introduced a consid- erable range of initiatives intended to discourage juvenile antisocial and offending behaviour, together with a growing understanding of the para- meters and requirements of appropriate provision to meet the individual needs of parents and diversity of family life. All the orders contained in the 1998 Act aim to reinforce parental responsibility and prevent young chil- dren, including those under the age of 10, from slipping into criminal ways. What is significant about all these measures is that they do not depend upon what would have been a criminal offence being committed had the child been aged 10 years or over, It is sufficient that the local community deems the behaviour disruptive or that the child is judged to be at risk of committing a criminal offence.

Corporate duty to prevent youth crime

Local authorities have a corporate responsibility to address the needs of children and young people living in their area. The Local Government Act 2000 sets out a broad expectation that there should be a concerted aim to improve the social and economic well-being of people and communities (section 2 Local Government Act 2000). To achieve this, there should be effective joint working by education, social services, housing and leisure, in partnership with health, police and other statutory services and the independent sector. The Children Act 1989 provides local authorities with a statutory mandate to call upon other departments within local govern- ment, such as any other local authority, any local education authority, any local housing authority and any health authority, special health authority, primary care trust or NHS trust to assist them in their duties to provide services for children and to prevent youth crime (section 27 Children Act 1989). This important provision of the Children Act 1989 seeks to ensure that the various arms of the public service should cooperate with each other. Any authority whose help is requested must comply with the request, provided it is compatible with its own statutory or other duties and does not unduly prejudice the discharge of any of its functions (section 27(2) Children Act 1989). In *R* v. *Northavon District Council, ex p Smith*[11] the word 'compatible' was given a limited interpretation, where it was held that the request must be compatible only with the duties of the department to which the request is made. In this case the housing department's primary function was to provide housing, therefore a request for accommodation for a child in need and his or her family cannot be incompatible with those functions. This provision does not require a housing authority to provide accommodation in these circumstances, but does impose a duty to ascertain whether it could provide a solution to the problems of homeless families so as to prevent children suffering from lack of accommodation. In *Re F; F* v. *Lambeth London Borough Council*[12] Munby J held that a local authority would be acting unlawfully if it failed to ensure effective inter-agency cooperation in the manner envisaged by the Children Act. The Children Act 2004 reinforces the need for closer joint working and better information-sharing between the various agencies involved with children. The Children Act 2004 establishes a duty on local authorities to make arrangements to promote cooperation between agencies in order to improve children's welfare. The 2004 Act also creates a duty for the key agencies that work with children to put in place arrangements to make sure that they take account of the need to safeguard and promote the welfare of children when doing their jobs. The 2004 Act defines children's welfare as specifically including their physical and mental health and emotional well-being; protection from harm and neglect; education, training and recreation; the contribution made by them to society; and their social and economic well-being (section 10(2) Children Act 2004).

When attempting to implement strategic approaches for providing support and services to prospective young offenders, local authorities should request the assistance of local education authorities (LEAs). The Education Act 1996 requires local education authorities to contribute towards the spiritual, moral, mental and physical development of the community by ensuring that efficient primary, secondary and further education is available to meet the needs of the population in their area (section 13(1) Education Act 1996). Engaging young people in suitable education is fundamental to preventing them from offending in the future. Each local education authority is under a duty to make arrangements for the provision of education, at school or otherwise, for children of compulsory age who are not receiving suitable education (section 19(1) Education Act 1996). Young people may not be receiving suitable education for various reasons. For example, they may be excluded, habitual non-attenders, suffering illness or injury, pregnant, or young mothers unable to attend ordinary school. In such circumstances the LEA may arrange admission to another school or provide home tuition. Arrangements may also be made for such children to receive education at a 'pupil referral unit' (section

19(2) Education Act 1996). Pupil referral units should offer a balanced and broadly based curriculum and, while they are not obliged to follow the National Curriculum, they should endeavour to meet the educational needs of their pupils. Local education authorities also have overall legal responsibility for special educational provision in their area (section 315 Education Act 1996). A child has special education needs, for the purposes of the Education Act 1996, if he or she has a learning difficulty that calls for special educational provision to be made for him or her (section 312(1) Education Act 1996).[13] Special educational needs cover a wide spectrum of needs, including emotional and behavioural difficulties resulting from abuse or neglect, physical or mental illness, psychological trauma, depressive or suicidal attitudes, school phobia, substance abuse, antisocial and offending behaviour, theft or violence (Department for Education and Employment 1996: 3.65, 3.66). Clearly, local education authorities have a pivotal role to play in preventing juvenile antisocial and offending behaviour.

Health authorities, primary care groups and NHS trusts also have an important contribution to make to helping local authorities prevent youth offending. Children and adolescent mental health services (CAMHS) provide a range of psychiatric and psychological assessment and treatment services for children and families. Local authorities may require specialist mental health services to become involved because of possible psychotic illness (for example, schizophrenia), suicide or risk of self-harm, hyperkinetic disorder, attention deficit disorder or any of the other mental health issues identified in Chapter 2 that are predictive of youth offending. A referral may also be made to specialist child mental health professionals for an assessment of family factors that are contributing to the child's disorder and to ascertaining the therapeutic needs of the child and family. Psychologists who work with children and their families are well placed to offer a range of services to support children in need and their families. In particular, educational psychologists working with children and schools to promote the child's social, emotional and intellectual development will have an important contribution to make. Educational welfare officers and educational psychologists will also be well placed to give a view on the impact on the child's behaviour of different types of treatment and intervention.

The principle of inter-agency cooperation is also reaffirmed in section 37 of the Crime and Disorder Act 1998, which places all those carrying out functions in relation to the youth justice system under a statutory duty to have regard to the new principal aim of preventing offending by children and young people.[14] Paragraph 4 of the 'framework document' for the Crime and Disorder Act 1998 explains the incorporation into statute of this aim. It argues that the youth justice system has for 'too long been seen to be separate from wider youth crime prevention work' and that the new statutory aim makes clear the 'important link that there should be between the work of the youth justice system and wider work to help prevent children and young people offending' (Home Office 1998). The Crime and Disorder Act places a statutory duty on all local authorities, police forces, police authorities, health authorities and local probation committees to work together in combating problems of crime and disorder in their locality (section 5 Crime and Disorder Act 1998), to ensure that, to such extent as is appropriate for their area, all youth justice services are available there (section 38 Crime and Disorder Act 1998), and to ensure that a youth offending team is in place (section 40 Crime and Disorder Act 1998). The youth offending team (YOT) comprises representatives from the police, probation, education and health authorities and the local authority, thus guaranteeing that teams of trained professionals with specific disciplines work together to tackle youth offending. The YOT works with young people aged 10–17 who are offending or at risk of offending, as well as those under 10 in order to prevent offending. The YOT has primary responsibility for coordinating youth justice services across a geographical area, providing a multi-agency service for children and young people at risk of offending, or who are involved in offending behaviour, and carrying out such functions as are assigned to them in the Youth Justice Plan formulated by the local authority (section 41 Crime and Disorder Act 1998). The YOTs aim to deliver a wide range of programmes that tackle offending behaviour at the different stages of its development. YOTs have taken the lead in creating schemes to provide purposeful and engaging activities for young people at risk of offending. Examples of such schemes will now be evaluated.

Youth Inclusion Programme

The Youth Inclusion Programme (YIP) works with young people who are most at risk of offending, because of either poor family support, lack of schooling or low self-esteem. YIPs put in place a structured and supervised environment to provide an alternative activity for young people who might otherwise become involved in crime. The programme is being implemented in some of the most deprived neighbourhoods in the United Kingdom. The Youth Inclusion Programme is expected to target its work on the 50 most 'at risk' young people aged 13–16 in these neighbourhoods. This group of young people are identified through a multi-agency consultation process, drawing on input from the youth offending team, police, local authority social services, education or schools, other local agencies and the community. While projects are intended to target the most 'at risk' young people in each area, they are also required to serve all young people in their neighbourhood. Indeed, the inclusive nature of project activities is central to their success in enrolling 'difficult to reach' young people. Participation is therefore voluntary, and any teenager who wants to can join, as the aim is to provide somewhere safe for young people to go where they learn new skills, take part in sporting or other activities, and benefit from educational support. The intention is to benefit all members of the local community who are available to participate in the activities. The rationale for doing so is that a fair and just society will not allow its young people to be marginalised, but will strive to include them so that they may enjoy opportunities and life chances similar to those available to other young people in society.

The YIPs cover a broad range of preventive measures, including after-school activities; teaching basic skills; life/social skills development such as drug and sex education and activities designed to teach relationship skills; youth work; mentoring; environmental work; and recreation. Team sports, debating society and creative classes aim to teach young people the value of working together, listening, cooperating with others and building self-esteem. Spending time with the positive role models of workers and volunteer mentors can help change young people's attitude to crime. Some Youth Inclusion Programmes provide a more innovative comprehensive source of help; for example, the Wyrley Birch Youth Inclusion Programme in Birmingham has set up a parenting group to provide full family support. These schemes seek to equip young people with the attitude and skills to develop a constructive lifestyle and resist the temptations of criminality; the aim of the project is to ensure that the most at risk young people are included in mainstream activities, by offering support to help them overcome a variety of social problems.

Splash schemes/Positive Activities for Young People

School holidays are traditionally considered a prime time for young people to become involved in antisocial or criminal behaviour. The absence of a structured day and, in many cases, the absence of a responsible adult to supervise their activities results in an increase in youth offending. The purpose of the Splash scheme is to reduce this offending in high-crime areas by engaging 13- to 17-year-olds in constructive activities during the daytime when they might otherwise be unoccupied and thus at risk of engaging in offending behaviour. Each Splash scheme provides five weeks of activity, engaging at least 100 young people, including a core group of 13- to 17-year-olds most at risk of offending. A multifaceted referral process is adopted through which formal referrals are sought from a number of agencies, including schools, youth offending teams, police, housing departments and local authority social service departments. Otherwise, referrals are on a broad self-referral neighbourhood basis. Activities range from reading and writing skills to sport, art, dance, computer skills, life skills, vocational skills as well as having talks on the realities of prison, health, substance misuse and sex education. Using this approach, the programmes aim to assist young people and their families to minimise the causal factors associated with involvement in juvenile crime and antisocial behaviour. Splash schemes have now been replaced by Positive Activities for Young People (PAYP). PAYP provides a broad range of constructive activities for young people at risk of social exclusion.

Mentoring programmes

Many young offenders lack a stable adult presence in their lives, someone who is prepared to provide them with the advice and support they need as they face the challenges of growing up. This could be due to the types of family problems examined in Chapter 2. By training adults to form relationships with young people who are at risk of offending or those who have offended, and supporting them in maintaining those relationships, YOTs can provide a healthy role model, sometimes for the first time in a young person's life. Such mentors can show young people that there are alternatives to offending. Mentors are expected to offer advice on key areas of the young person's life such as family issues, education and training. In 2001 the Youth Justice Board launched two more specialised mentoring projects:

- Mentoring Plus schemes offer more intensive mentoring for hard-to-reach and ethnic minority young people. Mentoring Plus schemes are more intensive, with mentors supporting and guiding young people back into education, training or employment. Most offer a residential experience, education and/or training opportunities and help with constructive use of leisure.
- Mentoring help with literacy and numeracy. Many young offenders (and those at risk of offending) have such poor basic skills that they are excluded from most employment opportunities. Many have had very negative experiences of education. This scheme aims to guide young people towards improved literacy and numeracy.

Parenting programmes

Parenting orders are an initiative, introduced in the Crime and Disorder Act 1998, that involve the court ordering parents of children convicted of an offence to go on corrective courses to learn to keep their children out of trouble, exert control and authority over their children (including operating curfews where appropriate) and ensure their school attendance. The parenting courses cover experiences of parenting, communication and negotiation skills, parenting styles and the importance of consistency, praise and rewards. The aim of the order is to support and encourage parents to address the child's antisocial and offending behaviour and to prevent offending. The court may impose a parenting order in the following circumstances: where a child safety order has been made in respect of a child; where an anti-social behaviour order, or sex offender order, is made on a child or young person; or where a person is convicted of an offence under section 443 (failure to comply with a school attendance order) or section 444 (failure to secure regular attendance at school of a registered pupil) of the Education Act 1996 (section 8(1) Crime and Disorder Act 1998). The relevant condition that has to be satisfied is that the parenting order would have to be desirable in the interests of preventing any repetition of the kind of behaviour that led to the order being made and the prevention of further offending by the child or young person. Should a parent fail to comply with the requirements of the order, he or she may be returned to court and will be liable on summary conviction to a fine not exceeding £1,000. Section 26(6) of the Anti-social Behaviour Act 2003 allows for a residential requirement to be attached to parenting orders. In the White Paper *Respect and Responsibility* (Home Office 2003a) the government expressed its belief that such a residential option would help parents experiencing problems to improve their parenting. In order to prevent juvenile offending behaviour from becoming entrenched, the 2003 Act gives YOTs powers to apply to the courts for parenting orders where the parent is not taking active steps to prevent the child's antisocial or criminal-type behaviour, and it is clear that this behaviour will continue. Local education authorities are also able to seek a parenting order where a child has been excluded from school for serious misbehaviour.

Developing the skills of parents to deal with the difficult and challenging behaviour of their children can be vital in restoring family relationships and providing the structure and support that a young person requires to change their behaviour and desist from engaging in offending behaviour. While the supportive aspects of the parenting order are attractive, it is surely questionable that using compulsion and the threat of fines and imprisonment will change the behaviour of parents (Arthur 2002, 2005a; Gelsthorpe and Morris 1999; Henricson *et al.* 2000). However, the parenting courses have proved so popular that some YOTs are offering them on a voluntary basis; in fact, about 60 per cent of participants are voluntary rather than on orders (Youth Justice Board 2002a). Parenting orders may therefore be appropriate for parents of young people who are engaged in offending behaviour or are at risk of offending. These orders enshrine in law the principle that young people's behaviour can be influenced by the kind of parenting they receive.

Youth offending teams are capable of acting speedily and effectively to prevent young people from offending by providing help with their physical and mental well-being and any family problems they are experiencing. The United Nations Committee on the Rights of the Child (2002: 59) welcomed the creation of these multidisciplinary teams to respond to juvenile offending behaviour. Youth offending teams offer a large selection of youth crime prevention programmes, which could prove to be a valuable and effective resource in helping local authorities to exercise their youth crime prevention functions.

Provision of family support services by other organisations

Not only do local authorities need to collaborate internally to fulfil their youth crime prevention duties, but external collaborations are also essential. Local authorities are required to facilitate the provision of family services by others, in particular voluntary organisations, and may make such arrangements as they see fit for others to provide such services (section 17(5) Children Act 1989). This is an extremely valuable power that could help to minimise damaging family factors and thus prevent children engaging in offending behaviour.

For example, in 1999 the Home Office set up a three-year programme called On Track, which is a £30 million project operating in approximately 25 deprived high-crime areas throughout the United Kingdom. On Track (now part of the Children's Fund) is a crime reduction programme aimed at children at risk of becoming involved in crime. The central aim of the programme is to identify those children aged between 4 and 12 who are at risk of developing patterns of antisocial or criminal behaviour and prevent them from doing so by providing them with a series of coordinated, multiple interventions to address their needs. Through the Family Support Grants, money is provided for projects that develop an enhanced range of evidence-based preventive services for children and their families. The core services include home visiting, structured pre-school education, parent training, home–school partnerships and family therapy.

Another noteworthy example is the Sure Start programme. Sure Start is an area based programme providing universal services for children under 4 and their families in some of the most disadvantaged communities. Sure Start provides an opportunity for early support and intervention and aims to ensure that health, education and social services are actively engaged in supporting the most vulnerable pre-school children. As early intervention is deemed to be the key to crime reduction, parents and schools are explicitly targeted in order to help prevent family break-up and tackle truancy and school exclusions.

Other notable examples of family-based youth crime prevention interventions include Home Start, NEWPIN and Connexions, to name but a few. Such programmes are primarily community-based preventive activities designed to alleviate stress and promote parental competency and behaviour that will increase the ability of families to successfully nurture their children; enable families to use other resources, especially informal support services and opportunities available in the community; and create social networks to enhance child-rearing skills. These types of interventions aim to ameliorate the damaging family conditions, examined throughout Chapter 2, that induce young people into engaging in offending behaviour.

Local authorities are required to publish information about the services they provide under the general duty (section 17 Children Act 1989), day care services (section 18 Children Act 1989), accommodation for children (section 20 Children Act 1989) and the availability of advice and assistance for certain children (section 24 Children Act 1989). Where they consider it appropriate they must publish information about similar services provided by others. They must also take such steps as are reasonably practicable to ensure that those who might benefit from the services receive the information relevant to them (schedule 2(1)(2) Children Act 1989). Additionally, the Children Act 1989 requires each local authority to prepare and publish a Children's Services Plan, which should bring together all aspects of local services for children (schedule 2(1)(A) Children Act 1989). The Children's Services Plan should look widely at the needs of local children and the ways in which local services, including statutory and voluntary services, should work together to meet those needs (Department of Health *et al.* 1999: 4.7). Other services should work in partnership with local authorities to produce Children's Services Plans, especially the health service and the youth justice service. Children's Services Plans should provide a local vehicle for determining how the contributions of all the relevant agencies fit together and support each other in delivering shared objectives for children in the local area (Department of Health 2000a: 6.9).

Compulsory state intervention

Although a wide range of assistance, guidance and help can be provided to children and their parents on a voluntary basis, it must be accepted that in some cases compulsion will be necessary to protect children and dissuade them from becoming involved in crime. For some children, a compulsory civil disposal may be appropriate where the child's offending is a symptom of wider family difficulties. This means early diversion of the child into the civil part of the system before the child becomes entangled in the criminal justice system (Department of Health 1991a: 6.46). The next section will investigate the range of compulsory orders available to the local authority and examine how these could be used to impact positively upon children's offending behaviour.

Care order

The care order is the most important order that a court may make in terms of the effect it has on the child, the child's parents, or persons acting *in loco parentis*, and indeed the local authority. A care order places a positive duty on the local authority, through the acquisition of parental responsibility, to ensure the welfare of the child and protect the child from inadequate parenting. Once the local authority has parental responsibility for the child, it can exercise almost all the rights, duties, powers and responsibilities that by law a parent has in relation to the child (section 33(3) Children Act 1989). This is not inconsistent with seeking to work in partnership with parents, since section 23 of the 1989 Act envisaged that the local authority could place a child with the child's parents under a care order. In fact, in 2000 11 per cent of children on care orders were placed with their parents, compared with 9.1 per cent for the year ending 1996 (Statistical Bulletin 2001).

Although, technically speaking, parental responsibility is not taken away from the parents when a care order is made, decision-making powers in relation to the child are firmly vested in the local authority. In fact, it is the local authority that has the power to determine the extent to which the child's parents may meet their own parental responsibility for the child (section 33(3)(b) Children Act 1989). However, section 33(4) directs that the local authority should not limit the extent to which the parents exercise their parental responsibility for the child unless satisfied that it is necessary to do so in order to safeguard or promote the child's welfare. The parental responsibility acquired by a local authority has some specific limitations. The authority must consult with the parents when making plans for the child, but it may override the parents' wishes (section 22(4) Children Act 1989). The local authority is not allowed to cause the child to be brought up in any religious persuasion other than that in which the child would have been brought up had no order had been made. It does not have the right to consent, or refuse to consent, to the making of an application for a freeing for adoption order, or to agree or refuse to agree to an adoption order or a proposed foreign adoption order. A local authority may not appoint a guardian (section 33(6) Children Act 1989). A care order lasts until the child is 18 unless it is brought to an end by a residence order (section 91(1) Children Act 1989) or by its discharge (section 39 Children Act 1989).

Availability of effective interventions for abusive families is a vital component of youth crime prevention services. The potential of the care order to protect children from damaged families is obvious, as care proceedings can be used to provide a legally protected space within which to assess and, if possible, work towards a resolution of family difficulties, or to demonstrate that this was not possible (Hunt 1998: 283). Although removing a young person from home is not a step to be undertaken lightly, where there are factors associated with the environment in which that person lives that are leading to, or encouraging, offending, it may be in the young person's best interests to move him or her away from this influence for a period of time. In an unsatisfactory home life the child may need the experience of foster or residential care in order to provide proper care and control. The introduction of a positive role model in a young person's life, such as a foster carer, is an important tool in changing troublesome and antisocial behaviour.

Supervision order

Section 31 provides for the making of a supervision order as an alternative to a care order. A supervision order is a form of compulsory intervention, although less draconian in its effect than a care order. A supervision order enables a local authority to arrange periodic visits to the child to ensure the child is being properly cared for and also to allow the local authority the opportunity to give any necessary advice regarding the care of the child. In this way the welfare of the child can be assessed and safeguarded with the making of directions if necessary, without the need to remove the child from his or her domestic surroundings. The Court of Appeal has emphasised the important difference between a supervision order and a care order. The former was to help and assist a child, leaving full responsibility with the parents,[15] whereas the latter places a positive duty on the local authority to promote the child's welfare and to protect the child from inadequate parenting.[16]

In *Re W (A Minor) (Interim Care Order)*[17] the court indicated that wherever possible a supervision order should be made rather than a care order; it is only if the supervision order appears unlikely to obviate the risk that the court should make a care order. Holmes J stated in *Re B (Care or Supervision Order)*[18] that 'a care order ... should only be made if the stronger order is necessary for the proper protection of the child'. Tyrer J concurred in *Re D (Care or Supervision Order)*,[19] and held that if the balance between a care order and a supervision order is equal, the court should adopt the least interventionist approach. He recommended that courts should not saddle local authorities with care orders, given that they have so many demands on their resources, if it is not really necessary to do so.[20] One of the advantages of the supervision order is that it is deemed to be 'less heavy handed'.[21] Indeed, Coningsby J recognised that a care order can scare a parent,[22] and that where cooperation between the local authority and parents has proved useful, then a supervision order will be preferable.[23] The care order is needed in cases where the risk to the child is grave, where intensive monitoring of the child is needed, where responsibility for safeguarding the child should be entrusted to the local authority and where the local authority needs to have parental responsibility so that it can remove a child from home without the need to go back to court.[24] A court may prefer a care order when it is afraid that the parents will not cooperate with the local authority without such an order, or where there is hostility towards the local authority.[25]

A supervision order may involve the supervised child complying with any directions given from time to time by the supervisor, normally the local authority (schedule 3(2(1)) Children Act 1989), which require the child to:

a live at a place, or places, specified in the directions for a specified period or periods
b present himself to a specified person at a place and on a day specified
c) participate in specified activities, such as education or training.

A supervision order may also require the supervised child to:

    a submit to a medical psychiatric examination
    b submit to such an examination from time to time as directed by the supervisor
    c submit to specified treatment in relation to his mental or physical condition.

The child may only be required to comply with such directions for a maximum total of 90 days (schedule 3(7) Children Act 1989). These provisions enable the local authority to require the child to participate in 'intermediate treatment' programmes that could involve residence away from home for up to 90 days. For example, local authorities have on occasion required as a condition of a supervision order that the child reside with a particular person, for example a grandparent. There is no necessity that the 90 days on which the child may be required to comply with the local authority's directions be a single period, and indeed that will rarely be the case (Bridge *et al.* 1990: 37). Such matters will be within the discretion of the supervisor (schedule 3(2(2)) Children Act 1989). The supervisor does not acquire parental responsibility for the child; the supervisor's main duty is to advise, assist and befriend the child concerned and to take such steps as are reasonably necessary to give effect to the order (section 35(1) Children Act 1989).

Obligations can also be imposed on a 'responsible person' as well as the child (schedule 3 Children Act 1989). A 'responsible person' in relation to a supervised child means any person with parental responsibility for the child and any other person with whom the child is living (schedule 3(1) Children Act 1989). With the consent of any responsible person, a supervision order may include a requirement that the 'responsible person' take all reasonable steps to ensure that the child complies with the supervisor's directions and to ensure that the child complies with any requirements contained in the supervision order concerning psychiatric and medical examinations or treatment (schedule 3(3) Children Act 1989). The responsible person may also be required to comply with any directions given by the supervisor for him or her to attend at a specified place to take part in specified activities either with or without the child (schedule 3(1)(c)(2) Children Act 1989). A supervisor could, for example, require a parent to attend classes in practical child care, or to bring the child to a family centre or to attend a therapeutic counselling group (Feldman 1992; Feldman and Mitchels 1990).

Supervision orders and care orders are powerful and valuable orders that have the potential to positively affect the child's experiences within the family and to reduce the child's propensity towards criminal behaviour. Hale J in *Oxfordshire CC* v. *L (Care or Supervision Order)*[26] stressed that the power to make a care or supervision order exists in the context of a statutory background that emphasises the preventive duties of the local authority. The Children Act was carefully structured to give effect to the policy that such intervention could not be justified simply on the basis that a court considered the state to be better able than the birth family to care for the child. Section 31 empowers the court to make a care, or supervision, order in respect of a child under 17 (or 16 if married) only if it is satisfied that certain threshold criteria are fulfilled.[27] Chapter 4 will illustrate that potential young offenders, as identified in Chapter 2, fulfil these threshold criteria and consequently that the making of a care or supervision order represents an appropriate means of preventing delinquency and youthful criminal activity.

Emergency and interim orders

In many cases there will be no necessity to take immediate action to remove the child from home. Conversely, there will be cases of extreme urgency where there is a risk to the life of a child or likelihood of serious injury, when immediate protection is required. There may be concerns about a child that are difficult to substantiate without access, which is being denied. In this regard there are a number of options available to the local authority, which I will now consider.

Emergency protection order

An emergency protection order authorises either the removal to, or prevention of removal from, accommodation provided by, or on behalf of, the applicant (section 44(4)(b) Children Act 1989). In the former instance the order operates as a direction to any person who is in a position to do so to comply with any request to produce the child to the applicant (section 44(4)(a) Children Act 1989). The court may also authorise an applicant to enter specified premises and search for a child, and may include another child in the order if it believes there might be another child on the premises (section 48(3) and (4) Children Act 1989). This does not give the power to make a forced entry. If the applicant is refused or likely to be refused entry, the court may issue a warrant authorising a police constable to assist in the execution of the order using reasonable force if necessary (section 48(9) Children Act 1989). The second circumstance is where the child is not living in a dangerous situation, but the applicant considers that an attempt may be made to remove the child to a situation where he or she may be at risk. This provision will be frequently used to retain children who are being accommodated on a voluntary basis by the local authority and whose return home is viewed with justifiable concern. Although commonly the applicant will be the local authority or NSPCC, any person may apply under this provision, including even a parent or relative. In such cases the local authority will also have to become involved, because under section 47(1) it has a duty to investigate upon being informed of the existence of such an order. When the applicant is a local authority the separate and additional ground that can be relied upon is that the court may make an emergency protection order if the local authority is making inquiries under section 47(1)(b) and those inquiries are being frustrated by access to the child being unreasonably refused and the local authority believes that access to the child is required as a matter of urgency (section 44(1)(b) Children Act 1989).

Section 44(4)(a) requires the local authority to raise the anxiety level of the court to the point where the court has reasonable cause to believe that the child is likely to suffer significant harm unless an emergency protection order is made. The test is prospective, so that evidence of past or even current harm is not sufficient unless it indicates that harm is likely to recur in the future (Bridge *et al.* 1990: 6.3.3). On the other hand, this prospective test can be satisfied even though the harm to the particular child has not yet occurred. The local authority must further persuade the court that there is a causative link between the harm being likely to occur and the child being removed from, or remaining in, his or her present accommodation. Once the emergency protection order is made it gives the applicant parental responsibility for the child (section 44(4)(c) Children Act 1989). However, the authority's parental responsibility is circumscribed by the duration of the order (eight days) and by section 44(13), which requires the authority to allow the child to have reasonable contact with his or her parents.

Section 44(1) is intended as an immediate short-term protection in genuine emergencies or in emergencies where inquiries cannot be completed because the child cannot be seen but there is enough cause to suspect the child is suffering, or is likely to suffer, significant harm. Such emergency interventions have enormous potential in reducing the likelihood of significant harm to the young person, who might otherwise demonstrate offending behaviour. In cases where there is a need for further investigation of a child's health and development but the child is thought to be safe from immediate danger, the proper order is a child assessment order.

Child assessment order

A child assessment order has the multiple effect of placing a duty on any person who is in a position to do so to produce a child to the person named in the order, to comply with such directions relating to the assessment as may be specified in the order (section 43(6) Children Act 1989) and of authorising any person carrying out the assessment, or any part of it, to do so in accordance with the order (section 43(7) Children Act 1989). The Children Act 1989 does not specify what kind of assessment may be involved with the child assessment order, so it could be assumed that assessment means anything that the court decides is assessment

(Mitchell 1991: 57). However, because the standard of proof that must be satisfied is one of reasonable suspicion, and because the order only gives the local authority a maximum of seven days in which to discover whether there is any real foundation to its suspicion, the type of intervention allowed is strictly limited.

As with applications for care and supervision orders, only the local authority and the NSPCC may apply for a child assessment order (section 31(9) and section 41(3) Children Act 1989). Under section 43(1) the court may make a child assessment order if it is satisfied that:

a the applicant has reasonable cause to suspect that the child is suffering or is likely to suffer significant harm
b an assessment of the state of the child's health or development, or of the way in which he has been treated is required to enable the applicant to determine whether or not the child is suffering, or is likely to suffer, significant harm, and
c it is unlikely that such an assessment will be made, or be satisfactory, in the absence of a child assessment order.

It must be emphasised that child assessment orders are not intended to be used in an emergency, or as a substitute for an emergency protection order. However, the court is empowered to treat an application for an assessment order as an application for an emergency protection order (section 43(3) Children Act 1989). Indeed, section 43(4) specifically enjoins the court not to make an assessment order if there are grounds for making an emergency protection order and the court thinks it ought to make such an order instead. However, the court has no power to make a child assessment order on an application for an emergency protection order. The fact that all parties have been given adequate notice and an opportunity to attend and be heard (section 43(11) Children Act 1989) further emphasises that child assessment orders are not designed to deal with emergencies.

Interim orders

Despite the statutory presumption that any delay in proceedings is likely to prejudice the welfare of the child concerned (section 1(2) Children Act 1989), there will be occasions when an adjournment of care proceedings is unavoidable. For example, the parties may need time in which to prepare their cases properly, or the guardian *ad litem* (guardian in law) may need time in which to investigate and report on the child's circumstances. It is important that in appropriate cases the court can control the case by way of interim orders until all the relevant material is before the court to enable it to make a final order. Section 37(1) provides for the making of an interim care order on the application of a local authority. The threshold criteria for care proceedings are applied, but the court has only to be satisfied that there are reasonable grounds for believing in, rather than be satisfied as to, their existence. An initial interim care or interim supervision order may be made for such period as the court orders but may not last longer than eight weeks; such orders may subsequently be renewed for a maximum of four weeks. It was established in *Gateshead Metropolitan Borough Council* v. *N*[28] that there is no limit in principle to the number of times an interim order may be renewed.

The legal consequences of an interim care order are identical to those of a full care order, except for the limited duration factor. The important and crucial effect of an interim care order is to vest parental responsibility in the local authority, with the result that it is in a position to exercise parental powers in relation to the child, subject to specified limitations. One of the key differences between a full care order and an interim order is that with the interim order the court may give directions as to the medical or psychiatric examination, or other assessment, of the child (section 38(6) Children Act 1989). In *Re C (A Minor) (Interim Care Order: Residential Assessment)*,[29] Lord Browne-Wilkinson held that this provision of the Children Act should be broadly construed to cover any assessment that involves the participation of the child. Therefore, the court could order a residential assessment of the child, or a joint residential assessment of the child and the parents together, and direct the local authority to fund any necessary placement (section 38(6) Children Act 1989). The court also has the power to incorporate exclusion requirements in an interim care order (section 38A Children Act 1989). This allows the court to make short-term ouster orders. It has long been recognised that in a situation which is actually or potentially abusive to a child, an outcome that may be less damaging to the child is for the abuser to leave the child's home, as opposed to the child's being removed. Interim orders may thus be used because of the flexibility which they give to the court.

These emergency and interim orders allow local authorities to intervene in damaged families, assess children and potentially discourage them from committing crime. These orders could therefore have a credible role to play in fulfilling the local authority's responsibility to prevent young people from offending.

Education supervision order and school attendance order

Chapter 2 documented the correlation between juvenile offending behaviour and school non-attendance, therefore reducing school exclusions, truancy and all forms of school non-attendance could have a very significant impact on preventing youth crime. The Children Act 1989 legislates against truancy by reinforcing parental responsibility to ensure school attendance. The 1989 Act empowers local education authorities to apply for an education supervision order where a child of compulsory school age is not receiving efficient full-time education suitable to the child's age, ability and aptitude and any special educational needs he or she may have (section 36 Children Act 1989). An education supervision order places the child under the supervision of the local education authority supervisor (education social worker or social worker), who must advise, assist and befriend the child and offer directions and support to the child and parents in order to ensure that the child is properly educated. The child will be required to attend school regularly, meet with the supervisor on a regular basis and discuss with the supervisor any problems that may be preventing attendance at school (schedule 3(12) Children Act 1989). If the child does not cooperate with the supervisor, the child will be referred back to the court, which could direct the local authority social services department to consider applying for a supervision or care order (schedule 3(19) Children Act 1989). Also, before instituting proceedings for an education supervision order, local education authorities are required to consult with local authority social services departments (section 36(8)(9) Children Act 1989). The local authority may decide that it would be more appropriate to provide some of the family support services considered earlier in the chapter, to apply for compulsory admission of the child to care or to apply for an ordinary supervision order. Although the child's parents will retain parental responsibility throughout the period of the education supervision order, they must ensure that their child attends school regularly, allow the supervisor reasonable contact with the child and meet with the supervisor on a regular basis. Failure to comply could result in the parents being referred to court, where they may be subject to a fine of £1,000. The education supervision order lasts for up to one year initially but may be extended for up to three years.

The aim of the education supervision order is to provide an effective means of guiding parents and children to ensure that all children receive a satisfactory education. Education supervision orders are most effective where a child has developed a pattern of poor attendance at school and the parents find it difficult to exercise proper influence over their child (Department of Health 1991d: 3.9). However, an education supervision order will not be effective if the parents are likely to be actively hostile to such intervention. In such situations a school attendance order or prosecution for irregular attendance under section 444 of the Education Act 1996 may be more appropriate.

If it appears to a local education authority that a child of compulsory school age is not receiving suitable education, the authority must serve a 'school attendance order' on the parent requiring the parent to cause the child to become a registered pupil at a school, or pupil referral unit, named in the order (section 437(3) Education Act 1996). The school attendance order will remain in force unless the parent convinces the authority that arrangements have been made to provide the child with suitable education at school or otherwise (section 442(2) Education Act 1996). Failure by a parent to comply with a school attendance order is an offence under section 443 of the 1996 Act (section 443 Education Act 1996). In section 443 proceedings the court may make a parenting order in respect of such a parent if the court believes that a parenting order will prevent further harm to the child, including preventing the child from becoming involved in offending behaviour. The court may also direct the local education authority to apply for an education supervision order (section 445(2) Education Act 1996). The local education authority is not bound to comply with such a request from the court if it decides that the child's welfare can be satisfactorily safeguarded without the making of an education supervision order (section 445(2) Education Act 1996). For example, the local authority may be able to provide family support services which render court proceedings unnecessary.

School attendance orders are effective only where a child is not registered at school. Where a child is a registered pupil and is failing to attend regularly, local education authorities should consider prosecuting under section 444 of the Education Act 1996. On conviction, the offence carries a fine up to a maximum of £1,000 for each absent child.[30] Although this offence is one of strict liability,[31] there are defences: for example, where the pupil was absent with leave agreed by school staff; or the pupil was ill or prevented from attending by some unavoidable cause; or the absence was on a day exclusively set aside for religious observance by the religious body to which the parent belongs; or the school is not within walking distance of the child's home[32] and the LEA has not made suitable arrangements for the child's transport to and from school, boarding accommodation at or near the school or enabling the child to attend a school nearer his or her home. Before instituting proceedings for an offence under either section 443 or 444 of the Education Act 1996 the local education authority is obliged to consider whether it would be more appropriate to apply for an education supervision order with respect to the child (section 443 Education Act 1996).

Section 19 of the Anti-social Behaviour Act 2003 gives local education authorities and schools powers to ask parents whose children do not attend school regularly or who have been excluded for serious misbehaviour to sign parenting contracts. Signing the contract will require parents to cooperate with support provided or arranged by the LEA or the school (such as parenting classes) and to take specified action to improve their child's attendance or behaviour. Where a child has been excluded for serious misbehaviour, LEAs will be able to apply for a parenting order if they consider that a parenting contract is not likely to be effective (section 20 Anti-social Behaviour Act 2003).

The education supervision order, school attendance order, section 444 of the Education Act 1996 and the powers created by the Anti-social Behaviour Act 2003 offer a potentially effective and enduring strategy for combating school non-attendance and associated behavioural problems such as juvenile antisocial and offending behaviour.

Children in care

For children who have been in local authority care, there is a remarkable body of pessimistic evidence to suggest that they are highly susceptible to being involved in delinquent and criminal activity.[33] The Children Act 1989 requires local authorities to act towards children in their care as any well-meaning natural parents would towards their offspring. If local authorities are to play a role in the long-term prevention of crime by young people, it is essential to examine their powers and duties towards children in their care, and investigate how they can intervene positively in such young people's lives and dissuade them from becoming involved in crime.

Children who are in the care of a local authority, or who are provided with accommodation[34] pursuant to any of the functions of a local authority, are 'looked after' by the authority.[35] In relation to such a child the authority has a number of primary duties. It is the duty of a local authority looking after any child to safeguard and promote the child's welfare and to make available such use of services as appears to the authority reasonable in the case of that particular child (section 22(3)(a) and (b) Children Act 1989). The local authority must ascertain as far as practicable the wishes and feelings of the child, the child's parents, any other person who has parental responsibility and any other person the authority considers to be relevant, before making any decision with respect to the child (section 22(4) Children Act 1989). Where an authority is 'looking after' a child it must provide him or her with accommodation while the child is in their care and must maintain him or her (section 23(1) Children Act 1989). In carrying out this duty the authority may place the child with a family member or relative, or any other suitable person, on such terms as to payment or otherwise as the authority determines (section 23(3) Children Act 1989). Placement may also be made in a community home, a voluntary home or a registered children's home, or by such other arrangements as seem appropriate to the authority (section 23(2) Children Act 1989). Section 59 of the Children Act 1989 requires voluntary organisations and children's homes to treat children accommodated there in the same way as a local authority would treat children whom it was looking after.

Where a child is being looked after by a local authority, the authority is required, unless it is not reasonably practicable or consistent with the child's welfare to promote contact between the child and the child's family, and must ensure that the family is kept informed of where the child is being accommodated (schedule 2(15) and sections 17(1) and 23(6) Children Act 1989). In keeping with this duty, the authority must ensure that the accommodation is near to the child's home and that siblings are accommodated together. Expenses may be paid for visits to or by children. If the child is neither living with his or her family nor being looked after by the local authority, such steps as are reasonably practicable should be taken to enable the child to live with his or her family or to promote contact between the child and his or her family, if in the authority's opinion it is necessary to do so (schedule 2(10) Children Act 1989). The authority is not required to disclose the whereabouts of the child if it has reasonable cause to believe that disclosure would prejudice the child's welfare. The authority has the right to exercise all its powers in a way that is inconsistent with these duties for the purpose of protecting members of the public from serious injury, and the Secretary of State may give directions to an authority in this respect (sections 22(6)–(8) Children Act 1989). These duties empower the local authority to promote the welfare of children in its care and to tackle some of the problems identified in Chapter 2 as being predictive of juvenile offending.

The local authority has the power under section 25 of the Children Act 1989 to keep a child whom it is looking after in secure accommodation if the child has a history of absconding and is likely to do so and suffer significant harm, or if the child would be likely to injure him- or herself or other people if kept in any other type of accommodation. Secure accommodation is defined by section 25 of the 1989 Act as 'accommodation provided for the purpose of restricting liberty'. Secure accommodation orders under the Children Act 1989 must be distinguished from a remand to a secure unit, prison or remand centre of a child or young persons institution under section 23 of the Children and Young Persons Act 1969. In *Re M (A Child) (Secure Accommodation)*[36] the Court of Appeal rejected the view that secure accommodation order proceedings under the Children Act involved a 'criminal charge', confirming instead that it is a benign jurisdiction to protect the child. Furthermore, Butler-Sloss P held, in *Re K (a child) (secure accommodation order: right to liberty)*,[37] that although a secure accommodation order under section 25 of the 1989 Act involved a deprivation of liberty, it was not incompatible with the European Convention on Human Rights, as any action must be limited to such reasonable restrictions as are necessary in order to protect the child from causing significant harm to him- or herself or others, or seriously damaging property.

A local authority may only keep a child in secure accommodation without the authority of the court for a maximum period of 72 hours in any period of 28 consecutive days.[38] The maximum period for which the court may authorise a local authority to keep a child is three months.[39] In reaching a decision whether to restrict a child's liberty by placing the child in secure accommodation under section 25, a local authority is required to have regard to its general duty to safeguard and promote the welfare of the child, but the child's welfare will not be the paramount consideration.[40] Schedule 2, paragraph 7(c) of the Children Act 1989 requires every local authority to take reasonable steps to avoid the need for children within its area to be placed in secure accommodation.

Secure accommodation seeks simultaneously to meet the needs of disturbed or unfortunate juveniles and to inject discipline and structure into the lives of deviant youth (Harris and Timms 1993: 5). Indeed, a Scottish decision, *Humphries* v. S,[41] held that being detained in secure accommodation may be in a child's best interest in order to prevent the child from worsening his or her position by committing offences. Secure accommodation may sometimes be an essential resource for local authorities and families trying to cope with the behaviour of young people who are troubled and troublesome.

Leaving care is a big step for most young people, so it is vital to prepare them well in advance, to let them know what to expect and to give them time to build up the skills and relationships they will need. Many researchers found that the plight of children leaving care was serious (Stein 1990; Pinkerton and Stein 1995). Many care leavers discover that independence for them means homelessness, poverty and vulnerability to crime. Section 24 of the 1989 Act confers powers and duties on local authorities to prepare the young people they are looking after for the time when they cease to be so looked after. If a young person of any age is being looked after by a local authority, it is the duty of the authority to advise, assist and befriend him or her so as to promote the young person's welfare when he or she ceases to be looked after by it. Section 24(1) is concerned not so much with the child who has left accommodation, but with all children currently being looked after by the local authority. The local authority must also provide after-care to certain other young people by way of advice and assistance. Such a young person who 'qualifies for advice and assistance' includes, according to section 24(2), any young person aged under 21 who ceased after reaching the age of 16 to be: (a) looked after by a local authority; (b) accommodated by or on behalf of a voluntary organisation; (c) accommodated in a registered children's home; (d) accommodated by any health authority, NHS Trust or local education authority, or in any residential care home, nursing home or mental nursing home (provided he or she was accommodated there for at least three months); or (e) privately fostered. This 'target group' consists of persons under 21 who were provided with section 20 accommodation at some time between the ages of 16 and 18 but who are no longer so accommodated. Local authorities have the power to advise and befriend such a young person, provided that the authority considers that the young person needs to be advised and befriended, the person who formerly looked after the young person does not have the necessary facilities for advising and befriending him or her, and the young person has asked for such help. There is no question of thrusting advice and friendship down the throat of an unwilling recipient. Some children who are leaving, or who have left, local authority accommodation may not want help from that particular quarter. For the same reason, there is no legal obligation on the authority's part to track down members of the target group and offer help (Allen 1992: 83).

Section 24 empowers local authorities to give assistance to the young people described above by contributing to accommodation expenses incurred in connection with employment, education or training. In such circumstances the local authority may also give assistance in kind or, in exceptional cases, in cash. This sort of help is designed to recognise the special needs of these young people; they do not have to qualify for income support to get it, and any financial help is in addition to whatever tested benefits or educational grants they may be getting. They may well not have the sort of family backing which it is assumed that other young people have, and local authorities are urged to be as generous as possible in helping them establish themselves in life.

Increasing the support offered to care leavers, including steps to prevent the inappropriate discharge of young people at the age of 16 and 17, is one of the priority areas under the Quality Protects Programme, thus ensuring that young people leaving care are not isolated and that they participate socially and economically as citizens (Department of Health 1991c: 7.72–7.73). Further progress is also being made in relation to preventing children leaving care from becoming involved in crime, in the form of the Children (Leaving Care) Act 2000, which provides for every 'looked-after' child to have a personal adviser and a pathway plan by the child's sixteenth birthday. The pathway plan will be informed by a multi-agency assessment of need, which effectively extends existing assessment and planning requirements to cover the child's transition to adulthood. The pathway plan maps out a clear pathway to independence, setting out the support and assistance the young person will receive. Support can include help with accessing leaving care grants and other forms of financial support, securing accommodation, furnishing and decorating a new residence, assistance with budgeting, offering advice in the role of a corporate parent, or liaising with the young person's family to encourage and maintain contact (Ward *et al.* 2003). These plans are about enabling young people to plan for their future and helping them to achieve their potential (Department of Health 1997: 3.6). The plan will be subject to regular review irrespective of whether the child remains looked after or has left care. The 2000 Act provides for the continuation of the plan and contact by the personal adviser until the young person reaches the age of 21. Thus, the whereabouts, activities and well-being of 'looked-after' young people will be kept under review until they are 21 years of age, or beyond if they are in an agreed programme of education or training.

The Home Affairs Committee in its Report on Juvenile Offenders published in July 1993 recommended that young people who leave care should not be abandoned by the system or they may fall more readily into the temptation to commit crime (Home Affairs Committee 1993). Although the legislative provisions of the Children Act 1989 and the Children (Leaving Care) Act 2000 are minimalist in terms of the support being made available to children leaving care, they nevertheless represent an admission on the part of the state that children leaving care may require a degree of support to ensure that they make a successful transition to the post-care environment. Leaving care schemes provide a valuable service helping young people to plan their futures, providing follow-up support and meeting accommodation needs (Biehal *et al.* 1995). Leaving care schemes and formal preparation and support can make a positive contribution in respect of accommodation, self-care skills and the furthering of social networks, developing relationships and building self-esteem; consequently, they may protect young people leaving care from becoming involved in criminal and delinquent activities.

What works in preventing youth offending: the Children Act 1989?

Evidence confirms that providing families with the types of support examined in this chapter and encouraging parents to make use of social services will help to ensure that family problems are dealt with before they develop into crises, and consequently reduce the levels of risk factors associated with youth crime (Olds *et al.* 1997; Welsh *et al.* 2001). Programmes combining early family support and education, serving low-income families and involving both a child-focused educational component and a parent-focused informational and emotional support component, have been proved to represent a promising method of preventing the early onset of chronic juvenile delinquency (Farrington 1996; Yoshikawa 1994). These forms of support, as available under Part III of the Children Act 1989, have the potential to achieve long-term prevention of antisocial behaviour and delinquency through their effect on multiple early risk factors such as parenting quality and family income.

For example, parents who have participated in the On Track programme reported an improvement in parental supervision, parental discipline and family conflict resolution. Consequently, the children identified as being most at risk of engaging in offending behaviour before the intervention showed a marked improvement in their behaviour after intervention and were deemed to be at a lower risk of engaging in offending behaviour (France *et al.* 2004). On Track is clearly making inroads into tackling levels of risk factors within the family environment. Parenting support was also shown to reduce childhood antisocial behaviour in an experiment conducted in London and Chichester. A randomised controlled trial involving 141 children aged between 3 and 8 years, all displaying high levels of aggression and other behavioural problems, found a large reduction in juvenile antisocial behaviour among those whose parents took part in the parenting support programme. The parenting support programme involved providing information and support to the parents to help them become more effective in raising their children and help them to learn family management skills, including non-violent discipline (Scott *et al.* 2001).

Pre-school programmes and day care have also been shown to lead to decreases in juvenile offending and antisocial behaviour, school failure and other undesirable outcomes (Farrington 1996; Smith and Stern 1997). One of the most successful delinquency prevention programmes has been the Perry Preschool Program, carried out in Michigan. The project targeted 3- and 4-year-old children in disadvantaged communities, who were allocated either to a control group or to an experimental group. The experimental children attended a daily pre-school programme backed by weekly home visits for up to two years. There was significant evidence that by age 19 those in the experimental group were less likely to have been arrested and more likely to have graduated from high school (Schweinhart *et al.* 1993). These results become more compelling when viewed in the context of ten other pre-school programmes followed up in the United States (Consortium for Longitudinal Studies 1995). With quite impressive consistency, all studies show that pre-school programmes have long-term beneficial effects on school success and offending behaviour: participating children exhibited fewer antisocial and negative behaviours and showed more positive social behaviour (Webster-Stratton *et al.* 1989). Furthermore, research suggests that the influence of pre-school education in disadvantaged children extends into adolescence and beyond, improving their chances of employment success and decreasing the risks of delinquency (Sylva 1994; Utting *et al.* 1993. After-school clubs also ensure that children are properly and safely supervised and reduce the risks associated with low income by enabling parents to work normal hours after school. Moreover, after-school clubs can exert a direct influence on attitudes, achievement and behaviour. By engaging young people in constructive leisure activities and providing opportunities to do homework, such clubs can tackle low achievement in school and early involvement in drug abuse and youth offending. Effective programmes, such as Splash schemes, for example, can help to encourage young people to develop their interest in sports, hobbies or other leisure pursuits. Research in Canada has demonstrated the potential value of after-school schemes. PALS (Participative and Learning Skills), an after-school recreation programme for young people aged 5–15 years living on a large, socially disadvantaged estate in Ontario, offered a wide range of leisure pursuits that involved learning a skill. An evaluation found a 75 per cent decrease in juvenile arrests by police in the experimental community compared with a 67 per cent increase in a similar control estate. Complaints to the police about delinquent behaviour declined significantly (Jones and Offord 1989; France and Wiles 1996).

The Children Act provides a framework for local authorities to provide these established types of family support and services to youth at risk of engaging in offending behaviour and their families. Part III of the Children Act 1989 empowers local authorities to provide young people and their families with a range of services, including family support; access to play and leisure opportunities; training parents in effective child-rearing methods; pre-school intellectual enrichment programmes; positive opportunities for physical, emotional, social and intellectual development in childhood; day care; and respite breaks and family holidays. The evidence verifies that Part III of the Children Act 1989 has the overwhelming potential to deter young people from becoming involved in crime as it compels local authorities to improve the chances for them to lead healthy, productive, crime-free lives by mitigating individual risk factors and reducing economic and social deprivation.

The Children Act 1989 and accompanying guidance also empower local authorities to use compulsory methods of intervention in families in the form of care orders, supervision orders, and education supervision orders for example. These compulsory orders provide an invaluable framework for action by local authorities that potentially can deal with troublesome or even dangerous children whose antisocial and offending behaviour needs to be addressed. For example, the Dartington Social Research Unit evaluated the effectiveness of a scheme that placed young people who had a history of antisocial and offending behaviour with foster families. Some 75 per cent of those placed on the scheme between 1993 and 1995 either committed no further offences or significantly reduced their rate of offending (Dartington Social Research Unit 1995).

Tremblay *et al.* (1992, 1999) evaluated a two-year intervention directed at disruptive kindergarten boys of low socio-economic background. The programme involved supervised home-based parent training that emphasised monitoring children's behaviour, effective and non-abusive punishment, and family crisis skills. By age 12, experimental boys were found to be 50 per cent less likely to have serious school adjustment problems and significantly less likely to have initiated delinquent behaviour. Furthermore, Kazdin *et al.* (1992) conducted an evaluation of a similar programme. They found that for boys and girls aged 7–13 years who were exhibiting antisocial behaviour, supervised parent training significantly reduced aggressive, antisocial and delinquent behaviour. Sherman (1997) also found that the most promising results in preventing youth offending are to be found in supervised home visitation programmes. These usually involve social workers, health visitors, nurses or mentors helping and training parents of young children. Sherman estimated that, on the basis of the evidence, a universal supervised home visitation programme throughout the United States would prevent at least half a million serious crimes committed by children.

Persistent truants and children who have been excluded from school because of their disruptive behaviour are at increased risk of engaging in youth crime. An evaluation carried out for the Department of Education and Employment judged the following to be the most promising solution: better registration procedures to ensure that unauthorised absence is systematically identified and addressed; action on the first day of unauthorised absence, including the use of education welfare officers to make contact with children and their families; and reintegration of persistent truants and excluded pupils into mainstream education with the help of tutoring and mentoring support (Learmouth 1995). The Education Supervision Order and School Attendance Order comprise all of these criteria.

The evidence examined designates local authorities as the lead agency in mitigating the risks for juvenile offending, particularly among abused and neglected children. However, the 1989 Act requires other agencies and organisations to assist local authorities in achieving this goal. We have seen in this chapter that youth offending teams also have an important role to play in preventing the onset of juvenile offending. Youth offending teams have developed Youth Inclusion Programmes, Splash schemes, mentoring programmes and parenting programmes. Ghate and Ramella (2002) evaluated the effectiveness of these parenting programmes. Around 800 parents and 500 young people provided information for the national evaluation. The researchers found significant evidence of positive change in parents who participated in the programmes, including improved supervision and monitoring of their children's activities, a reduction in the frequency of conflict with their children and an improved ability to cope with parenting in general. There was also considerable evidence of positive change for young people during the time their parents participated in the programme. Young people reported improved supervision and monitoring by their parents, reduction in the frequency of conflict with their parents, and improved relationship with their parents. In the year after the parents left the programme the reconviction rates of young people had fallen by over 30 per cent, offending had dropped by 56 per cent and the average number of offences per young person had fallen by 50 per cent. It seems that the parenting programme helped to 'apply the brakes' on a sharp downward course for young people (Ghate and Ramella 2002).

Findings from the national evaluation of the Youth Inclusion Programme showed that 73 per cent of the 'at risk' young people engaged by the project were not arrested after the project. Of those who were arrested after their involvement with the YIP scheme, the vast majority (75 per cent) were arrested for fewer offences. There was also a decrease of 27 per cent in the number of permanent school exclusions and a decrease of 12 per cent in the number of temporary school exclusions (Mackie *et al.* 2003). Mentoring programmes are also an important way of providing young people in difficulty with adult role models who offer friendship, support and reinforcement. Research by a team from the LSE sought to evaluate the role of mentoring by looking at the experiences of ten Mentoring Plus programmes (Shiner *et al.* 2004). Almost 400 young people between the ages of 12 and 19 were recruited on to the programme. There is little doubt that these young people were at significant risk of engaging in offending behaviour. Many had experienced substantial disruption in their family lives; many had left school without any qualifications; and levels of offending, illicit drug use and contact with the criminal justice system were much higher than in the general youthful population. The vast majority had persistently offended during the 12 months leading up to the start of the programme. Nevertheless, a sizeable proportion of these young people indicated that Mentoring Plus had helped to tackle their offending, and substantial reductions in offending were evident during the lifetime of the programme. By the end of the programme more than one in four (29 per cent) indicated that they had not offended during the 12 months covered by the programme. This represented an increase of almost 66 per cent compared with the 12 months prior to the start of the programme. Those who continued offending during the programme did so at a reduced rate. The general downturn in offending was particularly marked among members of the cohort who had offended persistently in the year before the programme, as on average they committed four times fewer offences during the following year. Consequently, the number of persistent offenders fell by more than 33 per cent. The reduced levels of offending that were evident during the lifetime of the programme were maintained in the six months that followed. Eighty-three per cent of the young people who had not offended while the programme was in place continued not to do so once it had come to an end, and 34 per cent of those who had committed an offence while the programme was running refrained from doing so in the following period. Furthermore, those who continued to offend did so at a relatively moderate rate. Consequently, while the proportion of non-offenders increased to almost one in two following the end of the programme, the proportion of persistent offenders fell to one in four.

The Youth Justice Board fully believes that the Splash schemes have also made a considerable impact upon crime rates (Youth Justice Board 2001). It reported that the summer 2000 Splash schemes kept 20,000 young people off the streets, and in areas where the schemes operated, the total crime rate fell by 6 per cent compared to a national increase of 3.8 per cent. Moreover, criminal damage fell by 14.2 per cent, compared with a national increase of 8 per cent and burglary fell by 26.6 per cent, compared to a national fall of 8 per cent. Splash 2002 has produced similar significant improvements: total crime was reduced by 7.4 per cent from June to August 2002 in those areas where a Splash scheme operated, compared to a 2.9 per cent national increase (Cap Gemini Ernst & Young 2003: 5.1).

The effectiveness of the Children Act 1989 in reducing offending behaviour is firmly established in empirical research. The efficacy of the 1989 Act is also recognised in the White Paper *Respect and Responsibility* (Home Office 2003a). In paragraph 2.22 the government pledges to encourage the development of an increased range of specialised, high-quality intensive support schemes to help parents and children in order to implement more effectively the provisions of the Children Act 1989. Similarly, in *Youth Justice: The Next Steps* (Home Office 2003b: 3) the government sets outs its vision of how the youth justice system will develop over the next few years. One of the key proposals is to strengthen parenting interventions. Also, the government's *Respect Action Plan* sets out wide-ranging programmes to tackle antisocial behaviour, including increased support to tackle poor parenting and establishing a National Parenting Academy to help families whose children are at risk of getting involved in antisocial behaviour (Respect Task Force 2006). The government recognises that these schemes will better support families where a lack of parental capacity or ability contributes to the child's offending behaviour. The task for local authorities is to develop coherent strategies of support in order to respond appropriately to local needs. The aim should be to strengthen families, enabling them to play a full part in controlling their children's behaviour (Audit Commission 1998).

Such an undertaking is also in line with Britain's obligations under the United Nations Convention on the Rights of the Child, the preamble of which recalls that the Universal Declaration of Human Rights proclaims, 'Childhood is entitled to special care and assistance.' Article 27 of the United Nations Convention provides for the right of every child to 'a standard of living adequate for physical, mental, spiritual, moral and social development'. Article 18.2 of the Convention sets out the obligations of the state to assist parents in raising their children: '[In order to] guarantee and promote the rights enumerated in this Convention, member states [must] provide appropriate aid to parents and legal guardians of the child in the exercise of the responsibility of raising the child.' Ratification of the United Nations Convention on the Rights of the Child is a commitment binding in international law; ratifying states are required, as a matter of legal obligation, to protect Convention rights in their law and practice. However, the Convention on the Rights of the Child is not a part of UK national law, therefore it is not possible to bring a challenge in the UK courts where there are grounds for believing that the state is violating Convention rights. This is not to say that the rights specified in the Convention are totally without protection: the Committee on the Rights of the Child monitors how states are making progress in securing the Convention rights for children within their jurisdiction.

The principles and provisions of the United Nations Convention are informed by a number of more detailed standards and guidelines to which the United Kingdom is formally committed, for example the United Nations Standard Minimum Rules for the Administration of Juvenile Justice (the Beijing Rules) 1985 and the United Nations Guidelines for the Prevention of Juvenile Delinquency (the Riyadh Guidelines) 1990. Although these instruments are purely recommendatory and are non-binding in that they have no direct legal impact upon either international or national legislative bodies, they serve to identify current international thinking on human rights for young people and they represent the minimum recommended standards on youth justice issues. The United Kingdom has committed itself to aspire towards fulfilling all the obligations outlined in these instruments. Article 1.2 of the Beijing Rules 1985 stresses the idea that the state should ensure a productive life for minors within the community such as to encourage in them a process of personal development and education 'during the stage of life where they are most exposed to deviant behaviour'.[42] These rules point to the important role that a constructive social policy for juveniles will play in the prevention of youth offending. These broad fundamental perspectives refer to comprehensive social policy in general and aim at promoting juvenile welfare to the greatest possible extent, which will minimise the necessity of intervention by the juvenile justice system, and, in turn, will reduce the harm that may be caused by any intervention. Such care measures for the young, before the onset of juvenile offending behaviour, are basic policy requisites designed to obviate the need for the application of the Rules (Arthur 2005c).

The 1990 Riyadh guidelines emphasise that policies should avoid criminalising and penalising a child for behaviour that does not cause serious damage to the development of the child or to others. The Riyadh guidelines stress that the successful prevention of juvenile delinquency requires efforts on the part of the entire society to ensure the harmonious development of adolescents with respect for, and promotion of, their personality from early childhood. By engaging in lawful, socially useful activities and adopting a humanistic orientation towards society, young people can develop non-criminogenic attitudes. The Riyadh guidelines recommend that policies and measures should involve the provision of opportunities to meet the varying needs of young people and to serve as a supportive framework for safeguarding the personal development of all young people, particularly those who are demonstrably endangered or at social risk and are in need of special care and protection. The guidelines support preventive policies that facilitate the successful socialisation and integration of all young people, in particular through the family. Article 33 provides that 'it is necessary that the community put into place or reinforce greatly varying methods of community assistance, recreational facilities and services designed in view of the special problems of children in a situation of social risk'.

At the 96th plenary meeting of the General Assembly of the United Nations Resolution 40/35 was adopted, *Development of Standards for the Prevention of Juvenile Delinquency*, which recognised that the prevention of youth crime includes measures for the protection of juveniles who are abandoned, neglected, abused and in marginal circumstances, and in general those who are at social risk. It was also acknowledged that one of the basic aims of the youth justice system is the provision of requisite assistance and a range of opportunities to meet the varying needs of the young, especially those who are most likely to commit crime or be exposed to crime, and to serve as a supportive framework to safeguard their proper development. Member states were requested to study the situation of juveniles at social risk and to examine the relevant policies and practices of prevention within the context of socio-economic development and to adopt distinct measures and systems appropriate to the welfare of juveniles at social risk.

The United Nations Committee on the Rights of the Child has repeatedly recommended that the United Kingdom establish a system of juvenile justice that fully integrates into its legislation, policies and practice the provisions and principles of the Convention, the Beijing Rules and the Riyadh Guidelines (United Nations Committee on the Rights of the Child 2002). In October 2002 the committee expressed continued concern that in England and Wales the treatment of children in conflict with the law has worsened. In particular, the UN Committee was concerned that the age at which children enter the criminal justice system is low; that the principle of *doli incapax* had been abolished; that increasing numbers of children are being detained in custody at earlier ages for lesser offences and for longer sentences; that children between 12 and 14 years of age are being deprived of their liberty; and that deprivation of liberty is not being used only as a measure of last resort and for the shortest appropriate period of time.

In addition to this wealth of material, the child's right to protection from involvement in antisocial and offending behaviour can be found in instruments of the Council of Europe. In 1987, Recommendation R(87)20, on social reactions to juvenile delinquency, was adopted by the Committee of Ministers of the Council of Europe. The Council of Europe recommended that each of the member states review their legislation and practices in view of putting into practice a global policy of prevention of maladjustment and delinquency. Similar to the various United Nations rules and resolutions, this recommendation places emphasis on the role of the family and society in the treatment of young people. The exposé of the motives summarises this orientation: '[I]ntervention with young people should, as far as is possible, take place in the environment of the young person, with the family being assisted adequately in order that it can contribute to the educational process.'[43] In 1996 the Council of Europe adopted a European strategy for children, urging member states to fully implement the United Nations Convention as well as relevant European Conventions to ensure children's rights.[44] Although the recommendations of the Council of Europe are not legally binding, they are adopted unanimously and so carry weight and indicate a common approach to policy and minimum standards (Van Beuren 1992: 388).

In England and Wales the state has both a legal and a conventional obligation to safeguard and promote the general health and welfare of its youngest citizens up to their eighteenth birthdays. The philosophy that directs the general principles of the Children Act, United Nations conventions and other international conventions is essentially based on the protection of the personality of the young person and on the mobilisation of existing resources within the community. This concurs with a philosophy that explains offending behaviour by reference to the nature of the negative family experiences of children. It also promotes the principle that in order to reduce the risk some children face of becoming offenders, the best strategy is to promote positive life and family experiences for all children.

Conclusion

The more that children live in a safe world where their physical, emotional, social, intellectual, sexual and spiritual rights are safeguarded, the more they will thrive in all aspects of living and develop into mature, law-abiding individuals. While parents have the primary responsibility for their children's welfare, the community as a whole has a vital role in supporting them to carry out this task. Society has an interest in fostering family structures that produce positive and socially beneficial results, which subsequently prevent the social costs of the dysfunctional behaviour of struggling adolescents from damaged homes. This chapter has conclusively established that progress towards complete implementation of the Children Act 1989 should progressively ameliorate the conditions that coerce children into engaging in antisocial and offending conduct by reducing the risk factors identified in Chapter 2. This chapter has identified a role for the state in creating the conditions in which families can flourish and all children have the chance to succeed. Common sense tells us that the economic and social costs of neglecting children and failing to promote their positive development are very high indeed.

Summary

This chapter comprehensively examined how the Children Act 1989 and related domestic and international legislation could be implemented in order to alleviate the problems and difficulties that were identified in Chapter 2 as contributing to the risk of young people engaging in offending behaviour. The chapter demonstrated that the 1989 Act legislates for the provision of a wide range of innovative family-based initiatives focused on improving parenting practices and promoting the welfare of children. By providing parents with support in bringing up their children the Children Act represents a move towards a proactive programme of support for children and families experiencing the problems identified in Chapter 2. The 1989 Act empowers local authorities to pursue youth crime prevention practices that are child centred; take account of children's vulnerability; prevent their exclusion from school; prevent their abuse and neglect; tackle poverty and social exclusion; provide a safety net for young runaways; and create opportunities for young people's participation in the community. Chapter 4 will investigate whether the children examined in Chapter 2 have any legal entitlement to the provision of resources and services studied in Chapter 3.

4 Young people at risk of offending
Children in need of protection

Introduction

Chapter 2 demonstrated that securing the well-being of children, protecting them from all forms of harm and ensuring that their developmental needs are responded to appropriately are all effective ways of inhibiting juvenile antisocial and offending tendencies. Chapter 3 established that the Children Act 1989 is an effective vehicle for protecting children from the disastrous consequences of their offending behaviour. The Children Act provides a coherent and comprehensive welfare safety net so that vulnerable children and families are protected from the adverse environmental, familial and socio-economic circumstances that can encourage criminal behaviour. However, most of the support and services in the 1989 Act are not intended as universal services for all children, but are selectively applied to those defined as 'children in need' or 'children at risk of suffering significant harm'. Although specific duties, like the duty to take reasonable steps to prevent the ill-treatment or neglect of children (schedule 2(4)(1) Children Act 1989), or the duty to provide family centres (schedule 2(9) Children Act 1989) and the duty to provide services so that children do not become involved in delinquency (schedule 2(7) Children Act 1989), extend to all children, even these are directed at a more restricted group since they exist for 'the purpose principally of facilitating the discharge of the general duty' (section 17(2) Children Act 1989) to safeguard and promote the welfare of children within their area who are in need, and to promote the upbringing of such children by their families. Thus, these duties are intended to prevent children from becoming children in need and suffering significant harm.

Chapter 4 will investigate whether the children examined in Chapter 2 qualify as either children in need or children at risk of significant harm, making them entitled to the support and services considered in Chapter 3. The first part of this chapter will examine whether children of the types identified in Chapter 2 can be considered as children in need within the terms of the 1989 Act, and the second part will determine whether such children satisfy the minimum threshold criteria justifying compulsory state intervention. Demystifying the concepts of children in need and the threshold criteria of significant harm is an essential foundation stone of any system designed to discourage juvenile involvement in crime. This analysis will enhance the supportive aspects of the child welfare system by endorsing a proactive use of the law that involves pushing the law's boundaries in order to secure services, to challenge the relevance of service provision as articulated through agency plans and to obtain redress at an individual level.

Eligibility for family support services under Part III of the Children Act 1989

Chapter 3 confirmed that family support services may usefully be employed to reduce the family stress that can lead to delinquent behaviour. The local authority must provide these services to children once it has been determined that a child is in need. Therefore, defining the referral as a potential 'case' of a child in need requiring a response by the local authority is the first milestone to be passed in responding to the needs of children at risk of engaging in offending behaviour and their families.

The criteria for defining a child as in need are set out in section 17(10) of the Children Act 1989, which states that:

> A child is in need if (a) he is unlikely to achieve or maintain, or to have the opportunity of achieving or maintaining a reasonable standard of health or development without the provision of services by a local authority, or (b) his health or development is likely to be significantly, or further, impaired without the provision for him of such services, (c) or if he is disabled.

This definition of children in need is wide enough to include all children who could potentially benefit from the provision of services, more children than any local authority will be readily able to serve. According to the Department of Health *Guidance* on the 1989 Act, the definition of 'need' is left deliberately wide to reinforce the emphasis on preventive support and services to families (Department of Health 1991b: 2.7). Yet the *Guidance* does not indicate which children or families should be given priority. Chapter 2 emphasised that children who experience poor parenting in the form of erratic and severe discipline, rejection and low interest in their development are at an increased risk of engaging in offending behaviour. These factors are more prevalent in children of teenage parents, or parents who abuse drugs or are mentally ill, and children in families where there is conflict in the home. Similarly, children who experience poor parental supervision, children suffering from mental illness, children who abuse drugs, low school achievers, truants, those living in circumstances of economic disadvantage and those living in unstable living conditions are all at risk of engaging in offending behaviour. Do these children qualify as children in need? The aim of the next subsection is to determine whether children who are at risk of engaging in offending behaviour, namely the kinds of children examined in Chapter 2, qualify as children in need of family services.

Children at risk of offending as 'children in need'?

One of the cornerstones of developing measures for preventing juvenile offending behaviour must be to provide child welfare practitioners with a basic understanding of children's developmental needs and the experiences they require in order to attain a reasonable standard of progress. Developing a detailed understanding of children's needs and best interests will enable local authorities to take the action required to meet and fulfil those needs, and consequently prevent those children from engaging in offending behaviour. However, 'need' is a complex and socially constructed concept that is imprecise and unpredictable, and is therefore challenging as an epidemiological identifier, as a target for policy and as a basis for developing a youth crime prevention strategy. Lord Lloyd of Berwick, in *R* v. *Gloucestershire County Council, ex p Barry*,[1] expressed the view that 'need' is properly applicable to the lack of what is essential for the ordinary business of living, albeit he was discussing section 2(1) of the Chronically Sick and Disabled Persons Act 1970.[2] Furthermore, as the Children Act *Guidance* observes, 'Sometimes the needs will be found to be intrinsic to the child, at other times however it may be that parenting skills and resources are depleted or under-developed and thus threaten the child's well-being' (Department of Health 1991b: 2.5). Such descriptions of 'need' are ambiguous and consequently of limited practical use in preventing youth crime. 'Children in need' is thus a concept in need of an analytical framework within which services may be mapped out and resourced according to the identified needs of families. Local authorities should be able to draw upon a knowledge base that helps them to understand what is a reasonable standard of health or development, how it is achieved and what are the factors that might cause impairment or prevent the child from achieving a reasonable standard of health or development. This knowledge could then be used by local authorities to promote learning opportunities for successful parenting and strengthen families in their role of guiding, disciplining, and instilling sound values in their children. The law explored in this chapter is intended to provide local authorities with such a knowledge base.

Health and development

Both section 17, which sets out local authorities' duties to families of children in need, and section 31, which defines the criteria for care proceedings, refer to the impairment of health or development as the basic condition that must occur in order to trigger local authority intervention. In section 17 a child is defined as in need if his or her health or development is likely to be significantly impaired, or further impaired without the provision of services. In section 31 harm is defined as ill-treatment or the impairment of health or development. The major difference in definition between the sections is that in section 31 the impairment of health or development must be attributable to unreasonable parental care or the child's being beyond parental control.

Development is widely defined to encompass physical, intellectual, educational, emotional, social or behavioural development.[3] The key parental tasks are demonstrating and modelling appropriate behaviour, control of emotions and interactions with others, and guidance which involves setting boundaries, so that the child is able to develop an internal mode of moral values, conscience and social behaviour appropriate for the society within which he or she will grow up. The aim is to enable children to grow into autonomous adults holding their own values and able to demonstrate appropriate behaviour with others. Achieving that aim involves not over-protecting children from exploratory and learning experiences, including social problem-solving, anger management, consideration for others, and effective discipline and shaping of behaviour (Department of Health 2000a: 2.10). Educational development covers all areas of a child's cognitive development, which begins from birth. It includes opportunities for play and interaction with other children, having access to books, acquiring a range of skills and interests, and experiencing success and achievement. It involves an adult interested in educational activities, progress and achievements, who takes account of the child's starting point and any special educational needs. Weak relationships between parents and children, little communication and affection, and a lack of child-rearing skills, such as the absence of appropriate discipline or rules, little interest in children's activities or schooling and ineffective supervision, are all related to impaired development; Chapter 2 clearly showed that these same factors are also associated with juvenile offending behaviour.

In July 1984 a governmental inter-departmental committee was set up comprising a Law Commissioner and officials from the Law Commission. The committee published its final report, *Review of Child Care Law*, as a consultation document in September 1985. This report informed and influenced the development of the provisions of the Children Act 1989 (Ball 1996). The *Review of Child Care Law* indicated that 'development' includes 'not only [the child's] physical progress but also his intellectual, emotional and social or behavioural development, so that it is clear that a child who is failing to learn to control his antisocial behaviour as others do is included' (Department of Health and Social Services 1985: 15.14). Thus, the inter-departmental committee believed that the child might display impairment of social or behavioural development through delinquent or antisocial behaviour. Such children are in need to the extent that their development will be significantly impaired if their families do not receive help.

Health includes physical and mental well-being, both psychiatric and psychological. Therefore, a child with a psychological disorder is entitled to have his or her needs assessed under section 17(10) of the 1989 Act. Maintaining a reasonable standard of health comprises providing appropriate advice and information on issues that have an impact on the child's health, including sex education, homelessness and substance misuse (Department of Health 2000a: 19). Health also incorporates 'sexual abuse and forms of ill-treatment which are not physical' (section 31(9) Children Act 1989). The 1989 Act does not define what comes within the term 'sexual abuse'. However, sexual abuse of children should not be confined to actual physical violation of a child by rape. Sexual assault could include allowing children to view sexual acts or be exposed to, or involved in, pornography, or exhibitionism and other perverse activities. A physical assault on a child may be manifested by bruising, fractures, tender and swollen joints, burns, scalds or intentional poisoning. In some cases physical abuse is an important sign of a number of other generally damaging circumstances, in particular of a harshly punitive, less reliable and less warmly involved form of parenting (Bates *et al.* 1997). These are the very family factors that, as Chapter 2 illustrated, expose children to an increased risk of engaging in offending behaviour.

Chapter 2 also convincingly confirmed that children who experience severe physical punishment are at greater risk of engaging in offending behaviour. Applying appropriate discipline, in the sense of responding consistently to a child's behaviour, and setting clear boundaries, is part of bringing up children. A failure to provide guidance and set boundaries is in itself a form of neglect that can be very damaging to a child. On the other hand, discipline that is harsh can be damaging to a child both physically and emotionally (Department of Health 2000b: 1.1). Protecting children from harsh or erratic discipline could steer youth away from criminogenic risks. In order to prevent the emergence of youth deviance, children experiencing such discipline should be regarded as 'unlikely to achieve or maintain a reasonable standard of health'. However, the protection provided to children by the law on assault and cruelty is qualified by the common law defence of 'reasonable chastisement'. Cockburn J described this defence in *R v. Hopley*,[4] in which he held that 'by the law of England, a parent ... may for the purpose of correcting what is evil in the child inflict moderate and reasonable corporal punishment, always however with this condition that it is moderate and reasonable'. Section 1(1) of the Children and Young Persons Act 1933 attempted to define the boundaries of 'moderate and reasonable punishment' by prohibiting the carer of a child from wilfully assaulting, ill-treating or neglecting the child in a manner likely to cause the child unnecessary suffering or injury to health. This broad standard allows for treatment and punishment of children involving physical and mental violence that may be in breach of Article 19 of the United Nations Convention Rights of the Child. Article 19 insists that children must be protected from all forms of physical or mental violence. Furthermore, in *A* v. *UK*[5] the European Court of Human Rights held that the United Kingdom was in violation of Article 3[6] of the European Convention of Human Rights by virtue of its failure to outlaw corporal punishment administered by a private individual acting *in loco parentis*, which amounted to 'degrading treatment'. *A* v. *UK* took the view that the English common law defence of 'reasonable chastisement' undermined the law's ability to protect children's rights. This ruling provided an opportunity for a radical overhaul of the English law relating to the corporal punishment of children, an opportunity that, sadly, was not seized (Arthur 1999, 2004a, 2005b). In January 2000 the government published the consultation document *Protecting Children, Supporting Parents* (Department of Health 2000b), which expressed the government's view that it would be quite unacceptable to outlaw all physical punishment of a child by a parent: '[T]here may be occasions when moderate and reasonable physical punishment of a child by a parent may be appropriate.' However, the consultation document did propose that the defence of reasonable chastisement be set out on a statutory basis, thus outlining in legislation the factors that should be taken into account by a court when considering whether physical punishment has been moderate and reasonable. In *R* v. *H (Assault of Child: Reasonable Chastisement)*[7] the Court of Appeal outlined which factors should be considered by a jury when considering the reasonableness or otherwise of the physical chastisement of a child. The court held that the jury must consider the nature of the defendant's behaviour, its duration, its physical and mental consequences in relation to the child, the age and personal characteristics of the child and the reasons given by the defendant for administering punishment. Rose LJ believed that this was an appropriate and accurate reflection of the current state of the common law in the light of Strasbourg jurisprudence to which the English courts by virtue of the Human Rights Act 1998 must now have regard.

However, the United Nations Committee on the Rights of the Child believes that the proposals to limit rather than to remove the 'reasonable chastisement' defence constitute a serious violation of the dignity of the child (United Nations Committee on the Rights of the Child 2002: 37). The committee expressed disappointment that the UK government failed to take significant action towards prohibiting all corporal punishment of children in the family (ibid.: 36). The United Nations Committee on the Rights of the Child urged the UK government to promote positive, participatory and non-violent forms of discipline and respect for children's equal right to human dignity and physical integrity (ibid.: 38). If children are to be inoculated against offending tendencies, then all discipline should be positive, and children should be taught pro-social values and behaviour, including non-violent conflict resolution skills (Brandon 1995). Emphasis should be placed on promoting better parenting skills and helping parents to find methods of getting children to cooperate and behave in an appropriate manner, using means other than physical punishment. This might include, for example, keeping the child in, sending the child to his or her room, or stopping the child doing something he or she likes (such as watching television) (Department of Health 2000a: 2.7). Although physical punishment *per se* is not regarded as amounting to impairment of a child's health or development, parents who use physical punishment excessively should be sounding warning bells to those engaged in the protection of children. If the changes to the law prove to be as minimal as the Consultation Document and *R* v. *H (Assault of Child: Reasonable Chastisement)* suggest, they will neither introduce real clarity into the law, nor protect children from unnecessary physical abuse, nor protect children from becoming involved in crime.

The definitions of health and development appear sufficiently broad to also include children living in unstable living conditions. An analysis of sections 17 and 20 of the Children Act 1989 reveals a statutory entitlement on the part of any 16- or 17-year-old who claims to be homeless, or at risk of homelessness, to an assessment. An assessment would give the young person an opportunity to prove that he or she was a child in need, as defined under section 17, and thus entitled to assistance as generally provided under that section. In addition, it could be used to prove more specifically that the young person's welfare would be likely to be seriously prejudiced if he or she were not provided with accommodation; this would result in an express entitlement to accommodation under section 20 of the Act (Brody 1996). All homeless 16- and 17-year-olds, and those 16- and 17-year-olds at risk of homelessness, should therefore be automatically assessed as children in need under the definition of the 1989 Act, since this group is not able to maintain a reasonable standard of health or development under the terms of the Act. By requiring local authorities to provide accommodation for such young persons 'in need', this provision offers the possibility of assistance being made available to those at risk of breaking the law and being drawn into the youth justice system.

'... likely to be significantly ... impaired'

It is evident from the definition of children in need that local authorities must concern themselves not only with those children who are already in need, in the sense that they already have a low standard of health or development, but also those who are likely to find themselves in that position if services are not provided. Through its reference to likelihood, the definition paves the way for important preventive functions to be given to local authorities, as the inclusion of the prospective element emphasises prevention rather than cure. This has particular significance in relation to the development of juvenile crime prevention programmes. Johnson and Parker's study revealed that persistent young offenders are children in need, as they are disaffected young people with a range of unmet needs.[8] These authors advocated that opportunities to support such children should be given higher priority (Johnson and Parker 1996). Their findings were based on the information provided by 11 London youth offending teams. Accordingly, if persistent young offenders are considered as 'children in need', those who are likely to find themselves in this position, namely the kinds of children examined in Chapter 2, ought to be provided with preventive services. The 'likelihood' factor accordingly underlines the local authorities' duty to invest resources on a youth crime prevention strategy.

Section 17(10)(c): A child is in need if he is disabled

A child is defined as disabled if he (or she) is blind, deaf or dumb, is substantially and permanently handicapped by illness, injury or congenital disability, or suffers from a mental disorder of any kind (section 17(11) Children Act 1989).

Do children at risk of engaging in offending behaviour constitute children in need?

Although the Children Act 1989 fails to provide a satisfactory definition of 'children in need', it is difficult to imagine more needing circumstances than those that were considered in Chapter 2. The analysis in the early part of this chapter has proved that the following categories of children should be regarded as in need within the terms of the 1989 Act: children at risk of abuse and neglect, children who are homeless, children with mental health problems, children who abuse drugs, children who are at risk of sexual abuse, children who experience harsh or erratic discipline, and children who may be broadly defined as living in poverty or at high risk of family breakdown. All these factors were highlighted in Chapter 2 as predictive factors for future offending behaviour. Significantly, children who are delinquent, or at risk of becoming so, were also considered to be 'in need' because their social or behavioural development has not reached an acceptable level. These interpretations of children in need maximise the opportunity for local authorities to prevent youths from committing offences and being drawn into the criminal justice system. An approach to the definition of need that fails to recognise that juvenile offending behaviour is rooted in the familial problems analysed in Chapter 2 effectively abdicates the local authority's responsibility for a specific group of children in need. A child who commits offences or is at risk of doing so should therefore be regarded as in need of proper direction and guidance.

Identifying children in need/children at risk of engaging in offending behaviour

The effectiveness with which a child's needs are assessed will be the key to the effectiveness of subsequent actions and services, and, ultimately, outcomes for the child. The 1989 Act requires local authorities to identify the extent to which there are children in need in their area (schedule 2(1)(1) Children Act 1989), to publish information about the services they provide (schedule 2(1)(A) and (1)(2) Children Act 1989), and to take reasonable steps to ensure that this reaches those likely to benefit. The Children Act *Guidance* also stresses local authorities' duty to identify the need for services in their area and to plan the types and level of services required to meet local priorities (Department of Health 1991b: 2.11; Department of Health *et al.* 1999: 3.2). Local authorities are thus required to develop strategies and systems that both seek out children in need and encourage such children and their families to come forward (schedule 2(1)(1), (1)(2), (2)(b) Children Act 1989). By targeting children presenting with a range of risk factors that are known to predispose them to future offending behaviour, it is intended to access such children into the mainstream services discussed in Chapter 3, which can respond flexibly and speedily to the needs of the target group.

The primary responsibility of the local authority in relation to identifying children in need and children at risk of offending does not diminish the role of other agencies and the need for inter-agency and multi-agency cooperation in the assessment of children and families. Sharing of information is important to assist the local authorities in their work with children and families (Department of Health 1991b: 2.11; Department of Health *et al.* 1999: 3.13). A child or young person may have a number of the key risk factors identified in Chapter 2 and because of a specific act or event come to the notice of an agency, voluntary-sector body or individual. Such agencies and professionals may be able to provide information they hold about the child or parents, contribute specialist knowledge or advice to local authorities or undertake specialist assessments. For example, education welfare officers will often visit homes and talk with students and parents about school problems. They may therefore be an important source of information in identifying children at risk of engaging in offending behaviour. Health authorities are also well placed to recognise when a child is in need of extra support or services to promote his or her health and development. General practitioners, nurses and primary health care teams are ideally positioned to recognise when a parent has problems that may affect his or her capacity as a parent or when the parent poses a risk of harm to the child. School nurses are also uniquely placed to identify risk factors to a child, such as impaired physical, emotional and social development. Where this is the case it will be the responsibility of the medical professionals to refer the young person to the local authority and to ensure that a multi-agency risk assessment is undertaken. Likewise, housing authorities may have important information about families that could be helpful to local authorities carrying out assessments under section 17 of the 1989 Act, therefore they also have an important contribution to make to the identification of children at risk of engaging in offending behaviour.

Many youth offending teams have developed projects to operate a rigorous multi-agency process to identify those most at risk of engaging in offending behaviour. Pre-crime risk panels are being set up in some areas under the supervision of the local YOT with the aim of identifying children as young as 8 who appear to be developing criminal behaviour and offering interventions to tackle this behaviour, including parenting support if this appears to be the problem. In October 2002 the Youth Justice Board announced the creation of pre-crime risk panels in the form of Youth Inclusion and Support Panels in areas with the highest levels of street crime. The panels comprise a range of experts, including youth offending teams, police, schools and local authorities, who will identify 8- to 13-year-olds displaying problematic behaviour and at risk of offending, direct them into mainstream social services and provide a key worker to offer the young people and their families help. The aim is to develop supportive mechanisms for families that will facilitate non-offending behaviour and strengthen the relationship between young people and their parents.

These are wide-ranging and ambitious programmes that enable a great deal of supportive, preventive and rehabilitative work to be undertaken for the local authorities. Assessments undertaken by youth offending teams are an important source of knowledge if the young person continues to be considered as a child in need under the Children Act 1989 or is referred back to local authorities for help following his or her involvement with the youth justice system.

The local authority has no power to compel families or children to accept services. There may well be cases where the parents' refusal to accept help for themselves, or their children, places the children at such risk that they are likely to engage in offending behaviour. In these cases care proceedings may be necessary. The next section will determine whether the children identified in Chapter 2 as being at risk of engaging in offending behaviour satisfy the threshold criteria for compulsory intervention.

Children at risk of significant harm

Given the relationship, firmly established in Chapter 2, between abuse and neglect and subsequent juvenile criminality, any programme that effectively reduces abuse and neglect could serve as a prevention strategy for juvenile delinquency. Committing an offence is no longer a ground for the making of a care or supervision order.[9] The *Review of Child Care Law* reported in 1985 that the existence of the 'offence ground' tended to focus undue attention on the child's offending and distract those concerned with the case from other relevant circumstances (Department of Health and Social Services 1985: 15.22). It was felt that once the 'offence' condition was satisfied, an order automatically followed, irrespective of whether such an order was in the best interests of the child's welfare. However, the *Review of Child Care Law* also stressed that care proceedings may still be an appropriate response to a child's offending behaviour. Where it is clear that a child's offending is harming his or her development to such an extent that compulsory care is the most effective means of promoting the child's welfare, then care proceedings are still available. Also, it is still possible for a juvenile offender whose home circumstances are thought to contribute to his or her offending to be placed in local authority accommodation for up to six months as an addition to a criminal supervision order (section 7(7)(b) and Section 12 Children and Young Persons Act 1969). Such orders should not be punitive but should be aimed at assisting the child to work through his or her problems and stop offending (Department of Health 1991a).

In relation to young people who have not offended but are at risk of doing so, the sole grounds for care and supervision orders relate to the welfare of the child. By dissecting the process by which child protection cases are brought to the courts under the Children Act 1989 I will verify that it would be both possible and appropriate to use care proceedings to respond to children who are at risk of committing crime, particularly where offending behaviour appears closely linked with some specific problem in their upbringing.

Threshold criteria

Parts IV and V of the 1989 Act contain carefully structured provisions designed to strike a balance between the need to protect vulnerable children from the consequences of inadequate parenting, and the need to protect the right to respect for family life free from interference by public authorities, a right that is guaranteed by Article 8 of the European Convention on Human Rights.[10] For example, compulsory intervention in a child's life has to be authorised by a court. Applications for compulsory orders to the court must be made only by a local authority or an authorised person as defined by section 31(9) of the 1989 Act, by the NSPCC or by any other person authorised by the Secretary of State, of which there are none as yet. Before taking proceedings, the authority seeking the relevant order should consider whether the child's welfare could not be better promoted by support furnished under Part III of the 1989 Act than by invoking its powers of compulsory intervention; only when voluntary methods of help are unable to provide adequate protection should the compulsory powers of Part IV of the Act be invoked (Department of Health 1991a: 3.10).

In order for a child to be eligible for care and supervision proceedings, the conditions in section 31(2)(a) and (b) of the Children Act 1989, known as the threshold criteria, must be satisfied. The threshold criteria are that:

a the child concerned is suffering significant harm, or is likely to suffer significant harm; and
b the harm or likelihood of harm is attributable to –
   i the care given to the child, or likely to be given to him if the order were not made, not being what it would be reasonable to expect a parent to give to him; or
   ii the child being beyond parental control.

The important question, in relation to this book, is whether the kinds of children investigated in Chapter 2 satisfy the threshold criteria and thus are eligible for the protective orders examined in Chapter 3. To answer this demands knowledge and understanding of the law and the accompanying government guidance.

Harm

Significant harm is a major site in the 1989 Children Act where the boundaries between state intervention and family life are drawn (Hardiker 1996). The risk of actuality of 'significant harm' lies at the heart of all the compulsory powers of intervention (Hoggett 1993: 180). The standard of 'significant harm' is therefore the determinant of whether prospective anti-social and offending behaviour will be considered by the legal system as more appropriately dealt with by care proceedings.

The forms of harm encompassed are extremely wide and cover all known forms of abuse or neglect (Bainham 1990: 98). Section 31(9) of the Children Act 1989 defines 'harm' as meaning 'ill-treatment or the impairment of health or development'. The definitions of 'health' and 'development' already examined in relation to section 17 are equally applicable in these circumstances. Ill-treatment carries an implication of abuse rather than neglect, of conduct towards the child which is in some way hurtful or damaging (Hoggett 1993: 180). The Lord Chancellor, Lord Mackay, described 'ill-treatment' as an imprecise term that could include 'instances of verbal abuse or unfairness' (Hansard H.L. vol. 503, col. 342). Ill-treatment is sufficient in itself and it is not necessary to show that impairment of health or development has followed, or is likely to follow, as a consequence, although that might be relevant to the question of whether the court should make an order. Neglect, which is a predictive factor for future offending behaviour, is not specifically mentioned in section 31. Even though the word 'neglect' does not appear in the legislation, it remains one of the categories for inclusion on the Child Protection Register. It is also clear from the *Guidance* that it is still intended to be recognised as a source of harm to children. Neglect is defined as

> the failure to protect a child from exposure to any kind of danger, including cold or starvation, or extreme failure to carry out important aspects of care resulting in significant impairment of the child's health or development, including non-organic failure to thrive.
>
> (Department of Health 1991e: 6.40)

Physical neglect occurs when the child's essential needs are not met, and this is likely to cause impairment to physical health and development. Such needs include food, clothing, cleanliness, shelter and warmth. Physical neglect may also include failure to secure appropriate medical treatment for the child, or when an adult carer persistently pursues or allows the child to follow a lifestyle that is inappropriate to the child's development needs or that jeopardises the child's health. Neglect may also include neglect of, or unresponsiveness to, a child's basic emotional needs (Department of Health *et al.* 1999: 2.7).

Ill-treatment also comprises all general forms of non-physical abuse such as emotional abuse.[11] Emotional abuse is stated to be the 'actual or likely adverse effect on the emotional development and behaviour of the child caused by persistent or severe emotional ill-treatment or rejection' (Department of Health 1991e: 49). Emotional abuse includes rejection, lack of praise, lack of comfort or love, lack of attachment, lack of proper stimulation (fun or play), lack of continuity of care, lack of appropriate handling, serious over-protectiveness and inappropriate non-physical chastisement (Department of Health 1988). Butler-Sloss LJ emphasised, in *R* v. *Hampshire County Council, ex parte H*,[12] that in the case of emotional abuse the harm must be caused by persistent or severe emotional ill-treatment or rejection. In this case there was evidence of stress within the family, but that could not on its own demonstrate significant harm. Regard could also profitably be had to the Scottish Office definition of emotional abuse (Scottish Office 1992), namely failure to provide for the child's basic emotional needs such as to have a severe effect on the behaviour and development of the child. This may include situations where as a result of persistent behaviour by the parent, or caregiver, children are rejected, denigrated or scapegoated, inappropriately punished, denied opportunities for exploration, play and socialisation appropriate to their stage of development, isolated from normal social experiences, prevented from forming friendships or encouraged to engage in antisocial behaviour. Such children are at high risk of engaging in offending behaviour; therefore, providing preventive intervention from emotional abuse could have a significant impact on preventing juvenile offending.

Long-term exposure to harrowing scenes of domestic violence may also emotionally affect a child. In *Re G (Domestic Violence: Direct Contact)*[13]

Butler-Sloss P ruled that domestic violence involves a very serious and significant failure in parenting, a failure to protect the child's carer and failure to protect the child emotionally.[14] Not only are children in domestic violence at a heightened risk of direct physical and sexual abuse, but the very experience of witnessing violence against their parent, usually the mother, is in itself emotionally abusive and the children can be considered in many cases to be suffering significant harm (Brandon and Lewis 1996; O'Hara 1995; O'Keefe 1995; Parkinson and Humphries 1998). This is noteworthy considering the research examined in Chapter 2, which resolutely established that children who witness or experience domestic violence can emerge severely damaged and engage in offending behaviour. Australian legislation, namely section 38F(2) of the Family Law Act 1975 as amended by the Family Law Reform Act 1995, requires the court in making decisions about children to consider a range of factors, including the need to protect the child from physical or psychological harm caused by being directly or indirectly exposed to abuse, ill-treatment, violence or other behaviour that is directed towards the child or that may affect another person, or any family violence involving the child or a member of the child's family. Likewise, in New South Wales the Department of Community Services states that 'children living in violent relationships are always at some risk physically, psychologically and emotionally' and that 'even if some children do not experience physical violence they may be harmed emotionally or neglected' (New South Wales Department of Community Services 1993: 10). The influence of these statutory provisions is evident in England and Wales in section 120 of the Adoption and Children Act 2002, which amended the meaning of harm in the Children Act to include 'impairment suffered from seeing or hearing the ill-treatment of another'. This amendment should improve the chances for young people to lead healthy, productive, crime-free lives by reducing individual risk factors.

In *Re O (A Minor) (Care Order: Education Procedure)*[15] the family proceedings court had to consider whether 'significant harm' was wide enough to include a child's educational development. The local authority applied for a care order, intending to remove a 14-year-old female truant from her family to a children's home from where she could be taken to school each day. It was argued on the girl's behalf that a care order was an inappropriate response to truancy, as section 36 of the Children Act 1989 provided the education supervision order for dealing with persistent absence from school. Ewbank J agreed that in an 'ordinary case' of this kind an education supervision order was the first step to be taken; however, he considered that everything that could have been done under an education supervision order had already been tried. Ewbank J believed that if the care order were granted, the child would be going to school and consequently improving her intellectual and social development. Accordingly, he granted the care order, because where a child is suffering harm in not going to school and is living at home, it will follow that either the child is beyond her parents' control or that they are not giving the care that it would be reasonable to expect a parent to give.

Persistent failure to attend school thus satisfies the threshold criteria for care and supervision proceedings.

Harm could also credibly include harm to the young person's development as a result of his or her offending behaviour and its consequences. A child's development is likely to suffer if the child is allowed to injure other people, and it will usually be better for the child to be prevented from injuring people than to face prosecution after the event.[16] These views are in accordance with the judgment of Waite J in *Re C (A Minor) (Care: Child's Wishes)*,[17] in which the threshold criteria were proved in respect of a 13-year-old girl because she was failing to thrive emotionally and was keeping unsuitable company. The girl continually associated with undesirable company from an unstable and criminal background. If the girl were returned to her father, she would remain at risk through exposure to undesirable companions from whom the father seemed unable to protect her. Furthermore, in *Re G and R (Child Sexual Abuse: Standard of Proof)*[18] Connell J held, at first instance, that the daughter was suffering significant harm because of the parents' erratic parenting and poor supervision, their failure to set proper boundaries and control their daughter.[19] In *Re G (Care Proceedings: Threshold Conditions)*[20] the threshold criteria were proved because of the child's impaired development, which was due to shortcomings in the mother's parenting, in particular the lack of physical, emotional and intellectual stimulation. Thus, these cases confirm that poor parenting and poor parental supervision satisfy the threshold criteria. These are also predictive factors for future offending behaviour.

In determining whether those at risk of engaging in offending behaviour are suffering significant harm, it may be useful to look at the law in other jurisdictions and examine how juveniles at risk of offending are construed by others. In Japan, for example, the Juvenile Act 1948 classifies delinquents into a number of categories, one of which is those under 20 years of age who have not yet committed an offence but whose tendencies indicate that they might commit offences in the future. This includes a juvenile who is prone to committing an offence or violating the criminal law in view of his or her character or environment, based either on habitually disobeying reasonable parental supervision, making repeated flights from home without reasonable grounds, associating with persons of criminal or dissolute propensity, frequenting places of dubious reputation, or engaging in habitual activity harmful to the development of his or her, or others', morals. Such juveniles will normally be referred to a Child Guidance Centre, whereupon they will receive measures under the child welfare law (Yokoyama 1992, 1996, 1997). A comparative study of the law in Canada also provides some useful insights on this subject. In Canada, section 13(2)(d) of the Child, Family and Community Services Act 1996 provides that a child is emotionally harmed if he or she demonstrates severe self-destructive or aggressive behaviour. A particularly instructive judgment is that of *Children's Aid Society of London & Middlesex* v. *S(M).*[21] Vogelsang J held that the continued exposure of the child to his father would eventually greatly increase the risk of the child adopting aggressive, antisocial and criminal characteristics. The combination of loose behavioural limits, the frequent lack of an effective response to early small transgressions, the presence of antisocial role models and the lack of emphasis on education and other community activities were issues of concern for the court.[22] The Canadian judiciary unequivocally held that because the child was at risk of engaging in offending behaviour, he was consequently in need of protection. The Canadian court believed that the child needed the chance to develop his educational potential to the fullest and to have the benefit of good role models who will provide him with sensitive and consistent structure and care. Accordingly, an order was issued making the child a ward of the Crown and committing him to the care of the Children's Aid Society to arrange an adoptive placement as quickly as possible. It is difficult to predict whether this instructive judgment will influence the English judiciary; however, in *Barrett* v. *Enfield LBC*[23] Lord Hutton observed that it is incumbent on courts in different jurisdictions to learn from each other, because they are all straining to achieve a careful analysis and weighing up of all the relevant considerations.

From this analysis of harm it can be inferred that the protective control of the Children Act 1989 could be exercised over children who are engaged in, or at risk of, offending if failure to intervene is likely to allow them to continue offending with a consequent significant impairment of either their health or their physical, intellectual, emotional, social or behavioural development.

'Significant'

With the very broad meaning attributed to harm in the Children Act 1989, some sort of qualifying term is warranted to prevent unnecessary interference. Minor shortcomings or trivial matters should not trigger the possibility of compulsory intervention unless they have serious and lasting effects on the child; thus, the harm that is caused must be significant (Department of Health 1991a: 3.21). The word 'significant' is not defined in the Children Act, but in *Humberside County Council* v. *B*[24] the dictionary definition of 'significant' was approved. Such an approach has long been taken in Canada, where the British Columbia Court of Appeal defined 'significant' as meaning 'harm that is more than trifling or transitory in nature; that is substantial enough to warrant government intervention, rather than government assistance through the provision of support services'.[25]

Significant harm can be thought of as a compilation of significant events, both acute and long-standing, that interact with the child's ongoing development and interrupt, alter or impair physical and psychological development. Significant harm represents a major symptom of failure of adaptation by parents to their role (Brandon *et al.* 1999: 2). Relatively minor family problems, although comparatively easy to prove, do not normally justify the draconian response of a care order, or even a supervision order. A court would expect the local authority to use its powers under Part III of the Children Act 1989 to deal with such situations.

Where a question of whether harm suffered by a child is significant turns on the child's health or development, this is to be compared with that which could be reasonably expected of a similar child. A 'similar child' is a child with similar physical attributes, not a child of similar parents (Hansard H.L. vol. 503, col. 354). According to *Guidance*, the meaning of 'similar' in this context needs to take account of environmental and social characteristics of the child (Department of Health 1991a: 3.20). Therefore, when comparing 'similar' children, features such as age, disabilities, ethnic and cultural background should be taken into consideration. This raises the contentious question of how far a disadvantaged child should be compared to a similarly disadvantaged child and how far he or she should be compared to a child who has benefited from greater material, social and intellectual advantages. For example, where children are living in deprived circumstances in an inner-city area, it might be expected that some such children will be poorly clothed, have few toys or books, be fed on a diet that is not very healthy, not receive much intellectual stimulus from those who are caring for them and be poorly supervised. It could conceivably be maintained that a child who is looked after in this way is being treated in no worse a manner than many other children living in deprived circumstances, and that the standard of care he or she is receiving amounts to good enough parenting in the light of the child's background. However, it is also true that deprivation and relative poverty do not provide a reasonable excuse for a child being dressed in filthy clothing, for complete lack of attention to his or her personal hygiene, for not seeking medical attention when the child is ill, for no interest being taken in his or her intellectual and emotional development, or for the child running out of control and becoming involved in offending behaviour. Thus, it is arguable that the child should not be compared with a child from a similar background or neighbourhood, since the similarity must relate to the child and not the child's home circumstances (Colton *et al.* 1995a: 14; Smith 1991: 409). In fact, the Lord Chancellor, Lord Mackay, believed that a similar child is a child with the same physical attributes as the child concerned, not a child of the same background (Hansard H.L. vol. 503, col. 354). However, such an approach ignores the fact that social and environmental factors contribute very significantly to what can be achieved.

'. . . is suffering' or 'is likely to suffer' . . .

The child must either be suffering harm or likely to do so. In *Re M (A Minor) (Care Order: Threshold Conditions)*[26] the House of Lords interpreted the phrase 'is suffering' as meaning that the court must consider the risk of significant harm to the child not just in the light of present events and circumstances, but also in relation to past incidents. The House of Lords held that the word 'is' in section 31 in fact meant 'was', in the sense that the child was suffering significant harm when the rescue operation was instigated: '[T]he relevant date with respect to which the court must be satisfied is the date at which the local authority initiated the procedure for the protection under the Act and from which the arrangements followed.'[27] The House of Lords expressly approved the earlier judgment of Ewbank J in *Northamptonshire County Council* v. *S.*[28] In that case, Ewbank J held that 'is suffering' relates to the period immediately before the process of protecting the child is first put into motion, so long as such protective arrangements have been continuously in place from the time of first intervention until the disposal of the case by the court.[29]

In care proceedings under section 31 of the 1989 Act it is not necessary for the local authority to prove that the child is suffering significant harm if alternatively it can be shown that the child 'is likely' to do so.[30] The House of Lords held, in *Re H & R (Child Sexual Abuse: Standard of Proof)*,[31] that the word 'likely' was being used in the sense of a real possibility that could not be sensibly ignored having regard to the nature and gravity of the feared harm in the particular case, rather than in the sense of more likely than not. This view caters for cases where, although an event of maltreatment itself was not proven, the evidence established a combination of profoundly worrying features affecting the care of the child within the family.[32] In such cases it would be open to a court in appropriate circumstances to find that although the court was not satisfied the child is yet suffering significant harm on the basis of such facts as are proved, nonetheless there is a likelihood that he or she will do so in the future.[33] The Children Act *Guidance* suggests that the 'likely to suffer' provision allows proceedings to be considered where, for example, the child has suffered significant harm in the past and is likely to do so again because of some recurring circumstance, such as abuse associated with bouts of parental depression or parental unemployment (Department of Health 1991a: 3.22). *Re H (A Minor) (Section 37 Direction)*[34] ruled that the likelihood test would be satisfied if the parent or carer would be unlikely to satisfy the emotional needs of the child, even some years in the future. In assessing the applicability of the threshold criteria to young offenders, it is worth noting that Department of Health *Guidance* suggests that 'a child who is failing to control his antisocial behaviour would . . . be included' (Department of Health 1991a: 3.2p). Thus, it can be inferred that local authorities should provide protective intervention where a child is likely to engage (or is at risk of engaging) in criminal behaviour. Clearly, it defies logic to wait for children to harm other people before they receive services.

Whatever the nature of the allegations against parents, the evidential test in care proceedings is the civil test of the balance of probabilities, not the criminal test of the court being sure beyond reasonable doubt. In *Re H (Minors) (Sexual Abuse: Standard of Proof)*[35] the majority in the House of Lords found that each factor which contributed to the conclusion that an order should be made, under section 31(2) of the Children Act 1989, had to be proven to the requisite standard irrespective of whether the court was deciding whether the child was likely to suffer, or had already suffered, significant harm.[36] If an alleged fact could not be proved to this standard then it could not be considered in assessing whether a child was at risk of harm: '[A]n alleged but non proven fact is not a fact for this purpose.'[37]

Section 31(2)(b)(i): 'attributable to the care given to the child'

Having satisfied itself that the significant harm has occurred, the court has also to be satisfied that it is attributable to the care given, or likely to be given, to the child not being what a reasonable parent would give to the child. Therefore, when adjudicating on significant harm, or likely significant harm, a court must be satisfied that the cause of the harm is linked to deficits in parental care or control. Section 31 requires a test to be applied as to what a hypothetical reasonable parent would provide.

In *Re B and W (Threshold Criteria)*[38] Walker LJ concluded that the 'attributable to' test cannot, and does not, necessarily import any degree of individual responsibility or culpability but an objective evaluation of parenting standards. The court must look to the standard of care that the child obtains, or is likely to obtain, if the protective order is not made and ask whether the standard provided is below that which it would be reasonable to expect the parent of such a child to give him or her. The parents may be doing the best they can, but if this is not what would reasonably be expected, then the condition is satisfied. Although the task of parenting may be undertaken in many different ways, nevertheless the very fact that children can be legally removed from parents who are seen to be acting unreasonably indicates some agreements as to a minimum standard for parental practice; reasonable parents do not want their children to become involved in antisocial and offending behaviour.

The reasonableness criterion makes no allowance for parents who, for one reason or another, are incapable of meeting the reasonableness hurdle. All parents come to the judgment seat of care proceedings on an equal footing, however unequal they are in the world outside the court, so that parents cannot argue that they have particular problems – that they are unintelligent, irresponsible, alcoholic, drug abusers, criminal, poor or otherwise disadvantaged – which justify them in providing a lower standard of care. To introduce these into the equation would result in the acceptance of lower standards of care for children of disadvantaged parents. This provision requires parents to provide the care their children need, even though they may lack the necessary resources, whether these be economic, emotional or intellectual. If parents are doing the best they can, but are nevertheless failing to meet the required standard of care, and as a consequence the child is suffering, or is likely to suffer, significant harm, the threshold criteria will be satisfied and an order may be made. This is not to say that the motive of the carer is irrelevant; clearly, harm that is caused intentionally or recklessly will be viewed with far greater concern than harm that occurred accidentally. This will be relevant to the question of whether an order should be made if the parents' problems could be ameliorated by the provision of family support services by the local authority, but such problems will not enable parents to avoid fulfilling the threshold criteria. Thus, the carer's motive is merely partly relevant to the second limb of the threshold criteria.

The standard of care should only be that which it is reasonable to expect for the particular child, rather than the best that could possibly be achieved. Applying a 'best' standard could lead to the risk of a child being removed from home simply because some other arrangement could cater better for that child's needs than care by his or her parents. However, reasonable parenting must be matched to the needs of the particular child. The focus of attention is on the care given, or likely to be given, to the child in question, and not to an average child. Children with emotional and behavioural difficulties will provide challenges to parents irrespective of the cause of the problems. If, for example, the child has particular difficulties in relation to his or her behaviour, the court will have to consider what a reasonable parent would provide for him. Volume 1 of the *Guidance* suggests that where the child's needs are complex or demanding, or the lack of reasonable care is not immediately obvious, the court may wish to seek professional evidence on the standard of care that reasonable parents could be expected to provide with support from community-wide services (Department of Health 1991a).

Section 31(2)(b)(ii): Child being beyond parental control

The threshold criteria will also be satisfied if the significant harm, or likelihood of it, is attributable to the child's being beyond the control of the parent. The 'beyond parental control' element demands the court to find the child is suffering significant harm because of decisions made autonomously by that child in contravention of the parent's wishes. The fact that a child is beyond parental control does not in itself indicate an absence of reasonable parental care. The child's carer may actually be offering extremely reasonable care but may still be unable to prevent the child from inflicting significant harm on him- or herself. Offending behaviour may result from loss of parental control, as such behaviour frequently stems from distorted or stressed relationships between parent and child (Department of Health 1991a: 3.25).

Butler-Sloss LJ acknowledged in *Re L (a minor)*[39] that there is almost no authority on the phrase 'beyond parental control'; however, examples of such conduct include where a child has become addicted to drugs,[40] is sexually promiscuous, is running away from home,[41] is assaulting other children,[42] is behaving at home in an unruly or disruptive manner,[43] or is engaging in offending behaviour and the parents are powerless to influence the child's behaviour (Kelly 1996; Stephenson 1995). External controls may therefore be necessary to protect the child from engaging in offending behaviour. Children who are beyond parental control often harm others, but that will not satisfy the threshold criteria unless it can be shown that the child him- or herself is also likely to suffer significant harm and that this is attributable to the child's being beyond parental control.

According to Stuart-White J in *M v. Birmingham City Council*,[44] the phrase 'being beyond parental control' refers to the parent of the child in question and not to reasonable parents in general. Important also is the control exercised by that parent in conjunction with a partner even if that partner is not the parent of the child. Parents cannot initiate an application for care proceedings, but they can request that the local authority provide accommodation for a child with whom they cannot cope (section 20 Children Act 1989). Where parents have truly tried their best to make reasonable arrangements for the child's upbringing, it is right that they should not be stigmatised as causing the child to suffer, or likely to suffer, significant harm because the care they have given the child is not what it would be reasonable to expect a parent to give. However, it is equally stigmatising for the child to be found to be beyond parental control in a case where the fault lies with those who have brought him or her up. Such a finding is likely to influence the arrangements that are made about how the child will be looked after if a care order is made, or the types of activities in which the child will be required to take part if a supervision order is made (Hayes and Williams 1999: 198). Where a child is engaging in offending behaviour, or otherwise beyond parental control, it may be comparatively easy to prove that the child is bringing harm upon him- or herself. It may be far more difficult to prove wrongdoing or other failure by a parent which has led the child to come to harm. There is a risk that the attribution of harm to the child, rather than the parent, might sometimes be selected as the basis for bringing proceedings, or making an order, because it is easier to prove. However, justice to a child requires that the child should be labelled as beyond control only where there is cogent evidence to support this allegation. Just as it is wrong to label a parent as having caused the child to come to harm unless there is evidence to substantiate this, so too it is wrong to label a child as being beyond parental control if the true cause of his or her coming to harm, by engaging in offending behaviour, is that the child's parents, or others, have failed to give him or her reasonable parental care.

Other relevant criteria

Even if the threshold criteria are satisfied, this does not necessarily mean that a care or supervision order will automatically be made. Instead the local authority could provide access to Part III services. The threshold criteria are the minimum circumstances that should always be found to exist before it can ever be justified for a court even to begin to contemplate whether the state should be enabled to intervene compulsorily in family life. Section 1(1) of the Children Act 1989 lays down the fundamental principle underlying child law in England, namely that 'when a court determines any question with respect to ... the upbringing of a child ... the child's welfare shall be the court's paramount consideration'. In upholding the welfare of the child as the paramount consideration, the court must have regard to the checklist in section 1(3):

a the ascertainable wishes and feelings of the child concerned (considered in the light of his age and understanding)
b the child's physical, emotional and educational needs
c the likely effect on him of any change in his circumstances
d the child's age, gender, background and any considerations which the court considers relevant
e any harm which he has suffered or is at risk of suffering
f how capable each of the child's parents, and any other person in relation to whom the court considers the question to be relevant, is of meeting his needs
g the range of powers available to the court under this Act in the proceedings in question.

Section 1(5) of the 1989 Act provides that the court will not make an order unless it considers that doing so would be better for the child than making no order at all. Therefore, local authorities will have to establish that the powers given to them by court orders will assist in the process of actually improving the child's situation and possibly changing the child's family condition. Also, section 121 of the Adoption and Children Act 2002 provides that no care order may be made until the court has considered the local authority's care plan, which outlines the proposed future care of the child.

The effect of these provisions is that a care or supervision order should only be made 'when there is some evidence that this would lead to an improvement from the point of view of the welfare of the child'.[45] Welfare is a very broad concept that incorporates the intellectual, physical, social and moral aspects of a child's upbringing. The promotion of welfare within the Children Act has several elements: understanding and helping to provide the necessary building blocks of optimal child development for a particular child, understanding the importance of children's families to their development, understanding how the environment in which a child is growing up can positively or negatively influence development, and understanding that the quality of experience in childhood will contribute to outcomes and life chances in adulthood (Aldgate and Statham 2001: 41). The welfare of the child must also be conflated with the prevention of juvenile offending.

Identifying children suffering significant harm/children at risk of engaging in offending behaviour

Local authorities have an active duty under section 47 of the Children Act 1989 to investigate any case where it is suspected that a child is suffering significant harm, or is likely to do so (section 47(1) Children Act 1989). *Guidance* provides that actions under section 47 should be seen as the usual first step when a question of child protection arises (Department of Health 1991a: 4.78). The investigation should provide evidence upon which to base judgments and make plans on how to safeguard the child, promote the child's welfare and support parents in promoting their children's welfare. If as a result of its inquiries the local authority concludes that it should take action in order to safeguard or promote a child's welfare, it must do so, so far as this is within its powers and is reasonably practicable (section 47(8) Children Act 1989). Action, for these purposes, can embrace many matters, and may simply involve the provision of advice and information, not necessarily by the authority, to the child and his or her carers. At the other end of the spectrum there is the compulsory intervention machinery which is expressly mentioned in section 47. Pursuant to schedule 2 of the Children Act, local authorities are under a duty to inform another authority if a child who the authority believes is likely to suffer harm lives, or proposes to live, in the area of that authority (schedule 2(4) Children Act 1989). In *Re C (Care Proceedings: Disclosure of a Local Authority's Decision-making Process)*[46] Munby J highlighted the principle that social workers also have a duty to notify parents of material criticisms and deficits in their parenting or behaviour, and to advise them how they might remedy or improve their parenting.

The local authority has the primary responsibility for initiating investigation proceedings. However, in discharging this duty local authorities do not work alone. Section 47 of the 1989 Act places a duty on any local education authority, housing authority and health authority to help a local authority with its inquiries. Indeed, in *Re E (Care Proceedings: Social Work Practice)*[47] Bracewell J emphasised that professionals such as health visitors and teachers were an important source of valuable information. As the *Guidance* states,

The authority cannot expect to be sole repository of knowledge and wisdom about particular cases. Full inter-agency co-operation including sharing information and participating in decision-making is essential whenever a possible care or supervision order is identified.

(Department of Health 1991a: 3.10)

In *R* v. *Local Authority and Police Authority in the Midlands, ex parte LM*[48] Butler-Sloss LJ stressed that 'the whole emphasis of the [Children] Act is on inter-agency co-operation'. She highlighted the need for a multi-disciplinary approach to the protection of the welfare of children. The main system facilitating such cooperation is the multi-agency 'Child protection conference'. The child protection conference provides a forum for analysing, in an inter-agency setting, the information that has been obtained about the child's health, development and functioning and the parents' capacity to ensure the child's safety and promote the child's health and development (Department of Health *et al.* 1999: 5.53). At this conference persons with knowledge of the child and the family pool information about the child and make recommendations for further action. *Guidance* describes the child protection conference as symbolising the inter-agency nature of assessment, treatment and the management of child protection (Department of Health 1991e: 6.1). If the child is at continuing risk then a child protection plan must be devised. The child protection plan identifies the nature of the risk of significant harm, the ways in which the child can be protected through inter-agency arrangements, short-term and long-term aims to ensure the child's safety, and ways of monitoring and evaluating progress against the plan. This plan itemises the steps that have been agreed about protecting the child and also decides whether the child should be put on a child protection register. The child protection register lists all the children in the locality for whom there is an inter-agency child protection plan. Registration is a record not of children who have been abused but of 'children for whom there are currently unresolved child protection issues and for whom there is an inter-agency protection plan' (ibid.: 6.36). The register is essentially a management tool that records the fact that a child has been, or is suspected of being, abused or is believed to be at risk of being abused.

Another important inter-agency forum for agreeing how different services and professional groups should cooperate to safeguard children and for making sure that cooperative arrangements work effectively is the Area Child Protection Committee (ACPC). The committee comprises senior officers and professionals from all the main authorities and agencies in the area that are involved in child protection, including local youth offending teams (Department of Health *et al.* 1999: 4.12). ACPCs provide a mechanism whereby whenever one agency becomes concerned that a child may be at risk, it shares this information with other agencies (Department of Health 1991e: 1.11). The functions of the ACPC include developing and agreeing local policies and procedures for inter-agency work to protect children; developing effective working relationships between different services and professional groups based on trust and mutual understanding; ensuring that there is agreement and understanding across agencies about operational definitions and thresholds for interventions; and communicating clearly to individual services and professional groups their shared responsibility for protecting children.

The Children Act 2004 imposes new duties on agencies to cooperate to improve children's well-being and to have in place arrangements to safeguard and promote the welfare of children (sections 10 and 11 Children Act 2004). Section 13 of the 2004 Act requires each local authority in England to establish a Local Safeguarding Children Board for its area. Local Safeguarding Children Boards (LSCBs) are designed to help ensure that the key agencies work effectively together by coordinating and ensuring the effectiveness of local arrangements and services to safeguard and promote the welfare of children. The 2004 Act effectively puts the area child protection committees on a statutory footing. LSCBs' membership will include local authorities, health bodies, the police and others as outlined in section 13 of the 2004 Act. Sections 18 and 19 of the 2004 Act require local authorities to put in place a Director of Children's Services and Lead Member to be responsible for, as a minimum, education and children's social service functions. Local authorities have discretion to add other relevant functions, for instance leisure or housing, to the role if they feel it is appropriate. These changes provide the opportunity to put in place more effective arrangements for local leadership, joint working and sharing of good practice. The 2004 Act places key agencies under a new duty to cooperate with local authorities to promote positive outcomes for children.

Promoting children's well-being and safeguarding them from significant harm and from becoming involved in offending behaviour depends crucially upon effective information-sharing, collaboration and understanding between agencies and professionals. The child protection conference, the child protection register, the Area Child Protection Committee and the Local Safeguarding Children Boards all aim to promote the dissemination of information about children among various agencies and to coordinate the work of these services. This function is crucial to the prevention of youth offending. With properly coordinated services there is a better chance of spotting warning signs of offending behaviour and of constructive action being taken before crisis points have been reached.

Restrictions on local authorities' powers

The provisions of the Children Act 1989 leave wide discretion to the local authority, since duties are expressed in terms of 'taking reasonable steps' (schedule 2(1)(1), (4)(1), (7)(1), (10) Children Act 1989) or providing 'as they consider appropriate' (schedule 2(8)(9) Children Act 1989) or as is 'reasonably practicable' (section 47(8), schedule 2(2)(2)(b) Children Act 1989). There are only two absolute duties: (1) to publish information about services provided; and (2) to open and maintain a register of disabled children. The authority could therefore decide that proceedings were necessary to safeguard a child, but not take them on the basis that it was not reasonably practicable to do so, what is practicable being influenced by considerations unrelated to the interests of the child. 'Practicable' is defined by the *Oxford English Dictionary* as 'capable of being carried out in action' or 'feasible'[49] and by Webster's dictionary as 'possible to be accomplished with known means or resources'.[50] 'Reasonably practicable' imposes a less strict standard than 'practicable'.

The most obvious obstacles to providing a comprehensive range of support in a strategic way are the problems of resources and competing priorities within local authorities. The courts do not proceed on the basis that there is an unlimited supply of funds available to maximise the protection of all children. For example, in *C (Family Assistance Order)*[51] Johnson J sought to make a family assistance order, which the local authority declined to implement because it lacked resources. The local authority argued that 'our resources are finite and ... we have to allocate our social services budget and personnel to meet the demands of many children and others. The allocation of resources is a matter for us as a local authority'.[52] Johnson J held that in the circumstances there was nothing he could do: '[I]t seems that I have failed and there is, I think, nothing further that I can do.'[53] Similarly, Thorpe J in *Re JN (Care: Assessment)*[54] took no action against a local authority for thwarting an assessment by refusing to finance it. The Court of Appeal in *R v. Cambridge Health Authority, ex parte B*[55] confirmed that the court could not make judgments about how local authorities decide to allocate a limited budget. The local authority was entitled to prioritise the services it was prepared to fund as it saw fit. Lord Bingham MR observed that local authorities are 'pressed to make ends meet' and concluded that 'difficult and agonising judgments have to be made as to how a limited budget is best allocated to the maximum advantage of the maximum number of patients. This is not a judgment which the court can make.'[56] These views are also consistent with the judgment of *R v. Gloucestershire County Council, ex parte Barry*,[57] in which the House of Lords confirmed that local authorities can properly have regard to the availability of resources when making assessments of the need for services and the necessity of their making arrangements to meet those needs. Lord Nicholls stated that it would be unreasonable for a local authority to fail to have regard to the availability of resources while endeavouring to discharge its duties.[58] Lord Nicholls held that 'needs for services cannot sensibly be assessed without having some regard to the cost of providing them' and that the weight to be given to that factor must depend on the means of the authority that has to meet the cost.[59] Their Lordships thus wished to avoid becoming involved in issues of public spending and the allocation of resources. In R v. *Sefton Metropolitan Borough Council, ex parte Help the Aged*[60] the Court of Appeal felt compelled in the light of *Barry* to conclude that resources are relevant to interpreting 'need' in section 2(1) of the National Assistance Act 1948.[61] Scott Baker J extended this view to include care proceedings in R v. *E Sussex County Council, ex p W*,[62] in which he noted that care proceedings were an expense on the public purse and that the local authority was entitled to ask whether a care order would bring any benefit. Likewise, in *In re S, W and Ors*[63] Lord Nicholls stressed that a court does not have the task of managing the financial and human resources available to a local authority for dealing with all children in need in its area. Such views are not confined to the English judiciary; the European Commission of Human Rights noted in *Osman* v. *UK*[64] that the state's obligations under the European Convention on Human Rights are dependent on the means available. Similarly, the European Court in *Osman* remarked that the obligations under the European Convention must be interpreted in a way that does not impose an impossible or disproportionate burden on the public authorities.[65] Furthermore, in *Re W & B, Re W (Care Plan)*[66] it was held that the duties of public authorities under the European Convention were limited by the many demands upon the resources of local authorities.

In circumstances where the demands placed upon local authorities outstrip their budgets, they must establish pragmatically defensible rationing schemes. However, the principles expressed in the case law allow for the local authority to fix eligibility criteria by reference to its resources. This can be read as supporting the proposition that local authorities are dutybound to meet only those needs in respect of which they can afford to provide services. Once the reasonableness of the actions of a local authority depends upon how scarce financial resources are applied, the local authority's decision becomes extremely difficult to review. The effect of the judgments I have outlined is that there is no duty to provide services if the provider considers that he does not have sufficient resources available to provide them. The logical inference of this is that in circumstances where there are no resources, it can legitimately be concluded that there are no needs.

By contrast, a different approach was adopted in R v. *East Sussex County Council, ex parte Tandy*.[67] Lord Browne-Wilkinson observed that 'to permit a local authority to avoid performing a statutory duty on the grounds that it prefers to spend the money in other ways is to downgrade a statutory duty to a discretionary power'.[68] This case concerned the issue of providing suitable education at school or otherwise than at school for children who, by reason of illness, exclusion from school or otherwise, might not receive suitable education without such arrangements being made (section 298 Education Act 1993).[69] Similarly, in R v. *Birmingham CC, ex parte Mohammed*[70] Dyson J held that an authority's resources were irrelevant in determining whether upgrading works are necessary and appropriate to meet the needs of the disabled occupant, for the purposes of section 24(3)(a) of the Housing Grants, Construction and Regeneration Act 1996.[71]

In two 1992 decisions, *Re O (Minors) (Medical Examination)*[72] and *Berkshire County Council* v. *C*,[73] the court held that a section 38(6) direction was binding upon the local authority and therefore amounted to an 'order' that must be obeyed, the lack of resources being no excuse.[74] Such a view is also in accordance with the House of Lords' judgment in *Re C (A Minor) (Interim Care Order: Residential Assessment)*.[75] Lord Browne-Wilkinson held that sections 38(6) and (7) conferred jurisdiction on the court to order or prohibit any assessment that involved the participation of the child, and was directed to providing the court with the material that was required to reach a proper decision at the final hearing. To allow the local authority to decide what evidence is to go before the court at the final hearing would allow the local authority by administrative decision to pre-empt the court's judicial decision. Therefore, the court had the power to override the views of the local authority. However, in exercising its discretion whether to order any particular examination or assessment, the court was required to take into account the cost of the proposed assessment and the fact that local authorities' resources were notoriously limited.

Moreover, local authorities cannot refuse to provide for an assessed need; in *R* v. *Bristol City Council, ex parte B Penfold*[76] it was held that it was not permissible for a local authority to refuse to carry out an assessment where a person appears to be in need of community care services, under section 47 of the National Health Services and Community Care Act 1990, simply because the authority doubts whether it will be able to afford to meet the need should the assessment demonstrate that it exists. Support for this perspective is also evident in the decision of *R* v. *Wigan Metropolitan, ex parte Tammadge*.[77] Forbes J expressed his belief that 'once the duty had arisen ... it was not lawful of Wigan to refuse to perform that duty because of a shortage of, or limits upon, its financial resources'.[78] Therefore, once Mrs Tammadge's need for larger accommodation was established, Wigan Council was obliged to make provision of such accommodation to Mrs Tammadge and her family. Thus, the opportunity for declining to provide a service would only arise if the requirement for a service were not identified by the local authority as a 'need' in the first place. In *Re F; F* v. *Lambeth London Borough Council*[79] Munby J acknowledged the desperate burdens that face overstretched and under-resourced local authorities, but nevertheless held that these issues cannot excuse the local authority's neglect, which resulted in the causing of serious harm to two boys in care.

Although local authorities have wide discretion to determine the range and level of services, the 1989 Act includes specific powers and duties that give some indicator for which support services should be provided; these are, among others, the prevention of ill-treatment and neglect, the reduction of the need to bring care or related proceedings, the promotion of family reunification and contact, and, most importantly, the reduction of delinquency and criminal proceedings against children (schedule 2 Children Act 1989). The effective deployment of support and protective services requires a systematic approach to the child protection system so that the relevant kind of assistance is brought into play at the point when the need arises. To do so local authorities require the necessary resources from central government. Central government therefore has to face the important question of the proper resourcing of the legislative duties imposed by the Children Act 1989.

Model systems for preventing juvenile offending

While recognising that neither child abuse nor delinquency can be legislated away, nonetheless this chapter has identified how most young people at risk of engaging in offending behaviour, and young offenders, could be appropriately dealt with as children 'in need' under Part III of the Children Act 1989, or as children at risk of 'significant harm' in care proceedings under Parts IV and V of the 1989 Act. Such views are also prevalent throughout legal systems in continental Europe and Scandinavia. For example, in France the Order of 2 February 1945 (*L'ordonnance du 2e février 1945*)[80] constitutes the fundamental text governing the penal code for juveniles. This law created a specialised jurisdiction with a specific juvenile court judge (*juge des enfants*) who has jurisdiction over both civil and penal matters.[81] In France the age of criminal responsibility is 13 years (compared to 10 years in England and Wales), therefore children under the age of 13 are considered too young to be held responsible for breaking the law and will not be prosecuted. Such children will usually be referred for social welfare provision. With regard to children over 13 and under 18 years who have broken the law, cases involving serious or persistent offending may be referred for trial. However, the vast majority of such cases are usually referred to the *juge des enfants* for social welfare support rather than punitive measures. Since the law of 1945 was passed, judges have tried to understand the juvenile offending behaviour in the context of the juvenile's life; the offending behaviour is thus considered as a sign of a need to intervene. Because of the court's dual jurisdiction for 'children in need of care' and 'juvenile delinquents', the juvenile court judge is in an unparalleled position to identify and react to the risk/needs factors most often associated with young offenders. The *juge des enfants* undertakes the criminal investigation; orders social psychological and family studies; and integrates educational, occupational, medical and psychiatric services for the young person and his or her family. Most of the procedures involving children and young people take place in the informal settings of the chambers of the *juge des enfants*, where the judge usually dispenses with the legal formalities that are obligatory with adults (Ely 1990). In France the view is that delinquency will be prevented, and the risks to vulnerable children reduced, if those condemned can keep or establish a place within conventional society (Blatier and Corrado 2001). Hence, the juvenile court judge is charged with the task of facilitating the young persons' 'inclusion' into conventional life by bringing their influence to bear on the education, social work, leisure, housing and other relevant systems (Ely 1990). The judge receives referrals from many sources: schools, social services, police, children's organisations, parents or even children themselves. While cases involving serious or persistent offending may be referred for trial (Garapon 1995), for the vast majority of cases the judge typically requests that a special educational worker assess the family environment in which the youth was raised (*investigation d'orientation éducative*). This inquiry focuses on the problem profile of the youth's family, the extent of the youth's criminal record, and the youth's school behaviour. The judge then has a wide range of options at his or her disposal to respond to the problem profile of the youth and the family. These options include, but are not limited to, placing the juvenile in a children's home; making a provisional order for the juvenile; appointing a social worker to assist the youth and family; placement in the care of a special educational establishment where the child may be ordered to see a psychiatrist, psychologist or vocational guidance expert; placements in local activity schemes designed to steer adolescents away from opportunistic petty offences; making a community service order for offenders between 16 and 18 years of age; or placing the youth in custody if necessary (Blatier and Corrado 2001; Blatier and Robin 2001). The most common outcome that results from the information provided to the juvenile court judge is Educative Action in an Open Environment (*action éducative en milieu ouvert*). This order requires that the child live with the parent(s), and that the family meet regularly with a social worker. The social worker evaluates the young person and the family and draws up a plan, then works directly with the young person to help him or her implement the plan. The situation is evaluated within six months after the order has been issued to determine whether the order should be extended or terminated. The focus is on evaluating the risk posed to the child if he or she remains within the family. Where it is deemed necessary, experts will also be consulted to assess the specific risk factors in health, mental health and school. In addition, the juvenile court judge has the option of retaining the youth under the court's protective care until age 21. During this period the judge considers the specific problems that are inhibiting the youth's ability to reintegrate into the community. The judge also has the authority to devise, implement and monitor a plan of intervention that can include, but is not limited to, foster care, special education, and training programmes (Blatier 1998, 1999a).

The French approach to juvenile crime is imaginative and flexible, and could be a model for a humane and effective treatment for young offenders

(Ely 1990). The French model has many advantages. It is based on informal procedures and powers that maximise the quantity and quality of information the judge is able to utilise in devising, implementing and monitoring the outcome of individual cases. The French youth justice system places priority on understanding the juvenile's actions and offering therapeutic interventions rather than condemning the child (Blatier 1999b, 2000, 2002). The aim is to take into consideration the personal situation of the juvenile in order to prevent further offending behaviour. The extraordinary powers of French *juges des enfants* allow them to influence and direct access to state resources or programs. The youth court judge in conjunction with social workers acts at a critical moment of the young person's life 'when destiny is still flexible' (Garapon 1995). The focus of judicial intervention is on the family, rather than on ascertaining the precise actions that have taken place and on characterising specific acts as criminal or as child abuse.

In the Scandinavian countries and Finland the age of criminal responsibility is 15 years, and offenders under 18 years of age are subject to a system of justice that is geared mostly towards social services, with incarceration as the last resort. For example, in Finland the offending behaviour of children between 15 and 18 years of age is managed within the child welfare system. This system is very clearly based on the assessment of the needs of trouble-making children, and the norms of curbing offending youth are formally seen in the context of young offenders being in need of care, supervision and protection. Thus, young offenders are seen not as objects of punishment, but as being in need of supervision and control (Pösö 1991: 99). Similarly, in Denmark and Sweden, when juveniles under 18 years of age commit offences, the social welfare authorities intervene (Sarnecki 1991; Svensson 1995; Vestergaard 1991). Youth crime is seen as a social problem, and young offenders are regarded as in need of protection and support. Therefore, when the social welfare authorities make a decision regarding a suitable measure as a reaction to offending behaviour, the decision is based solely on the young person's social and family situation. Typical interventions include meeting with a social worker, family therapy, or intermediate care that involves structured activity with the young person in his or her home (Socialstyrelsen 2000).

Scotland has one of the lowest ages of criminal responsibility in Europe, 8 years of age, but the consequences of youth offending are almost all framed within the welfare system. The origins of the Scottish system of juvenile justice date back to the Kilbrandon Report (1964). The Kilbrandon Committee believed that in terms of the child's actual needs, the legal distinction between juvenile offenders and children in need of care or protection was very often of little practical significance. Kilbrandon argued that, more often than not, the problems of the child in need and the delinquent child can be traced to shortcomings in the normal upbringing process in either the home, the family environment or the school. Kilbrandon described such children, whether they were children in need or offenders, as 'hostages to fortune'. It was considered essential to extend to this minority of children the measures that their needs dictate and of which they have previously been deprived. Furthermore, since the incidence of delinquency, the forms and patterns it takes and, in many cases, the combination of factors underlying it vary widely from area to area, these problems must be tackled at local level.

Cases are initially referred to a Reporter from a range of bodies, including social work departments, the police and education authorities. The Reporter must decide whether referrals should be discharged with no further action or whether they should be referred to a social work department or to a children's hearing. The main grounds for referral to a children's hearing are that the child is in need, has offended, has been offended against, has truanted, has misused drugs or alcohol, has been physically, emotionally or sexually abused, has fallen into bad associations, is in moral danger, needs care and protection, or is out of control (section 52 of the Children (Scotland) Act 1995). No distinction is made between children referred because of an allegation that an offence has been committed and the other grounds. When a case reaches a children's hearing it is deliberated upon by three lay panel members who are selected to be reasonably representative of the community in terms of age, ethnicity and occupational background. The hearing can only proceed if guilt is admitted. If a child or parent denies the commission of an offence, then the case is referred to the sheriff's court for the offence to be proved. If it is proved, the child is referred back to the children's hearing. The children's hearing is solely concerned with deciding a future course of action. The hearing takes account of all aspects of a child's conduct, not simply the offence that has been committed. The panel considers many different facts in reaching its decision, including findings from social workers, school officials, children's homes and psychiatrists. The panel also considers what other people have done and neglected to do for the child. It recognises that the incident of an offence for which a child might be referred may be only one of several aspects involved in relation to a child's welfare (Hogg 1999: 63). Following a children's hearing, a limited number of options are available: the referral can be discharged; a supervision order may be made; or the panel may make a residential supervision order requiring the child to live at home or some other specified address.

The Scottish system has won praise throughout the world for the relaxed and informal way in which it deals with children who have committed crimes (King 1997; Whyte 2003). The advantages of the Scottish juvenile justice system and the other systems I have examined include their child-centredness, their focus on welfare and the avowed avoidance of punishment. These youth justice systems all adopt a holistic approach, looking beyond the deeds of young offenders, and provide a multidisciplinary assessment of children under the age of 18 years that looks beyond their offending behaviour to assess the nature of the intervention needed.

In all the jurisdictions examined the criminal justice system is not considered an appropriate response to a child's offences. Instead, the prevention of delinquency and juvenile criminal activity is seen in relation to a general concern for the mental and physical health of children as a means of promoting in the long term the mental and physical health of the community (Arthur 2004b). In England and Wales the White Paper *Justice for All* proposes granting the youth court power to direct a local authority to undertake a section 47 investigation into the circumstances of any child convicted of an offence, in order to ascertain whether grounds exist to justify applying for a care or supervision order (Home Office 2002: 5.58). This power would be similar to that which family proceedings courts currently have under the 1989 Children Act (section 37 Children Act 1989). The effect of this proposal is that the youth court will have to consider both criminal justice and social welfare issues when making decisions concerning children and young people (Home Office 2002: 5.59). This proposed reform would not only bring the youth justice system in England and Wales in line with the jurisdictions examined in this chapter, but also acknowledge the Children Act as an effective strategy for reducing the impact of risk factors and enhancing the influence of protective factors in the lives of youth at greatest risk of delinquency.

Conclusion

Chapters 3 and 4 have argued that in England and Wales there exists an agency and a legislative framework, similar to the French, Scandinavian and Scottish examples, that has the power to assess the nature of intervention needed by children at risk of offending, and children who have offended, and that has the authority to require that appropriate welfare or support services be provided. The Children Act provides a framework for local authorities to implement strategic approaches for providing support and services to youth at risk of engaging in offending behaviour and their families. The 1989 Act obliges local authorities to seek the cooperation of the police, schools, youth offending teams, local education authorities, health authorities, family centres, day care providers and also parents in identifying children at risk of becoming offenders. Local authorities must then assess the level of intervention needed by such children and provide, or arrange the provision of, the necessary welfare support. Thus, the potential of the Children Act 1989 is immense, as it provides a single system for assessing and providing the assistance needed by young people at risk of engaging in juvenile offending. How far the youth crime preventive aspects of the Children Act 1989, and the other programmes identified in Chapter 3, will fulfil these aspirations will depend on the resources made available, the kind of policies and programmes local authorities develop and how the services are delivered to families. This is a crucial question, which will be examined in Chapter 5.

Summary

This chapter investigated the formal assessment procedure adopted in defining priorities within the parameters of the Children Act 1989. This chapter established that children at risk of engaging in offending behaviour (as identified in Chapter 2) are 'children in need' and children at risk of 'significant harm', and therefore are legally entitled to the youth crime prevention support and services examined in Chapter 3. However, local authorities have a very wide discretion in determining how they will discharge their statutory duties. Chapter 5 will therefore examine how local authorities interpret and perform their youth crime prevention duties under the Children Act 1989 and consider whether in practice local authorities are implementing the youth crime prevention provisions of the Children Act 1989.

5 Local authorities' interpretation of their youth crime prevention duties

Introduction

As was evident from Chapters 3 and 4, the Children Act 1989 represents the linchpin for the development of an effective multi-agency youth crime prevention strategy. However, the effectiveness of the Act is unfortunately limited by the all-embracing vagueness of its provisions, which leave it to each local authority to define and finance the work they undertake. Each day, local authorities and their child welfare professionals translate the words of the 1989 Act and its related *Guidance* into practice by engaging in the process of supporting families and protecting children. Each local authority must determine issues such as whether the child is 'in need'; whether the child is suffering, or is likely to suffer, significant harm; what action must be taken; whether courts should be petitioned; and whether out-of-home placements are necessary. These decisions determine whether services are delivered or denied, whether children stay in foster care or return to once-abusive parents, whether families are housed or not, and whether troubled teenagers are sent to counsellors or to court. How these decisions are made will inevitably influence how local authorities discourage and divert children from engaging in offending behaviour. Given their impact on youth crime prevention, it is important to understand these decision-making processes as they occur in practice.

The question that this chapter will address is whether local authorities interpret their youth crime prevention duties in accordance with the analysis of Chapter 4. How child welfare decisions are made and how agencies use resources are the key issues that will be dealt with by this chapter. First, I will investigate how local authorities have interpreted the concept of children in need and evaluate whether local authorities consider the kinds of children examined in Chapter 2 as being children in need. Next, I will examine whether local authorities consider children at risk of engaging in offending behaviour as fulfilling the threshold criteria of section 31 of the Children Act. I will then consider how local authorities are implementing their duties in relation to looked-after children and investigate whether local authorities are fulfilling their youth crime prevention duties by developing inter-agency cooperation and facilitating the provision of preventive services by other agencies such as health authorities and youth offending teams. The central focus of this chapter will be the degree of concordance between the preventive perspective of the Children Act 1989 and the child welfare professionals' actions and motivations during the child care and protection process.

Local authorities' interpretation of 'children in need'

The effectiveness with which a child's needs are assessed will be the key to the value of subsequent action and services, and ultimately whether youth offending will be prevented. Because the definition of children in need is in the 1989 Act, a local authority cannot lawfully substitute any other definition. However, the criteria for determining need are wide and prospective, and could stretch to every child. Consequently, the legal definition requires operational interpretation. This section will examine how local authorities interpret their duty to safeguard the welfare of children with family support needs, and will thus verify whether the local authority's view is consistent with the analysis of Chapter 4.

Research findings expose local authorities as taking a rather less proactive approach than the architects of the Children Act 1989 may have hoped.[1] Two principal impediments have emerged which are hindering the implementation of the preventive provisions of the Children Act 1989:

- The evidence warns that in general there is very little consistency of approach to children in need between different local authorities: similar children are being treated very differently by different authorities. Decisions about who might access services are not transparent and are likely to vary from agency to agency, according to individual judgements of workers processing requests for services and the services available on the day. Thus, the principle of needs-based assessment is not being translated into practice.

- The research findings also suggest that there is a disproportionate distinction in respect of children considered in need and children considered to be at risk of significant harm. Protection issues consume the greater part of social service resources in England and Wales, with little left for the broader duties of prevention. Even for those considered to be at risk of significant harm, the focus is often too narrowly on the child and the child's immediate environment, with insufficient attention paid to the wider family context or the past social history.

In order to assess how these problems are affecting the way local authorities implement their statutory duties, I will examine each of these problems and their impact on how local authorities perform their youth crime prevention role.

Inconsistent interpretation of 'children in need'

There is a large body of research and experience which shows that the quality of assessments under section 17 of the Children Act 1989 needs to be improved, as assessments frequently do not have sufficient synthesis and analysis of data to support decision-making and the forming of long-term plans. For example, Gardner's study (1992: 141) found that section 17 has been poorly understood, resulting in many problems in its implementation. Gardner questioned 40 workers in fieldwork teams and family centres about their background legal and policy knowledge, the kind of tasks they undertook to prevent family breakdown, and tasks or activities they would have liked to have embarked on but were unable to do so, with the reasons. Detailed interviews were undertaken with 15 senior and middle managers in social services housing departments and 15 social workers in fieldwork teams and family centres. Gardner found that the majority of managers and workers interviewed were not aware of departmental policy on the subject of prevention. Between 33 per cent and 50 per cent of interviewees, both workers and managers, did not know the current legal provisions for preventing the need for children to enter care or go before a court. It took senior managers some time to discover written statements on these issues, but the majority of people had not seen them at all, and only two team leaders out of the whole group had discussed prevention and family support in a management context. These findings resonate with the results published by the Audit Commission (1994), which concluded that local authorities seem unsure how to identify children in need as required by the Children Act, and few have agreed definitions, assessed the extent of need, set priorities or planned services based on an assessment of needs.

Brandon *et al.* (1999) also found that social workers do not routinely refer to the legislation and are unfamiliar with the 'in need' definition. They identified a sample of 105 cases and followed them through for a year. Information was collected from case files and interviews with social workers at the time the child was identified for the study and again a year later. Brandon found that despite being clearly told that they may not rewrite the 1989 Act's definition of 'in need', local authorities, influenced by individual environments, politics and resources, drew up their own threshold procedures for prioritising the provision of services to those who crossed the 'in need' threshold, rather than the language of the Act. Very soon it was these procedures that were referred to by social workers when making decisions.

Similarly, Sinclair and Carr-Hill (1995: 3) formed the opinion that most local authorities have devised their own criteria for assessing who is a child in need. They surveyed 86 local authorities in England and Wales, which were asked to provide their current criteria for classifying a child as in need. The overall categorisations included children in need as a result of breaking the law; their own physical condition, disability or developmental difficulties; deprivation, poverty or social disadvantage; abuse or neglect; living within unstable, stressed, conflictual, emotionally or developmentally damaging families; or rejection from, estrangement from, or collapse of their own family. However, there was great variation in how these categorisations were applied in particular circumstances. Such variations reflect different political priorities and professional values, which are in turn reflected in local authority resourcing, organisation, management and coordination of services for young people. Sinclair subsequently undertook a follow-up study five years later and arrived at similar conclusions (2001: 99). This second study consisted of interviews with social workers in respect of 40 children with whom they were currently working.

Furthermore, research by Thoburn *et al.* (1997, 2000) indicated that few social workers turned regularly to the legal definition of 'in need'. Thoburn *et al.* explained that local authorities offered very little, if any, guidance to social workers on how to interpret the concept of 'children in need' in practice. In the absence of such guidance, social workers tended to fall back on their own individual value systems and experience, or resorted to readily available material designed for use in child protection work.

Colton *et al.* (1995a: 18) also found that the policy documents concerning children in need varied considerably in length and context. Some were brief, containing no reference to many of the duties required by local authorities under Part III of the Children Act, while others were comprehensive, covering almost every duty. The Victoria Climbié Inquiry noted that Haringey local authority had produced over a dozen documents containing policies, procedures and guidance for staff in relation to children's services (Department of Health *et al.* 2003). The inquiry found the material provided to be of a vast and dense nature and therefore recommended that staff be provided with guidance which would be of a 'real and practical help and of manageable length, the test being whether the material actually helps staff do their job' (ibid.: 14). Local authorities need to provide clear and succinct statements for workers and users alike of their family support strategy and its legal basis if they are to be effective in preventing juvenile offending.

Reports of the Social Services Inspectorate (1997, 1999a, 2002) have been very critical of the failure of local authority social services departments to meet the aims and objectives of section 17. The Social Services Inspectorate, having studied the responses of eight local authorities to requests for services from children in need and their families, found that the overall impression was of a lack of strategic planning and that most local authorities did not have a shared agency definition of children in need (Social Services Inspectorate 1997, 1998, 1999b). Hence, agencies sometimes provide services to families that may not need them and at the same time fail to provide other, higher-risk families with the resources needed to protect children adequately, thus rendering access to services something of a lottery. The Social Services Inspectorate concluded that assessment, planning and review systems were not in place in most social service departments and that while some social service departments had good services, overall they had not been well thought out and were not making the most effective use of resources (Social Services Inspectorate 1996).

The central philosophy and preventive principles of the Children Act 1989, including youth crime prevention, are being undermined because the family support aspirations and provisions of the 1989 Act are being implemented partially and not prioritised. Society expects that professionals, by virtue of their knowledge and skill, will make decisions carefully and in an informed and rational manner. Yet the picture that emerges is of social workers relying mainly on their common-sense understanding of people, enriched by some theoretical ideas from their training courses and insights gained from practical experience. It is important for local authorities to select the right strategic objectives to avoid these pitfalls if juvenile offending behaviour is to be seriously addressed. The value of services for young people and their families should be recognised as an investment for the future of the families involved and the community as a whole. If efforts were focused on providing help to troubled children, there should be less need to punish children in trouble.

Thresholds for Part III services are too high

Another problem, inextricably linked with the issue of inconsistent interpretation and implementation of section 17, is that there remains a remarkable unwillingness to equate need with anything other than the identification of serious child maltreatment. It seems that families that require help where children are in need for reasons other than child maltreatment are not always getting access to services. The fear is that child protection is taking increasing priority over child care, with family support and preventive services viewed as some kind of optional extra to be offered if resources allow rather than as part of the same continuum of services for children in need. Comprehensive needs assessment of children in each local authority should be undertaken, based on a broad interpretation of needs that looks at causes as well as symptoms of need. Failure to adhere to these basic principles increases the likelihood that individual beliefs, biases and political and financial considerations will shape implementation decisions. In this situation the ongoing issue of youth crime prevention can become marginalised.

Aldgate and Tunstill's study (1995a, b) provides a reliable measure of local authorities' attitudes towards defining children in need. They endeavoured to obtain a national picture of the range of approaches that local authorities were adopting to implementing section 17. Their findings were based on the results of a postal survey sent out in autumn 1992 to all 108 social services departments in England, of which 82 replied, and on in-depth interviews with senior and middle management in ten local authorities. The researchers looked at four main topics: how local authorities assessed the extent of need; which children and families were given priority for receiving services; what kinds of services were offered; and how far local authorities had collaborated with other agencies in defining and meeting need. The findings indicate that the criteria that determined why some children were sent down a 'child protection route' and other children were assessed as in need of Part III services were not necessarily based on children's needs.

For example, over 75 per cent of local authorities gave high priority to children at risk of harm or neglect, or children looked after, indicating that there was a common misperception that the statutory duty to provide for children in need referred only to these cases. When asked to consider characteristics of individual children which would lead to high priority for access to services, only 39 per cent of local authorities responded that children at risk of offending would constitute a high priority. Only 10 per cent believed that children in low-income families, children in one-parent families and children in families characterised by marital problems were a high priority within the community. Children who were homeless or those living in poor housing conditions were even less likely to be given a high priority for services.

This latter finding corroborates a 1993 study, which found that the majority of local authority social services departments in England and Wales did not consider homelessness alone as a sufficient reason to be accepted as 'in need' (McCluskey 1993), a finding that is clearly inconsistent with the analysis of Chapter 4. Tunstill summarised these findings as illustrative of the fact that section 17 is 'primarily designed to legitimate resource rationing' (1997: 56). Thus, local authorities are using the provisions of the Children Act to assess children as in need in a way that narrows and stigmatises the provision of family support services. This reality makes it practically impossible to carry out the necessary interventions to support and facilitate the family-strengthening philosophy of this book. Emphasising child protection work to the detriment of fulfilling the preventive duties of the Children Act places social workers in the position of doing more investigation than relationship-building, relying more on tools and instruments than on professional integrity and assessments, attending more to the needs of the organisation in order to avoid scandal than to the needs of families and children, and generally reacting after family breakdowns rather than engaging in interventions to prevent family crisis and subsequent delinquency.

The second *Safeguarding Children* report found that because some social service departments used inappropriately high referral thresholds they were failing to respond to the needs of children and families needing support (Social Services Inspectorate 2005). Because of social services' inadequate responses, other agencies do not always refer children when concerns about welfare emerge. Consequently, families are being subjected to avoidable pressure, and children may be experiencing preventable abuse and neglect. Thus, the language of practice needs to go beyond the limits of 'protection' to account adequately for the therapeutic process of self-healing that can, and should, be promoted through effective interventions. What is required is a shift beyond protecting children in their own families to protecting families from the social, economic and political forces that conspire to induce children into engaging in antisocial and offending behaviour.

Aldgate and Tunstill's findings are not just indicative of English local authorities. A study by Colton *et al.* (1995a, b) of children in need in Wales paints a similar picture. This study examined the provision of services for children in need and their families under Part III of the Children Act 1989. The first phase of this project was based on an analysis of local authority policy documents and interviews with leading child care managers in all eight social service departments in Wales, before their reorganisation into 22 unitary authorities.[2] The progress of the Welsh local authorities in implementing Part III of the 1989 Act was later compared with the progress made by eight similar authorities in England. This analysis of policies and plans was followed by a thorough study of two Welsh authorities on how need was actually assessed and responded to in practice. This involved interviewing over 100 child care managers and social workers. Child care managers were asked to rank nine categories of need in order of the actual service priority that each category receives, and then in the order that each category should ideally have, in the manager's opinion.

Actual rankings given by managers indicate that local authorities in Wales were clearly concentrating their efforts on children at risk of abuse and neglect. Social workers tended to construct definitions of need closely aligned with notions of minimum human rights and requirements such as adequate food, warmth, clothing, education, hygiene, appropriate developmental progress and a childhood free from abuse and neglect. However, when asked how they would prioritise under ideal circumstances, proactive prevention work came much higher up in the managers' 'ideal' list. This difference between actual and ideal rankings reflected the desire of child care managers to give equal priority to all children's needs. Thus, although family support services were desirable to lower the threshold of significant harm, resource constraints precluded offering these services to any other than those already defined as being high-risk cases.

Such practice reflects an imbalance between child protection and family support services. If local authorities act in the spirit of the Children Act 1989 they should prioritise children in need and match them to appropriate services, which would enable them to achieve better outcomes. While there should remain a clear focus on safeguarding children at risk of significant harm, nonetheless the consequence of emphasising protection rather than prevention means that local authorities will be obliged in the future to protect those children for whom they fail to provide preventive services at present (Colton *et al.* 1995a: 25). Interestingly, the study by Colton *et al.* also found that 11 per cent of parents were frustrated by the social workers' inability to solve children's delinquency problems and wanted information in this area (1995d: 99). These parents believed that social services were pushing back on to them responsibilities that should belong to the state, namely responsibility for delinquent youth – and, as I hope Chapter 4 convincingly determined, the parents were correct in their belief.

Aldgate and Tunstill's and Colton *et al.*'s findings are confirmed in other research. For example, Farmer and Owen's study (1995) found that there is intense concentration on protecting children, and in the process the wider welfare needs of children and their parents are given relatively little attention by professionals. This research was conducted in two local authorities in England. After attending at 120 initial child protection case conferences, Farmer and Owen drew up an intensive sample of 44 children on the child protection register from the 73 cases that were newly registered at these conferences (this corresponds to 60 per cent of the registered cases and was a representative sample). The parents, older children and key social workers were interviewed after the initial conference and again 20 months later. In addition, a scrutiny of the case files was undertaken at the end of the study. The study confirmed that too much emphasis is still being given to child protection investigation at the expense of family support services. The Social Services Inspectorate (1997, 1998) concluded from similar findings that eligibility criteria for family support services were poorly developed, and used to exclude people rather than to make services more widely available. As a result, some families that needed support were inappropriately caught up in the child protection system, while in other situations obvious risks to children were overlooked.

A Department of Health study (1994, 1995a) also found that it was noticeable that in some areas assessment procedures seem to be over-elaborate and unduly influenced by child protection, with children at risk of abuse or neglect and those in care or accommodation ranked highest. Some support was being provided to families below the threshold for full child protection procedures, but it was likely to be subordinate to the demands of child protection work, and such families had to be exceptionally demanding and persistent. The Department of Health recommended that family support services should be more readily available to children not identified as needing protection. Otherwise, local authorities are in danger of limiting resources simply to children on the child protection register. However, the definition of children in need is much wider than just children at risk of harm or abuse, and *Guidance* makes it plain that interpreting a 'child in need' solely in terms of the risk of significant harm would be unlawful (Department of Health 1991b: 2.4).

The research reviewed by the Dartington Social Research Unit (1995) also suggests that much work under the Children Act is performed under the banner of child protection. They believed that there was room for improvement in assessment procedures, particularly a more discriminating matching of children's needs to services (Department of Health 1995b: 7.9). It was found that some children were subject to section 47 inquiries because professionals believed that this increased their chances of getting resources for services (Brandon *et al.* 1999). Social workers and families were trying to get around narrow eligibility criteria set by individual social service departments by interpreting concerns about impairment as border-line concerns about possible significant harm. Thus, some social workers were deliberately manipulating the system to ensure that the children they judged to be in need gained access to services. The Department of Health (1998: 1.33) confirmed that other agencies also frequently referred children in child protection terms, as the referrer knew this was the most certain way to achieve an effective response. If agencies could establish that the family posed a substantial risk to the welfare of the children, this often increased the chance of accessing services for that family. It is not acceptable for child protection investigations to be used as a gateway for family support services. The effect of this is that through pressure of circumstances and in a family crisis, families become caught up in a child protection system that is more attuned to assessing risk than to bringing out the best in parents struggling in adversity.

An exclusive focus on identification of whether maltreatment has occurred can be deleterious to the child's welfare by allowing needs to go unnoticed, allowing problems to recur, or by dealing with cases via a section 47 investigation that do not warrant it, and families that might otherwise have used services to enhance their welfare become alienated (Waterhouse 1997: 192). If this overemphasis on investigations of child abuse were redressed, some of the resources that are consumed in often rather heavy-handed investigations of mild or minimal abuse could be redirected at helping families and consequently preventing juvenile offending. This broader approach to needs involves rebalancing children and family work and investing more in 'universal' provision such as playgroups, childminding and the development of a range of family and community support resources. Making this difference could have a positive impact on the lives of the most vulnerable children in England and Wales and thus on the generation to come. Such a view is advocated by the Audit Commission in an influential report published in 1994 that criticised local authorities for failing to develop adequate management information systems in relation to children in need. The report called for better use of risk assessment systems to achieve improved targeting of interventions on the most serious cases. The report argues that this approach would release resources, which would enable family support services to be developed and this would result in a reduction in the need for crisis intervention.

The research findings strongly signal that in practice local authorities are not complying with the analysis of Chapter 4. The evidence suggests that local authorities do not see their duty to assist children in need as directly connected to their responsibility under the 1989 Act for preventing delinquency and that not all local authorities have identified the children examined in Chapter 2 as being clearly within their responsibilities for children in need. Effectively, local authorities are abdicating responsibility for a specific group of 'children in need'. Although the Children Act 1989 represents a leap forward in the emphasis placed on providing support for families under stress, the legislation has not resulted in appropriate preventive work reaching the broad band of families in 'need' that was envisaged. Achieving the youth crime prevention objectives outlined in this book requires clear and unambiguous rules to guide those responsible for implementing them. Section 17 and Part III of the Children Act 1989 should be prioritised in terms of helping and supporting families with children in need and thereby keeping notions of policing, surveillance and coercive interventions to a minimum.

Child protection procedures and prevention of juvenile offending

This section will investigate whether local authorities consider that children at risk of engaging in offending behaviour fulfil the threshold criteria of section 31 of the Children Act 1989. Like the previous analysis, this section will examine how local authorities interpret the threshold criteria in practice and then examine the impact of their practice on the local authorities' youth crime prevention functions.

It has already been noted that a substantial proportion of local authority resources are being directed into child protection assessment. Unfortunately, this does not necessarily mean that children and their families will receive appropriate help. The seminal research of Gibbons *et al.* (1995) provides an illuminating illustration of how local authorities' implement their child protection duties under the Children Act 1989. This 1992 study was based in eight local authorities. Gibbons and co-workers identified all children referred for a new child protection investigation (1,888 cases) and tracked their progress through the child protection system for up to 26 weeks via social work records and minutes of case conferences. Of the original 1,888 allegations, 42 were lost from the outset and could not be traced. At the first stage about 26 per cent of cases were filtered out by social work staff without any direct contact with the child or family. This process may have involved discussions with the senior social worker and telephone calls to other agencies. Cases were more likely to be filtered out at this initial stage if the allegations concerned neglect rather than physical or sexual abuse, if the abuse was thought to be physically less serious, if the alleged perpetrator was not in the household, or if the source of the allegation was anonymous or from a lay person and there had been no previous contact with social services. This is in spite of the fact that juvenile offending behaviour is generated in the type of family that often comes to the notice of the local authority because of suspected child neglect.

A high proportion, approximately 44 per cent, of cases actually investigated[3] resulted in no further action at all: there was no intervention to protect the child, nor were any services provided. Moreover about 66 per cent of the cases investigated never reached an initial child protection conference. Gibbons *et al.* concluded that approximately six out of every seven children who entered the child protection system were filtered out without being placed on a child protection register. Thus, the most common outcome for children who entered the child protection system was case closure without any services being provided. This approach leads to large numbers of children being drawn into the child protection system, with their need for services being ignored once it is established that protective intervention is not required. If a large proportion of referrals receive no intervention, this raises questions as to the benefit for families of reporting or turning to local authorities. The children ejected from the system probably had no need for specific protection, but in most cases they appeared to fit within the definition of children in need, as they belonged to multi-problem families living in severely deprived circumstances. Thus, they were eligible for family support services, but these were rarely offered. Gibbons *et al.* also estimated that the proportion of unsubstantiated allegations – those that were assessed as untrue or having alternative explanations or insufficient evidence – was, remarkably, 49 per cent of the total. These findings indicate that resources are expended on investigating cases but identified needs are not met.

Similar results have been found in other studies. For example, Giller (1993) investigated four Area Child Protection Committees and found that over 75 per cent of cases 'dropped out' of the child protection system between the time of becoming a referral and the conclusion of a case conference with a view to registration. Giller noted that this represented a considerable volume of child protection work, even though registration was not the end result. The high rate of screening out may be attributed to the weakness of the original referrals or, more plausibly, to the failure to invest in prevention when earlier opportunities arise. Another closely linked factor is the critical atmosphere that surrounds child welfare workers. There is a tendency among social workers and other professionals to consider all children as potential victims of abuse and to adopt a 'safety first' approach, with both referrers and receiving social workers erring on the side of caution, fully recognising that there will be some false positives – that is, children deemed to be at risk and subjected to investigations when the likelihood of any abuse occurring is remote (Munro 1996). For staff there is always the anxiety that this referral may be the one that will attract attention, regardless of the details available at the time of the referral (Devaney 1999). The fear of a child abuse scandal influences the dominance of this type of work at the expense of supportive services where there are finite resources.

The Audit Commission report *Seen but Not Heard* (1994) argued that the amount of time and resources used up by investigating and responding to child protection referrals could be controlled and better managed by the use of clearer guidelines and by developing tighter risk indicators that trigger a full child protection investigation. The Audit Commission recommended specifically that ways should be found to screen out the high proportion of child protection cases that are not pursued after the initial time-consuming investigation. The productivity gains that would eventually follow from better focusing could free resources for social workers to specialise in more proactive interventions, for example in family support work or possibly preventive work with children at risk of engaging in offending behaviour.

Clearly, many cases initially seen as possible child protection cases receive no service after the initial investigation. But what about those children who are not filtered out of the child protection system after the initial assessment? Are these cases processed in accordance with the analysis of Chapters 3 and 4? An overview of the findings of the research studies suggests that local authorities are intervening and invoking child protection procedures solely on the basis of physical injuries to children without paying proper regard to the child's wider situation. Studies looking at families referred into the child protection system show that the daily routine of most child care social workers is dominated by such tasks as risk assessment, the collection of evidence and the surveillance of children considered to be at risk of abuse, and that the wider needs of children, beyond simply being protected, are often not identified or addressed. The legislation requires local authorities to establish whether or not the child is suffering or is likely to suffer significant harm, and whether any action should be taken to safeguard and promote the child's welfare. Such action includes exercising any of their powers under the Children Act 1989, among which are providing services to children in need. However, the much-needed provision of support services under Part III of the 1989 Act was observed in a number of studies to have been ignored while the social workers concentrated on a bureaucratic response to the injuries sustained.

In 1995 the Department of Health published a report entitled *Child Protection: Messages from Research* (Department of Health 1995b), which gave details of the key messages arising from 20 individual studies of research into child protection. *Child Protection: Messages from Research* noted the tendency for protection concerns to trigger an over-zealous interest in gathering evidence of physical harm to children without always addressing the needs of the child and the family. In many cases the emphasis on investigation meant that children clearly in need received no services because the physical maltreatment had not occurred or was only a minor incident. One of the conclusions reached from the research was that real benefits could arise if there were a focus on the wider needs of children and families rather than a narrow concentration on the alleged incident of physical abuse. These findings substantiate other researchers' opinions. For example, Aldgate and Tunstill (1995a: 35), through interviews with local authority managers, confirmed that children at risk of physical and sexual abuse were ranked as the highest priority. Brandon *et al.* (1999) also found that there was a continuing focus on acts of abuse rather than on its effects on the child.

The therapeutic and welfare orientations of the Children Act 1989 have been replaced by the forensic gaze of the child protection system, so that prevention is not able to force its way on to the agenda. This creates the serious risk that social workers will miss the chance to support parents by focusing narrowly on alleged incidents of physical abuse rather than looking at the child's needs within a child development and family context. Long-term youth crime preventive strategies must address the social and familial context in which children find themselves. Child protection inquiries should therefore not just be about whether or not an incident of physical maltreatment has occurred. Assessments should also take account of parents' situations and consider what help they might need to safeguard and promote the children's development.

Long-term difficulties for children are more likely to be a consequence of living in an unfavourable environment, particularly one that is low in warmth and high in criticism. Unfortunately, the research suggests that these are just the situations where the current operation of the child protection system, seems to be least successful, in the sense that such children are likely to be filtered out of the child protection system receiving few protective interventions or support services (M. Smith *et al.* 1995). Children at risk of emotional abuse or experiencing psychological difficulties appear to remain largely undetected by the child protection system, in part because of the uncertainty and confusion about what constitutes emotional abuse; it may be that it is considered too contentious to deal with unless it is very extreme, and perhaps also because it is not a category of abuse that is well understood by the legal system. The Social Services Inspectorate report *Someone Else's Children* (1998: 3.8) found that in cases of emotional abuse, even when the children concerned were on the child protection register, staff were unsure about the level of current or future harm that might be caused by such abuse and were subsequently unsure of the appropriate intervention to make. Some children were being left in emotionally abusive situations for too long, while too many other children were the subject of unnecessary inquiries under section 47. This report highlights the need for greater understanding of the impact of emotional abuse on children and the appropriate intervention mechanisms that need to be put in place. Fischer *et al.* (1995) noted the lack of attention paid in case conferences to the emotional environment in which the child grows up. This approach seriously inhibits parents seeking help and accurate professional understanding of parent–child relations. These findings prompted O'Hagan to describe the emotionally abused child as the 'least heard [and] the most easily ignored' (1993: 101).

Neglected children, too are often not regarded by social workers as suffering significant harm (Steele 2000: 318). Much evidence to the National Commission of Inquiry into the Prevention of Child Abuse (1996: 8.13) suggested that the neglect of children has itself been neglected by the statutory services. Gibbons *et al.* (1995) found that although 21 per cent of referrals to the child protection system were for neglect, ultimately only 7 per cent were registered. Many of those not registered failed subsequently to receive support. The Social Services Inspectorate's inspections of children's services in 32 local authorities between August 2000 and July 2001 found that there was a marked reluctance to intervene in long-term cases of chronic neglect (Cooper 2002: 3.46). Yet such families often have major material and other needs that social services neglect to attend to. Consequently, emotional abuse and neglect remain the smallest categories of child protection conference registrations (Department of Health 1991e: 6.40).

These findings are not indicative of trends elsewhere in the world. For example, in the New South Wales and Victoria emotional abuse is the highest registration category (Broadbent 1997). Research in the late 1980s in New South Wales indicated that the category of emotional abuse is used as a generic category for all cases where the child is deemed to be 'at risk' in a non-coping family (Craig *et al.* 1990). However, the small number of case conferences for neglect or emotional abuse, and the fact that they appear to be brought for conference as a last resort, and when registration is inevitable, suggests that the child protection system in England and Wales is much more sensitive to physical and sexual assaults on children than to the physical or emotional neglect of children. This confirms that local authorities will intervene to protect children from their families, but are more reluctant to intervene to promote parents' capacities to protect their children for themselves.

Claussen and Crittenden (1991) studied a sample of 175 cases of reported abuse in 2- to 6-year-olds, as well as a large sample of child psychiatry patients, and found that physical abuse and physical neglect, whenever they occurred, were almost always accompanied by forms of emotional abuse and neglect. Minty and Pattinson (1994) found that emotional neglect was an essential feature of all neglect, so that although emotional neglect is often found by itself, this is rarely true of physical neglect. Thus, in all except a tiny minority of the most serious cases of neglect and emotional maltreatment, both family support and child protection services are needed (Thoburn *et al.* 2000: 2). These findings should lead local authorities to take seriously the emotional, cognitive and behavioural consequences of uncaring parenting and extremely poor child management. A revised system, focusing on the need for assessments to address the full range of the needs of children and their families, rather than focusing solely on whether children are at risk of suffering physical or sexual harm, is more likely to tackle the adverse effects of emotional abuse and neglect. Preventing youth offending entails focusing on the child's emotional well-being as well as on the signs and symptoms of assaults; emotional harm must therefore be treated as 'significant'.

Farmer and Owen (1995: 79) found that social workers frequently had a poor understanding of the symptoms of mental illness, problem drinking and drug use among children, and their impact on the family. Consequently, social workers were hampered in working in partnership with families and responding to children's needs. Farmer and Owen also directed criticism at social work practice in the area of domestic violence. Watching repeated parental violence may lead to as much childhood disturbance and distress as physical abuse to the child; however, it is an aspect of family life that seems to receive little attention in child protection investigations. Farmer and Owen found that case conferences were often conducted in ignorance of whether or not children lived in violent families. In fact, they found that the level of domestic violence discovered during the research interviews was twice that known at the initial case conference. Daniel's findings also indicate that social workers do not pay sufficient attention to issues of domestic violence. Daniel (1999) explored 128 social workers' and students' beliefs and opinions about 'good enough parenting' and about decision-making in child protection. Violent marital conflict, a factor closely associated with juvenile offending behaviour, was present in nearly half of the cases and was an important factor contributing to significant harm to the child, but was overlooked in most child protection plans (Brandon *et al.* 1999). Further criticisms include social workers' tendency to focus on the woman's 'failure to protect' rather than appropriately challenging the man's violence (Lloyd 1995; Milner 1993), and the slippage towards emphasis on other problems such as parental mental health or alcohol abuse, so that domestic violence becomes invisible as an interconnected or coexisting issue (Humphreys *et al.* 2001). Local authorities must therefore consider domestic violence as a child protection, and by inference a juvenile delinquency, issue.

The Crime and Disorder Act 1998 supplements the protective provisions of the Children Act by providing local authorities with the power to intervene and prevent young people from offending (Home Office 2000). For example, local authorities can tackle the causes of youth crime by applying for an anti-social behaviour order, child safety order or a child curfew order. Yet these powers have been used sparingly; between April 1999 and June 2002 only 380 anti-social behaviour orders were made in respect of young people aged under 18 years (Campbell 2002b), only 12 child safety orders have been declared, parenting orders are rarely used and no child curfew zones have been introduced (House of Commons Research Paper 2001; Joint Committee on Human Rights 2003; Walters

2002). The courts have been less than enthusiastic in imposing parenting orders: between 1998 and 2003 only 3,106 parenting orders were made under the Crime and Disorder Act 1998.[4] There also appears to be a wide variation in the use of parenting orders by the courts. In some areas, fewer than 10 orders were made between spring 1999 and the end of 2001 (Holdaway *et al.* 2001; Youth Justice Board 2001). The criteria for recommending an order appear to lack consistency both within and between YOTs, and in some areas they are not supported by adequate resources (Audit Commission 2004). It seems that opportunities for local authorities to divert and discourage young people from engaging in offending conduct are not taken as often as they might be.

In general, the research findings suggest that local authorities operate with too strong a distinction between children perceived to be at risk of significant harm and other children deemed only to be in need. Social workers were found to have little spare time to organise support for families whose needs are not in crisis, and regard 'children in need' as a separate group with a low priority. Field social workers in particular appear to have insufficient time to undertake more proactive work in support of children in need and are giving less priority to the relationship skills which are so valued by teenage children because of the pressures of child protection work (Department of Health 1996, 2001a; Horwath 2002). Services for children at risk of significant harm should not be just about protective work, but should be truly supportive of children and young people in their families and in the community. The child's interests must come first, but this priority can be meaningful only if the climate of professional intervention allows for an objective and comprehensive appraisal of the child's needs and for those needs to be matched to resources with parental agreement whenever possible. Procedural guidance that stresses detection and monitoring without sufficient attention to support may serve to drive a wedge between parents and professionals to the detriment of children. This is not to suggest that physical, sexual or psychological harm to children should be ignored; on the contrary, supporting children and parents is likely to improve assessment and to target resources where they count. If the youth crime prevention provisions of the Children Act 1989 are to be realised, then what is needed is a more even approach that sees protection and prevention as part of a continuum whereby concern for a child should also call forth an assessment of family support needs. Such a scheme might prevent more serious outcomes, such as the child becoming an offender and incurring costly and harmful interventions.

Children leaving care

Looked-after children are three times more likely to receive a final warning, caution or conviction than young people generally (Department of Health 2002: 4.12). It is generally recognised that support for young people leaving care at the age of 16 has been underdeveloped, resulting in these young people frequently being left isolated, abandoned and at risk of engaging in offending behaviour (Audit Commission 1999b: 37). For instance, Marsh and Peel (1999: 102) conducted research into how local authorities were fulfilling their duties under section 24 of the Children Act 1989 to promote young people's welfare when they leave care. The study involved 87 young people who were about to leave care and who were not going home. Social workers admitted that the majority of care leavers were emotionally unprepared for leaving care (47 out of 81 responses) and merely adequately prepared for the practicalities of leaving care (49 out of 81 responses). Broad's study (1998) also provides clear evidence of the wide variation in social work support and in the range of financial assistance received by care leavers. This study comprised a questionnaire survey of 46 leaving care projects working with 3,308 young people throughout England. In this wide-ranging survey of the views of staff in leaving care projects, Broad concluded that support for young people in care is still very patchy and that policies on leaving care or accommodation are frequently not followed.

Robbins (2000: 1.6.3) found that the prevention of offending was found to be integrated into social work with looked-after children in only a few areas. Robbins's report was a synthesis of the evidence collected about how far 150 councils in England had met their targets for transforming children's service in Year 2 of the Quality Protects programme. Quality Protects was the government's five-year programme (1999–2004) for transforming the management and delivery of children's social services. It was a key element of the government's strategy for ensuring better life chances and improved outcomes for the most vulnerable children, such as children in need, children in need of protection, looked-after children and, by inference, children at risk of engaging in offending behaviour. From the mass of data collected, both qualitative and quantitative, evaluators were able to assess the extent of local authorities' achievements. Good work with care leavers of all ages was being done in all regions, but evaluators found that it was particularly concentrated on the older age groups, rather than on preventive and preparatory work with younger children. All councils were collaborating in one way or another with the development of the local youth offending teams; some had good information about offending among looked-after children, some were targeting young offenders with a range of projects and others were working on a prevention plan, again targeting the behaviour of potentially problem children. But few had got to the stage of requiring social work staff in all their contacts with looked-after young people to deal with the possibility, or fact, of offending as an issue potentially affecting the rest of their lives.

This evidence indicates that the duty to advise, assist and befriend children and young people who are no longer being looked after by the local authority is more often honoured in the breach than in the observance. The logical conclusion from this is that local authorities' duties towards children leaving care aged 16 or over, under the Children Act 1989 and the Children (Leaving Care) Act 2000,[5] are not being directly linked to their duties to discourage children from committing crime. Leaving care programmes need to take their place as part of a developing politics of child welfare capable of contributing to debates about wider youth policy issues, such as the prevention of youth offending behaviour. Meeting the needs of this highly vulnerable group of young people will require a comprehensive strategy addressing the resourcing of services, including an understanding of the dynamics of social exclusion and the need for 'joined-up' inter-departmental policy responses, the development of preventive services for vulnerable young people, as well as more focused substitute care, leaving care and after-care policy and practice responses.

Inter-agency cooperation

Local authorities have the lead role in responding to children in need, protecting children from significant harm and preventing juveniles from engaging in antisocial and offending behaviour. However, Chapters 3 and 4 established that ensuring inter-agency cooperation is an essential foundation stone of any youth crime prevention strategy. For example, the Crime and Disorder Act 1998 requires youth offending teams to undertake work to prevent juvenile offending and thereby help the local authority to discharge its duty to prevent juvenile offending under Schedule 2 of the Children Act 1989 (section 17 Crime and Disorder Act 1998). The youth crime prevention role of the YOT is underlined by the Youth Justice Board's stated twin objectives of reducing the number of young people who offend and ensuring that young people most at risk of offending are targeted by mainstream services (Youth Justice Board 2002b). Local authorities have been assisting youth offending teams to develop and provide schemes for identifying and supporting young people at risk of engaging in offending behaviour. For example, in 2001, local authority social services provided 56 per cent of funding to YOTs and in 2004–05 local authority social services provided 37 per cent of funding to YOTs (Youth Justice Board 2005b). Could this constitute evidence that local authorities are in fact actively discharging their duty to discourage juveniles from involvement in offending conduct by facilitating the provision of youth crime prevention services by other agencies in accordance with section 17(5) of the Children Act 1989?[6]

Youth offending teams have many statutory duties to fulfil. For example, they are required to coordinate the provision of youth justice services for those in the area who need them (section 38(4) Crime and Disorder Act 1998). This includes:

• the provision of appropriate adult services under the Crime and Disorder Act final warning scheme provisions (section 65 Crime and Disorder Act 1998);

- assessment and intervention work in support of final warnings given by the police to young people who admit offending;
- the prompt provision of pre-sentence reports required by courts in criminal proceedings against young people; participation on youth offender panels;
- preparation of youth offender contracts;
- supervision of young people sentenced to an action plan order (sections 69 and 70 Crime and Disorder Act 1998), reparation order (sections 67 and 68 Crime and Disorder Act 1998), supervision order (section 71 Crime and Disorder Act 1998), community rehabilitation order (sections 41–45 Powers of Criminal Courts (Sentencing) Act 2000), community punishment order (sections 46–50 Powers of Criminal Courts (Sentencing) Act 2000) or combination order (section 51 Powers of Criminal Courts (Sentencing) Act 2000);
- coordination and provision of effective support for young people on bail, through care and post-release supervision for young people sentenced to a detention and training order or other custodial sentence.

Thus, much of youth offending teams' core work is with known offenders, and it is a matter for local decision how far YOTs are involved in preventing offending by young people who have not yet committed offences (Home Office *et al.* 1998: 32).

Evidence suggests that much of the work of YOTs is concerned with those young people who have come to the notice of the criminal justice system and that preventing youth crime is a low priority (Wiles *et al.* 1999). Overall, a mere 2.5 per cent of the overall Youth Justice Board budget is being spent on preventing offending (Morgan 2005). For the period 2002–05 the Youth Justice Board spent just 0.28 per cent of its total budget on directing young people at risk of offending to mainstream services; a further paltry 0.83 per cent of its budget for this three-year period was allocated to reducing the number of young people who offend (Youth Justice Board 2002b). In 2005–06 the Youth Justice Board allocated just £9 million of its total budget of £383 million to preventing offending; 70 per cent of the Youth Justice Board's budget is spent on secure accommodation (Youth Justice Board 2005b). The Youth Justice Board plans to increase its spending on youth offending prevention to £33.8 million by 2008 (8 per cent of its total budget), while still spending approximately 65 per cent of its budget on secure facilities (ibid.: 27).

The effect of this budget allocation is that the youth crime prevention schemes devised by YOTs, studied in Chapter 3, are being developed and implemented in a piecemeal and incremental fashion. Splash schemes were guaranteed funding for 2003–04. They have now been replaced by Positive Activities for Young People (PAYP). PAYP were introduced in 2003 and aim to build on the success of Splash schemes by providing a broad range of constructive activities for 8- to 19-year-olds at risk of social exclusion.

However the future of PAYP is also in doubt, as this scheme is guaranteed funding only until the end of 2006. The Youth Justice Board is currently funding about 84 mentoring programmes, of which 34 involve intensive mentoring for ethnic minority and other hard-to-reach young people and the remainder involve mentoring help with literacy and numeracy. Only 1.11 per cent of the total budget will be allocated to these projects over the next three years. There are 72 Youth Inclusion Programmes (YIPs), all of which have been guaranteed funding until 2008. The government has indicated its aim for a 50 per cent expansion in YIPs by 2008, increasing the total number to approximately 108 (Home Office 2004). Yet in October 2002 the then Chairman of the Youth Justice Board, Lord Warner, conceded that to have a real impact on youth crime prevention 300–400 of such schemes were needed across England and Wales (Warner 2002). Lord Warner also highlighted the need for three times as many parenting courses as have been offered up to now. As a result of lack of resources, effective procedures for the establishment of social programmes to provide necessary support for children at risk of engaging in offending behaviour and their families are not being adequately developed. Furthermore, the YOTs' lack of preventive focus creates difficulties in engaging cooperation from education and health sectors in the prevention of youth offending.

Health services have also been slow to recognise the contribution they can make to youth crime prevention strategies. The national survey of mental health services for young people carried out in 1993 found wide variations in health authorities' willingness to cooperate with other agencies (Kurtz *et al.* 1994). The Audit Commission report *Children in Mind* also found that the amount spent by health authorities on specialist Child and Adolescent Mental Health Services (CAMHS) varied by a factor of 7 from area to area (Audit Commission 1999a: 31). The Audit Commission audited 59 health authorities and 147 NHS trusts between 1997 and 1999, thus, by 1 June 1999 it had reviewed approximately 60 per cent of the health authorities commissioning CAMHS in England and Wales and over 90 per cent of the NHS trusts providing CAMHS. The main part of the audit was carried out by means of questionnaires, and extra information was collected directly from professionals, who provided details of their work by completing a diary over a four-week period. This variation in service provision showed little relation to local needs and frequently resulted in a mismatch between needs and resources. In fact, one in ten CAMHS could not offer a first appointment for non-urgent cases within six months, and referrals were frequently allocated on the basis of which professionals had the time available, rather than their particular skills. The Audit Commission report also found that 33 per cent of health authorities did not have a complete understanding of the sources of income or their expenditure for their specialist CAMHS. If health authorities are to assist local authorities in their duty to discourage and prevent juvenile offending, there needs to be greater awareness of how much is being spent on these services, and separate budgets must be set up where none currently exist.

The Audit Commission asked the health trusts about their working arrangements with education, social work and youth justice services. One-quarter of health trusts delivering CAMHS had no joint working arrangements with GPs. More than 33 per cent of CAMHS trusts disclosed that joint working with the youth justice system was inadequate, and 66 per cent of youth offending service managers reported problems gaining access to mental health services. Only 14 per cent of referrals to CAMHS came from social services and education combined. The report suggests that social workers make few referrals to CAMHS because they are concerned that the child will have to wait a long time for an appointment and that the child will be seen in a health service clinic rather than in a setting that he or she is used to and may find more acceptable. Overall support for other agencies involved just 1 per cent of mental health professionals' time. Better inter-agency collaboration and joint planning are needed to respond to the mental health needs of children at risk of engaging in offending behaviour. Research also indicates a lack of communication and coordination between education and social service departments (Harker *et al.* 2003). Many social service departments do not hold central records of the schools that 'looked-after' children attend, and schools are unaware that they may have 'looked-after' pupils attending, or of whom to inform if they have concerns about the performance and behaviour of 'looked-after' pupils (Social Services Inspectorate and Office for Standards in Education 1995).

The Area Child Protection Committee (ACPC) has primary responsibility for ensuring and coordinating inter-agency cooperation in protecting children. The Social Services Inspectorate inspected the inter-agency arrangements for safeguarding children in eight ACPC localities between December 2001 and March 2002 and reported its findings in *Safeguarding Children* (Social Services Inspectorate 2002). This report found that the eight ACPCs were not actively addressing the needs of young offenders and young people at risk of offending, youth offending teams were working in relative isolation from other services, there was no regular inspection of the work of youth offending teams, and few ACPCs had representatives from youth offending teams on them. *Safeguarding Children* also found that local agencies did not generally accept that they were accountable to the local ACPC for safeguarding arrangements. Consequently, there were very few formal agreements between agencies about how and when information should be shared. In most areas the ACPC had not initiated, supported or endorsed joint information sharing protocols between agencies. Although at the time of the inspection some areas were working on draft protocols, most staff did not know about these. Only two areas had developed effective joint funding arrangements that would enable the ACPC to fulfil its responsibilities. The report recommended that strong leadership of the ACPC needed to be combined with the commitment of all local agencies to support its work. The second *Safeguarding Children* report in 2005 found that other agencies still did not understand the role of social workers (Social Services Inspectorate 2005). Agencies other than social services are often unclear about how to recognise the signs of abuse or neglect and are uncertain about the thresholds that apply to child protection. Also, there is still considerable variation in the membership and effectiveness of ACPCs, and arrangements for sharing information and joint working between agencies do not always work well. Consequently, there are delays in addressing risk factors, health issues and educational needs. These findings highlight the need to undertake further work to clarify roles and responsibilities across agencies when developing Local Safeguarding Children Boards (the successors to ACPCs).

The Social Services Inspectorate's inspections of children's services in 32 local authorities between August 2000 and July 2001 also highlighted the poor communication that existed when implementing child protection procedures (Cooper 2002). A number of Area Child Protection Committees had lost impetus, met only six-monthly and experienced problems regarding the poor attendance of agencies at review child protection conferences. The report recommended that in these areas there was a need to relaunch the ACPC in order to raise its profile and include it in the planning process. The Social Services Inspectorate was also concerned about delays in holding child protection conferences, which were frequently not held at regular intervals and frequently not minuted. Lord Laming's inquiry into the circumstances surrounding the death of Victoria Climbié found that the ACPCs involved in this case had become 'unwieldy, bureaucratic and with limited impact on front-line services' (Department of Health *et al.* 2003: 7). Lord Laming recommended that all workers involved in child protection investigations should be required to demonstrate that their inter-agency working practices are up to date.

These findings indicate that there is a need for inter-agency guidelines on delinquency prevention. These guidelines must provide a shared understanding of the links between delinquency and child abuse, a comprehensive overview of prevention planning, and protocols for developing and incorporating these plans in practice. In tandem with this, Local Safeguarding Children Boards (LSCBs) should ensure that their constitution, membership, level of representation and funding arrangements are adequately resourced for the purpose of leading the children's safeguarding agenda across the area in all relevant settings. Most importantly, LSCBs must guarantee that concerns about young people at risk of offending are identified and addressed in partnership with the local youth offending teams (YOTs) and invite all local YOTs to become full members of all LSCBs. Endorsing these recommendations will remove the current 'luck of the draw' situations many families are faced with when seeking local authority assistance.

Resources

The provisions of the Children Act 1989 represent potentially a very responsive and effective framework for preventing juvenile offending behaviour by adopting the philosophy of family support and family empowerment. It is evident from the analysis of this chapter that local authorities are not implementing the Children Act 1989 in accordance with the philosophy of Chapters 3 and 4. However, this is an expensive philosophy to put into practice, and the Children Act 1989 is not prescriptive, requiring only that local authorities set the level of services they consider appropriate for the children in their area. Each local authority must decide for itself how much it will spend on children's services. In 1999–2000 net expenditure for children and families was £2,760 million, 27 per cent of local authorities' total expenditure on personal social services of £10,050 million (Department of Health 2001b: 11.2). In 2000–01 the net expenditure for the same category was £2,840 million, 27 per cent of the total personal social services expenditure of £10,700 million. The proportion of local authorities' budgeted net expenditure on children and families for 2002–03 was £3,240.8 million, 26 per cent of total budget net expenditure of £12,622 million. Although the total personal social services spending increased by 18 per cent, expenditure on children's services increased by only 14 per cent. In 2003–04 local authorities' expenditure on services for children and families accounted for 24 per cent of their total expenditure. Local authority funding dictates a much narrower interpretation of need and tighter criteria for service provision (National Commission of Inquiry into the Prevention of Child Abuse 1996: 8.32). Therefore in practice, local authorities are defining 'appropriate' in a manner that matches their resources rather than the needs of children and families.

In order to gain a clearer picture of actual service provision, Colton *et al.* (1995a: 41) asked child care managers and social workers to state whether they felt that provision was adequate. The overwhelming majority (95 per cent) felt that, in general, the available services were inadequate. Services deemed to be least adequate were family centres; occupational, social, cultural or recreational activities; accommodation for children and families; day care; and out-of-school and holiday activities. There was a particular lack of services for children with emotional and behavioural problems in the 7–12 age group. The most requested form of help, social work support, was least likely to be met. Managers and social workers were next asked which categories of children they felt were most affected by inadequate services. Not surprisingly, the children least likely to be affected by inadequate services were children at risk of physical abuse. The categories of children identified by both social workers and managers as most likely to be affected by inadequate services were children living in poverty and children in unsatisfactory home conditions. Families whose main category of need was social deprivation were also least likely to get help.

These findings are replicated in other studies. For example, Tunstill and Aldgate (2000) found that the existence of a broad range of services for children in need remains patchy and does not have the universal endorsement of every social services department. Their study revealed a dearth of family support services for children in their teenage years. The Social Services Inspectorate report *Safeguarding Children* (2003) observed that in all areas, staff were concerned at the limited resources to provide support to families under stress. The Social Services Inspectorate study *Delivering Quality Children's Services: Inspection of Children's Services* found that arrangements to deliver child and adolescent mental health services on an integrated basis were poorly developed (Cooper 2002). These findings are of concern because it means that there is very little early intervention to address the problems of this age range, such as mental health, substance abuse or offending behaviour. If such problems are not addressed at an early stage, the children and young people in question may find themselves precipitated into care or into juvenile offending systems.

Although day care operates as a valuable addition to the range of services local authorities can offer children in need, in most local authorities independent day care places are arranged on an *ad hoc* basis; they are used for relatively few children and their use is often not planned or organised as part of a strategic approach to children's services. The picture that emerges from Dillon and Statham's national overview of the use of sponsored day care (1998: 121) is that there is little consistency in the organisation of sponsored day care placements between different areas and that rather than being multi-functional in approach, most day care services are mainly in the business of performing one function, be it care, education or support. The main data were drawn from questionnaires sent in October 1996 to all 118 English local authorities, 83 per cent of which were returned. Most of the questionnaires were completed by managers of early years or under-eights services, or by senior officers with knowledge of local authority policy on services for children in need and the use of day care to support such children.

Cannan demonstrated that other forms of child care provision in Britain, such as extended family care, childminders and playgroups, are also of variable quality '[T]he consequence for children is that the public care system, and its relations in the private, informal and voluntary sector is highly variable in quality' (1992: 158). Schweie (1994: 211) also observed that British child care facilities are 'inadequate, piecemeal and scarcer than in other EU countries'.

Britain's poor showing in terms of public day care is particularly striking in the case of under-threes (Candappe *et al.* 1996; Ruxton 1996: 156). The principal aim of Sure Start is to improve early years services for children living in the most disadvantaged neighbourhoods and communities, and it received £452 million over 1999–2001 with a further £580 million pledged for 2002–04. Initiatives such as Sure Start and On Track have proved to be an effective way to target limited resources to those most at risk (Audit Commission 2004). However, while the integrated and well-funded support systems offered by Sure Start have been welcomed, there has been a simultaneous criticism over the limited scale of its target group (Henricson *et al.* 2001). Many disadvantaged areas fall just short of its qualifying criteria: rural populations in particular are under-represented because of the dispersed nature of rural deprivation, and there are many poor families who live in averagely affluent areas. Not all programmes have clear guidance and support to ensure that they are developed locally according to a consistent national model (Audit Commission 2004: 200). It has taken longer than expected for Sure Start programmes to be implemented and to deliver a full range of services (Tunstill *et al.* 2002). If preventive activity is to continue to be funded through government initiatives it needs to be better coordinated and overseen from a single source.

Staff shortage is also a serious problem undermining the delivery of services to young people at risk of engaging in offending behaviour. The second *Safeguarding Children* report found regular difficulties in recruiting and retaining skilled and experienced social workers (Social Services Inspectorate 2005).

As a result of the shortage of resources, local authorities are having to operate high thresholds and small safety nets, turning away people who desperately need help. Several studies drew attention to the fact that families were sometimes offered services inappropriately, drawing from a pool of existing services that did not meet families' needs rather than providing services based on assessment of needs (Packman and Hall 1998; Statham *et al.* 2001). This pattern might be called a 'sticking plaster' approach to assessment, based on what services might be in the medicine box (Aldgate and Statham 2001: 120). A prudent manager has little alternative other than to draw attention to serious resource deficiencies and to ensure efficient management of what is available (National Commission of Inquiry into the Prevention of Child Abuse 1996: 5.9). Resource constraints compel managers to target particular groups, and children at risk of physical harm are inevitably afforded first priority. Consequently, local authorities do not have the resources to provide the assistance many children need; family support regularly comes too little, too late, and the reasons behind children's offending behaviour are not addressed.

The Social Services Inspectorate found that all departments inspected undersold family services. Local authorities were failing to ensure that social workers took such steps as are reasonably practicable to ensure that those who might benefit from the services receive information relevant to them, reflecting many managers' fears of a deluge of service requests that could not be met (Social Services Inspectorate 1998: 7.3). Progress was also less advanced in the area of seeking out the extent of children in need and developing services to meet them (Department of Health 1994). This points to the need for social services departments to consider how to better inform the public about their facilities, in order to raise public understanding. Improved information would enable families in need of services to select the most appropriate resources to meet their needs and, where necessary, approach departments before they reached a crisis. More attention needs to be given to improving the range and quality of information at local and national level to support the development of services and strengthen the effectiveness of the Children Act.

Conclusion

In July 2002 the Institute for Public Policy Research published an influential report on the criminal justice system in England and Wales (Sparks and Spencer 2002). The report recommended that the government should establish a unified juvenile justice system, based on the Scottish Reporter system, for assessing the nature of intervention needed by young offenders and those at risk of offending. This system would receive referrals from police, schools and parents and have the authority to require that services be provided. I have argued throughout this book that such a system already exists in England and Wales in the form of the Children Act 1989 and that there is no need for a new system to be established. However, this chapter has illustrated that local authorities are not complying with the analysis of this book and are very much failing to fulfil the youth crime prevention duties of the Children Act 1989. Therefore, the problem is a matter not of law, but of its implementation.

The child care and protection system as a whole operates against a background of conflict and uncertainty. There are dilemmas over what constitutes abuse and over the relative weight to be given to the welfare of children, their rights and wishes, and the rights and responsibilities of their parents. Most local authorities have not developed clear priorities for allocating resources or determining who is eligible for services. Decision-making is compromised by factors such as time pressure, lack of resources, internal politics and fear of child abuse scandal. Local authority practice has consequently become preoccupied with child rescue and insufficiently attentive to providing supportive and preventive services. Local authorities are not working in cooperation with other agencies such as local youth offending teams and education and health authorities. Local authorities are hesitant to commit expenditure to prevention, even though this will be more economical and effective in the longer term. The potential savings to victims, society, the criminal justice system and the local authority from effective youth crime prevention measures are surely immeasurable.

What is required is the development of a more robust network of family support services to try to ensure that they do not once again end up subservient to child protection services, and also better targeting of child protection endeavours, resulting from improved practice and procedures. A more balanced service for vulnerable children would encourage professionals to take a wider view; there would be efforts to work alongside other agencies and organisations, to strengthen and support families in their parenting responsibilities, to raise families' self-esteem rather than reproach them, and to promote family relationships where children have their needs met, rather than leave untreated families with an unsatisfactory parenting style. A comprehensive service for vulnerable children would enable professionals to look at protection concerns in the context of other needs, considering the overall needs of families rather than concentrating on the alleged incident of abuse. Local authorities need to devote far more attention to prioritising resources in the direction of preventive services, including youth crime prevention.

The reality is that the Children Act 1989 has been seriously under-resourced, and this has presented a range of difficulties for all professionals concerned with responding to the problem of the prevention of juvenile offending behaviour. In an era of scare resources it would seem that local authorities are misdirecting too many resources to cure rather than prevention. Until the approach outlined in Chapters 3 and 4 is adopted, local authorities will continue to disregard their statutory functions and fail in their duty to discourage juvenile involvement in crime. The next chapter will examine how the gap between the analysis of Chapters 3 and 4 and the local authorities' practice, discussed in this chapter, can be redressed.

Summary

Chapters 3 and 4 established that the Children Act 1989 contains provisions that potentially can prevent children who are at risk of engaging in antisocial and offending behaviour (as examined in Chapter 2) from becoming offenders. This chapter has demonstrated that the youth crime prevention provisions of the Children Act are not being implemented. There are many reasons for this. For example, services are crisis oriented, communication among service agencies is lacking, local authorities are overburdened and existing services are not adequately funded. Chapter 6 will examine the extent to which local authorities can be compelled to fulfil their youth crime prevention role, and hence will determine whether the disparity between my analysis of local authorities' youth crime prevention duties (Chapters 3 and 4) and the actual everyday practice of local authorities (this chapter) can be bridged.

6 Enforcing the role of local authorities in preventing youth crime

Introduction

This book has conclusively argued that the predictive factors for likely future involvement in juvenile crime are not conditions for which the child is directly responsible but reflect familial, economic and social deficits that must be rectified. Young people should not be punished for what their family environment makes of them; instead, they should be protected from the factors that contribute to offending behaviour. It has been shown that the Children Act 1989 entitles all children to an experience of good parenthood and that the responsibility for ensuring that young people are protected from criminogenic influences rests with the local authority. However, as is evident from the previous chapter, some local authorities operate a very narrow interpretation of the 1989 Act, with the result that young people in trouble and their families are not receiving the services they require and are entitled to under the legislation. It therefore seems fair to assume that local authorities have been unable to fulfil their youth crime prevention responsibilities.

This final chapter will examine to what extent the disparity between the preventive analysis of Chapters 3 and 4 and the local authority practice analysed in Chapter 5 can be overcome. The question that this chapter will address is whether a young person at risk of involvement in criminal activity can compel the local authority to provide preventive services. This chapter will consider whether 'children in need', in accordance with section 17 of the Children Act, can enforce their right to receive Part III services. I will also consider whether children who are being abused and neglected or at risk of being abused and neglected and not receiving help from social services have any avenues of redress. I will examine each possible avenue of redress and determine which, if any, is the most appropriate means of enforcing the youth crime prevention powers and duties of the Children Act 1989.

Complaints procedure

Complaints procedures were introduced into the Children Act 1989 as a means of ensuring 'justice, quality and efficiency in public administration' (Lewis and Birkinshaw 1993). The principle that underpins the complaints procedure is that 'vulnerable people' need protection and that service quality may be improved by encouraging consumers of social services to 'challenge or question the system' (Department of Health 1991f: 1.5). Every local authority must therefore have a procedure for considering representations and complaints made by children it is looking after, any young person qualifying for advice and assistance, or any child to whom it owes a duty as a child in need, which, as seen in Chapter 4, includes those children who are at risk of engaging in offending behaviour. Complaints may also be made by parents or anyone else with parental responsibility, local authority foster-parents and others whom the local authority recognise as having a sufficient interest in the child's welfare (section 26(3) Children Act 1989). Children's access to the complaints procedure is dependent on their knowledge of its existence and the provision of support for those wishing to make a complaint, therefore the local authority must publicise its procedures for considering any complaints.

Can young people at risk of engaging in offending behaviour, as identified in Chapter 2, use the Children Act complaints procedure to compel a local authority to provide them with the youth crime prevention services examined in Chapter 3? The Children Act *Guidance* specifically details the areas in which a complaint can be made as including the provision of day care services, support to children within their family home and accommodation of a child (Department of Health 1991f: 10.8). Section 24(14) of the Children Act 1989 allows young people to complain if they consider that the local authority has not given them adequate preparation for leaving care or adequate after-care. Although the Children Act *Guidance* indicates that the complaints procedure should be used primarily by children and their families under Part III of the Children Act 1989, it is a matter of good practice for authorities to extend the provision of a complaints procedure to complaints concerning protection issues. In *R v. East Sussex County Council, ex parte W*[1] Scott Baker J confirmed that where someone was aggrieved at the failure of a local authority to apply for a care order, the complaints procedure would in ordinary circumstances provide a suitable remedy. He observed that under section 26(2) the local authority must review certain matters, including whether to apply for the discharge of a care order. He concluded that once decisions about the discharge of a care order come under Part III, it would seem difficult to construe a decision to apply for an order as relating solely to Part IV. Thus a decision whether or not to mount care proceedings is one that is capable of falling within the remit of the statutory complaints procedure. Children who have not received Part III services or children aggrieved by a local authority's failure to apply for a care or supervision order can use the Children Act complaints procedure to give voice to their grievance. These are the same children identified in Chapter 2 as being at risk of engaging in offending behaviour. Does this mean that such children can enforce the local authority's youth crime prevention powers and duties?

The complaints procedure must ensure that an 'independent person', someone who is not a member or officer of the authority, is involved in the consideration of the complaint and any discussions about what action is to be taken (section 26(4) Children Act 1989). Independent persons are expected to be 'neutral and identified with neither the local authority nor the complainant' (Bridge 2001: 220; Social Services Inspectorate 1991: 21). If the complainant is dissatisfied with the proposed result, he or she can insist that the complaint is referred to a complaints panel of three people, at least one of whom must be independent. This independent person may not necessarily be the same independent person as at the first stage of the procedure. It would seem preferable to have a different person at the second stage regardless of whether the independent person at the first stage has supported the local authority's position (Ryan 1999: 183).

Section 26(7) of the 1989 requires the local authority to have 'due regard' to the findings of those considering the complaint. This does not mean that the local authority must abide by the recommendations of the complaints panel; it simply means that the recommendations must be looked at and not ignored. In *R* v. *Brent London Borough Council, ex parte S*[2] the Court of Appeal acknowledged that it could not compel a local authority to accept panel recommendations. It went on to say, however, that it would be an unusual case when an authority acted contrary to the recommendations, the criterion being whether the departure from a complaints panel's recommendations is reasonable. Therefore, while the complaints procedure allows young people at risk of engaging in offending behaviour, and young offenders, a means of voicing their criticisms, it does not necessarily guarantee that local authorities will be forced to adopt a more proactive approach to youth crime prevention.

If the complainant is still dissatisfied with how the authority has handled the process, he or she could complain of maladministration to the Local Government Ombudsman. The Local Government Ombudsman, also called the Local Government Commissioner, is completely independent and may inquire more widely into discrimination, incompetence, delay or other maladministration. The jurisdiction of the Ombudsman extends across the broad range of local authority functions, including education functions. The Ombudsman can examine all the papers in a case and require people to give evidence by issuing a subpoena. The Ombudsman has the power to determine whether maladministration has taken place and whether there has been an injustice from which someone has suffered as a result. Maladministration relates only to the manner in which the decisions are reached and not to the quality or reasonableness of the decision itself.[3] Examples of maladministration include failure to follow an authority's agreed policies or rules of procedures, failure to have proper procedures, failure to tell people of their rights, failure to provide advice or information when reasonably requested, or the provision of inaccurate or misleading advice. If there has been an injustice, the Ombudsman may recommend that a local authority should pay compensation, but cannot enforce an award of compensation. Indeed, a recalcitrant local authority could ignore the Ombudsman's report altogether, the ultimate sanction being bad publicity as a result of the publication of the Ombudsman's findings (Daly 2000). The voice of the child is also strengthened by the establishment of a Children's Rights Director, under the Care Standards Act 2000. The Children's Rights Director's functions include ensuring that the Care Standards Commission safeguards the rights and welfare of children receiving regulated services and gives proper consideration to the views of children and their parents. Also, the Children Act 2004 created the role of the Children's Commissioner in England; Scotland, Wales and Northern Ireland had already appointed Children's Commissioners. The Commissioner's remit is to promote awareness of views and interests of children. The Commissioner is expected to raise the profile of the issues that affect and concern children, and promote awareness and understanding of their views and interests among all sectors of society, both public and private.

As a last resort, a complainant may have recourse to section 84 of the 1989 Act and ask the Secretary of State to find that the authority has failed without reasonable excuse to comply with its duties under the 1989 Act. The Education Act 1996 confers general default powers upon the Secretary of State to intervene where local education authorities have failed to discharge any statutory duty (sections 496 and 497 Education Act 1996). The Secretary of State may invoke this power irrespective of whether any complaint or representation has been made; conversely, the Secretary of State is not obliged to act even if a complaint has been made.[4] If the decision of the Secretary of State finds the local authority in default, he can direct it to comply within a stated time, and seek an order of 'mandamus' against the authority if it does not do so (section 84 Children Act 1989). Simon Brown LJ pointed out, in *R* v. *Devon County Council, ex parte Baker*,[5] that where ministers have default powers, application to them will generally be a better remedy than bringing an action to court. The minister has the means to conduct an appropriate factual inquiry and can bring the department's expertise to bear upon the problem. Moreover, unlike the court, the minister can direct a solution, rather than merely leaving the local authority to re-determine the question. Recourse to the Secretary of State might provide a useful remedy for general rather than particular issues. For example, if a local authority decided that it would not provide, nor purchase, a service for deaf children, it might be possible to ask the Secretary of State to intervene, because the authority would be failing in its duties under section 17 of the Children Act 1989 (Daly 2000). Section 84 of the 1989 Act could also be used if the local authority failed to provide any day care for under-fives, or if it failed to publicise services, or if it failed to make requisite provision for a class of children. Accordingly, if a local authority decides that it will not be providing services to discourage those at risk of engaging in offending behaviour, this could credibly be grounds for a complaint under section 84.

The benefits of the complaints procedure are that it is a low-cost, informal procedure which can provide the solution actually sought by the complainant. In R v. *Kingston-upon-Thames Royal Borough, ex parte T*[6] the High Court emphasised the scope of the complaints procedure as well as its speed, convenience and cheapness. However, the complaints procedure is internal to the local authority and therefore not entirely independent, and only results in recommendations, not binding decisions. Also, there is no general complaints procedure against local education authorities; such complaints can only be made to the Local Government Ombudsman or the Secretary of State. There are procedural advantages in going to the Ombudsman in terms of speed, cost and informality. The notion of injustice in maladministration is also more malleable than the recognised heads of loss in a negligence action, with *ex gratia* compensation often being paid for feelings of anxiety and uncertainty and 'time and trouble' in pursuing maladministration. However, the Ombudsman service also has a considerable disadvantage compared with other remedies. Not only is the local authority's compliance with the Ombudsman's decision voluntary, but also any compensation paid will be small compared with damages in tort. The welfare of the child will not be the Ombudsman's paramount consideration, and he or she may not have any particular expertise in child care matters. The process of complaining to the Ombudsman is lengthy and there is no power to require a local authority to alter its decision. As for complaining to the Secretary of State, it is unlikely that the Secretary of State will regard this procedure as an avenue for complaint about how individual cases have been handled; rather, it seems likely that it will apply to an absence of services to a group of children. Thus, although the complaints procedure, the Ombudsman service and the Secretary of State's powers all provide a means of enforcing the local authority's youth crime prevention duties, nevertheless, owing to the shortcomings and disadvantages of these procedures, it is imperative to consider other avenues of redress.

Judicial review

In administrative or public law terms a failure on the part of the local authority or local education authority to fulfil or perform a statutory duty or power may be investigated and enforced by way of judicial review. Judicial review is a means by which members of the public can seek to ensure that public bodies observe the law. If the local authority has acted in breach or disregard of its statutory responsibilities, or in a way in which no reasonable authority could have acted, the remedy of judicial review should ensure the actual performance of the duties breached. Will this procedure provide an effective remedy for those at risk of engaging in offending behaviour who have not received the family support services that Chapter 4 determined they are entitled to, because of the reasons identified in Chapter 5?

The purpose of judicial review is to ensure that the individual is given fair treatment by the authority. The focus is on the decision-making process and whether the authority has approached its decision legally, rationally and with procedural propriety, and not on the facts or merits of a decision. Relief will only be granted if a decision can be shown to be *ultra vires* (beyond the authority's legal powers), based on a misinterpretation of the law, procedurally incorrect, contrary to the rules of natural justice or unreasonable. The unreasonableness test, as laid down in the landmark case of *Associate Provincial Picture House Ltd.* v. *Wednesbury Corporation*,[7] establishes two criteria upon which a local authority may be said to have acted unreasonably: (1) because the local authority has taken into account matters that should not have been taken into account; or, conversely, (2) it may have failed to have regard to relevant matters. If the applicant succeeds in establishing any of the above grounds, the High Court may at its discretion set aside the decision that has been made, thus requiring the local authority to reconsider the care arrangements made, or the failure to carry out a duty; or it may order the authority to rectify the omission. The court can quash the local authority decision, it can order the local authority to stop the action it is taking, or order the authority to act or make a decision where it has wrongfully failed to do so, but the court cannot substitute its own decision for that of the authority and the court cannot direct a local authority to implement a particular course of action.[8] The function of the court is only to see that lawful authority is not abused by unfair treatment and not to attempt itself to fulfil the task entrusted to the local authority by the law.[9]

In order to deter frivolous or inappropriate claims, an applicant for judicial review must obtain preliminary leave from the High Court (section 31 Supreme Court Act 1989). The High Court will wish to ensure that the applicant has sufficient standing to commence the application, and that the case has some prospect of success. Where there has been a genuine and fair consultation by the local authority, it is unlikely that judicial review will be successful.[10] Leave to apply for judicial review will not normally be granted if there are more suitable methods of redress that have not been pursued by the applicant. Thus, there is an expectation that the complaints procedure will be used first.[11] In *R* v. *Brent London Borough Council, ex parte S*[12] the Court of Appeal held that 'if a statutory right of appeal has been provided but not pursued or exhausted it is only in exceptional circumstances that the court would entertain an application for judicial review or grant relief'.[13] In *R* v. *Kingston-upon-Thames Royal Borough, ex parte T*[14] the High Court emphasised that 'the door of the court is the last door that should be opened'.

Once these hurdles have been overcome, there is still no guarantee that judicial review will be of any assistance to children at risk of engaging in offending behaviour who have not been provided with Part III or Part IV services under the Children Act. In *R* v. *Harrow London Borough Council, ex parte B*[15] the court held that recourse to judicial review ought to be rare in the field of child protection. Butler-Sloss LJ stressed that 'all concerned in this difficult and delicate area should be allowed to perform their task without looking over their shoulder all the time for the possible intervention of the court'.[16] Thus, the success of such proceedings would be dubious save in the most clear of cases and extreme of circumstances.

For example, it was established in *Nottingham County Council* v. *P*[17] that the court does not have the power to direct a local authority to apply for a care order. Moreover, it would be difficult to judicially review a decision in the case of an individual child by reference to the general duty contained in section 17 of the Children Act 1989, as section 17 is wide and leaves a generous margin within which the local authority can operate (Everall 1991: 213). Lord Hope in *A* v. *London Borough of Lambeth*[18] held that the duty owed by local authorities to children in need under section 17 of the Children Act 1989 was a target duty owed to children in general and was not justiciable by judicial review.[19] The House of Lords believed that section 17 is directed to a wide section of the community, namely children in need within the authority's area, and it is therefore owed collectively rather than individually. Section 17 was considered by the court to be a hybrid provision: it is on the one hand more than a mere power, but on the other, less than a specific duty to, and enforceable at the behest of, individuals. A child in need is eligible for the provision of these services but has no absolute right to them.[20] This view was confirmed by the Court of Appeal in *The Queen on the Application of* W v. *Lambeth London Borough Council*.[21] Brooke LJ held that section 17 merely confers a 'target duty' and that in relation to individual children the local authority has only a power. Because there was no enforceable duty, and owing to the wide discretion conferred upon local authorities in determining what course of action to pursue under section 17 of the Children Act 1989, the court had no power to intervene and compel the performance of a duty under section 17.

This echoes the language of Woolf J in *R* v. *Inner London Education Authority, ex parte Ali*.[22] In this judicial review application concerning the duty of a local education authority, under section 8 of the Education Act 1944, to provide primary school places of a sufficient number, character and equipment to afford all children optimum opportunities, Woolf LJ drew attention to the fact that this duty could be described as a target duty and the standards to be achieved were for the local education authority to determine as long as they did not go outside the tolerance provided by the section. He added that even if the education authority was not meeting the required standards it would be meeting its statutory duty if it was taking steps to meet the required standards.

Judicial review was unsuccessfully employed to complain that a local authority was failing to provide a day care facility in *R* v. *Barnet London Borough Council, ex parte B*.[23] All six applicants were children in need within section 17 of the Children Act 1989, attending a day nursery school provided by the council pursuant to its responsibilities under sections 17 and 18 of the 1989 Act. Their application was for judicial review of a decision made by the council to close the school. Auld J held that sections 17 and 18 imposed on the council a general duty to provide day care for children in need; nonetheless, this left the council with a measure of discretion.[24] It was therefore for the council to decide the weight to be given to the circumstances of any individual child in the context of the general range of services provided, and to balance those considerations against its financial and budgetary constraints. Auld J recognised that there will inevitably be instances where the overall provision is appropriate, yet not ideal for certain individual children. Deciding what considerations and what weight should be given to the interests of any child when his or her needs or interests may conflict with the appropriate provision overall is essentially a matter for the local authority and not the court.

These rulings will be of particular significance to those children in need or suffering significant harm (and thus at risk of engaging in offending behaviour) who have not been provided with the protective (and youth crime preventive) services of Parts III and IV of the Children Act 1989. However, a shift of emphasis towards recognising the effectiveness of judicial review in the context of section 17 of the Children Act 1989 is evident in *Re J (Specific Issue Order: Leave to Apply)*,[25] in which Wall J emphasised that Parliament envisaged that the exercise of the duties imposed on local authorities under Part III of the Children Act should plainly be susceptible to judicial intervention by means of judicial review. This was also the view of Potter LJ in *R* v. *Kensington and Chelsea Royal London Borough Council, ex parte Kujtim*,[26] in which he categorically stated that there was nothing in the judgment of *R* v. *Inner London Education Authority, ex parte Ali* that prevented an aggrieved individual from seeking, or obtaining, by judicial review an order requiring the local authority to carry out its duties. In *Queen on the Application of A* v. *Lambeth London Borough Council*[27] Laws J went even further and stressed that a decision by a local authority not to exercise its powers under section 17 is also open to judicial review.[28] In *R (on the application of G)* v. *London Borough of Barnet; R (on the application of W)* v. *London Borough of Lambeth; R (on the application of A)* v. *London Borough of Lambeth*[29] Lord Nicholls, dissenting, asserted that section 17 imposes a duty in respect of each individual child within the local authority's area who is in need. Lord Nicholls believed that the generality of an obligation in respect of children in a local authority's area is not of itself inconsistent with the obligation being a duty in relation to the needs of individual children in the area. An obligation in respect of the general may include an obligation in respect of the particular. A duty in respect of an entire class or group as a whole may include a duty in respect of the individual members of the class or group, depending on the language read in its context. Lord Nicholls asserted that there is nothing in the language of section 17 which suggests that the duty is not a duty in respect of each child within the local authority's area who is in need. The phrase 'children within their area who are in need' refers to all the children in need within the local authority's area. Section 17(1) is intended to be wide in its scope because the needs of children vary widely. Lord Nicholls believed that local authorities must provide an appropriate range and level of services, whatever those services may be. The duty to promote the welfare and upbringing of all such children makes little sense unless it is a duty in respect of the welfare and upbringing of each such child. Indeed, if this were not so, section 17(1) would be a poor general duty.

Thus, from the recent case law it seems that a failure by a local authority to exercise its powers or duties under section 17 could be susceptible to judicial review. Any other view would mean that a local authority is not under any duty to assess the needs of any child under section 17. Such an approach would blunt the whole purpose of Part III of the Children Act 1989. It is implicit in section 17(1) that a local authority will take reasonable steps to assess the needs of any child in its area who appears to be in need. The first step towards safeguarding and promoting the welfare of a child in need by providing services for the child and his and her family is to identify the child's need for those services. If section 17(1) imposes a duty on a local authority to assess the needs of an individual child, then it equally imposes a duty to provide a range and level of services appropriate to those needs. Actions or omissions by a local authority in the exercise of its child care functions should therefore be capable of being subject to judicial review. Consequently, the children identified in Chapter 4 as children in need and at risk of engaging in offending behaviour should be able to use judicial review to compel a local authority to fulfil its youth crime prevention role.

Examples of the successful use of judicial review in respect of local authority child care functions include *Re T (Accommodation by Local Authority)*,[30] in which it was held that the court could quash the refusal of a Director of Social Services to ratify the decision of a complaints panel that a child should be accommodated under section 20(3) on the basis that her welfare would otherwise be seriously prejudiced. Likewise, in *R v. Avon County Council, ex parte M*[31] judicial review was granted when the authority failed to deal properly with the recommendations of a complaints panel. In *R* v. *Hampshire County Council, ex p K*[32] the local authority failed to disclose to the parents medical reports relating to their children, who were the subject of the proceedings, and refused to permit the parents to allow their own medical consultant to examine the children. Both of these decisions were subject to judicial review and quashed. A similar result occurred where a local authority decided to close children's homes without sufficient regard to the interests of the children living in them[33] or where an education authority arbitrarily reduced the provision of home tuition.[34] Decisions taken at case conferences are subject to judicial review when the question is whether the conduct of the conference was unfair or unreasonable.[35] Sedley J pointed out, in *R* v. *London Borough of Islington, ex parte Rixon*,[36] that a failure to comply with the statutory guidance is unlawful and can be corrected by means of judicial review. Non-compliance by local authorities with section 17 of the Crime and Disorder Act 1998 could also provide grounds for judicial review against the authority (Boys *et al.* 2001). In *R* v. *Wandsworth London Borough Council ex p S*[37] the High Court held that judicial review is clearly available where local authorities blankly refuse to assess whether a child is a 'child in need'. Judicial review provides a means of questioning how local authorities exercise their child welfare powers and duties, and therefore could potentially provide a remedy to those children in need who are at risk of engaging in offending behaviour and have not been provided with the youth crime prevention support and services of the Children Act 1989. Chapter 4 established that all children at risk of engaging in offending behaviour enjoy the right to receive youth crime prevention services, and judicial review provides a means of questioning why some young people are not receiving these services. Judicial review could galvanise a local authority from the dormancy evident in Chapter 5 into compliance with its youth crime prevention powers and duties. Even if the legal outcome is not as the complainant desires, the publicity generated could prove to be to a complainant's advantage (White and Liell 1992).

Though judicial review has proved to be increasingly far-reaching in questioning how local authorities are fulfilling their youth crime prevention role, it is limited in its effectiveness and it does not provide a source of compensation. Judicial review is a cumbersome and expensive way of challenging local authorities' decisions. Judicial review is only effective for challenging local authority actions at the time they occur, and does not provide redress in relation to decisions made in the past. Another major problem with judicial review as a method of challenging local authorities is that the court is only looking at the way in which the decision has been made, and not at whether the decision itself is right or wrong. A complainant may win the legal argument but the court may exercise its discretion not to grant relief. Even if an order is made which requires a local authority to take a decision again and change a policy that fetters its discretion, that will not necessarily mean a different outcome for the families involved. Given these limitations, it is to be hoped that a more effective means of enforcing local authorities' youth crime prevention role is available.

Action for damages

Money damages are at the heart of the common law system. Where the plaintiff is damaged by a negligent action, the ordinary rule is that the negligent actor must compensate the victim for the losses incurred. This section will consider whether dissatisfied complainants can bring civil proceedings for negligence against a local authority which, they allege, has failed to discourage them from engaging in offending behaviour. Can children who have not received the support and services that Chapters 3 and 4 established they were entitled to, and subsequently engaged in offending behaviour, hold the local authority liable for failing to fulfil their youth crime prevention role as prescribed in the Children Act 1989?

A young person seeking to claim compensation from a local authority for loss or damage that he or she has suffered as a result of something the local authority did, or failed to do, would have to answer three questions: (a) was there a duty of care; (b) was there a breach of that duty; and (c) was there damage caused by the breach of that duty? Damage, which includes physical, emotional and psychological harm, is the essence of a cause of action in negligence, and the critical question in a particular case is whether the scope of that duty of care in the circumstances of the case is such as to embrace damage of the kind that the plaintiff claims to have suffered. Where damages are felt to be too remote from the event causing the damage, the victim's right to recovery will be limited. As Lord Bridge stated in *Caparo Industries Plc v. Dickman*,[38] 'It is never sufficient to ask simply whether A owes B a duty of care. It is always necessary to determine the scope of the duty by reference to the kind of damage which A must take care to save B.' The House of Lords in *X (A Minor) v. Bedfordshire County Council and Others*[39] clarified the scope of the private law remedy of an action for damages for breach of duty in the context of alleged failures by a local authority in connection with its child protection duties. This case concerned a local authority that failed to take appropriate action to protect the five child plaintiffs against parental neglect and the risk of abuse. The local authority had received reports from relatives, neighbours, the police, the family's general practitioner, a head teacher, the NSPCC, a social worker and a health visitor that if the plaintiff children continued living with their parents they would be at risk of abuse, including sexual abuse, that their living conditions were appalling and that the children were hungry and dirty. Despite these reports, the defendant local authority took little or no action with regard to the children from 1987 until 1992, when it finally decided to seek care orders in respect of them. In 1993 the children brought an action against the local authority claiming damages for breach of statutory duty and negligence. It was argued that the local authority should be held liable for breach of a duty imposed by statute, as the authority had failed to have regard to the children's welfare as required by the Children and Young Persons Act 1969, the Child Care Act 1980 and the Children Act 1989. The children also alleged that there was a breach of a duty of care owed by the local authority to the children.

In order for damages to be claimed for breach of a statutory duty, the statute must be designed to protect a limited class of the public and it must be clear from the terms of the Act that Parliament intended individuals to have a right to claim damages for breach of any of the duties imposed by the Act. It was accepted that the Children Act 1989 was designed to protect a specific group of people; however, it was not accepted that the Children Act 1989 afforded a right to claim damages for breach of a duty. The House of Lords considered that the child protection legislation operates in an 'extraordinarily delicate' sphere where exceptionally clear statutory language would be necessary to indicate the existence of an action, and that the words of the relevant primary legislation are inconsistent with any such intention.[40] The House of Lords found that the duty imposed upon the local authority in relation to the welfare of children was so general and unspecific that it conferred a wide scope to exercise subjective judgment. Lord Browne-Wilkinson insisted that where a public authority enjoyed such a statutory discretion, it was for that body and not the courts to exercise the discretion. Therefore, nothing that the body did within the ambit of its discretion could give rise to an action at common law. The plaintiffs, in seeking to show that the authority acted outside its discretion, would have to prove that it acted manifestly unreasonably so that its actions fell entirely outside the ambit of statutory discretion. The same test would similarly apply in cases concerning careless and negligent exercise of a statutory power as well as a duty.

In the decision of *Stovin* v. *Wise*,[41] it is clear from the majority judgment given by Lord Hoffman that the courts will only rarely impose a duty of care on a public body in the context of a claim concerning the omission to exercise a statutory power. Lord Hoffman expressed the view that the fact that Parliament has conferred a discretion must be some indication that the policy of the Act in question was not to create a right to compensation.[42] Two minimum conditions were laid down for basing a duty of care on the exercise of a statutory power in respect of an omission to exercise the power: (1) it must have been irrational for the authority not to have exercised the power, so that there was in effect a public law duty to act; and (2) there must be exceptional grounds for holding that the policy of the statute conferred the right to compensation on those who suffered loss if the power was not exercised. The doctrine of general reliance developed in the Australian High Court by Mason J in *Sutherland Shire Council* v. *Heyman*[43] was accepted in limited circumstances by Lord

Hoffman. This doctrine, as propounded by Mason J, is based on the idea that the legislature may well have conferred powers on a public body in relation to matters that were of such complexity or magnitude that individuals could not be expected to take adequate steps for their own protection. Such a situation generates a general expectation on the part of the individual that the power will be exercised, and a realisation on the part of the public authority that there will be general reliance on the exercise of that power. Lord Hoffman held, in *Stovin*, that it was essential to this doctrine that the benefit or service provided under statutory powers should be of a uniform and routine nature, so that one could describe exactly what the public authority was supposed to do.[44] Thus, if a service was provided as routine, it would be irrational for a public authority to provide it in one case and arbitrarily withhold it in another. Therefore, X v. *Bedfordshire* and *Stovin* v. *Wise* create quite an obstacle to enforcing the youth crime prevention powers and duties of the Children Act 1989.

The second action brought against the local authority in X v. *Bedfordshire* was breach of a duty of care owed to the children. The House of Lords accepted that there was a relationship of proximity between the local authority and the plaintiffs, and that the damage suffered by the plaintiffs was foreseeable. Nevertheless, the House of Lords held that public policy considerations negated the imposition of a duty. Lord Browne-Wilkinson identified five such considerations, namely:

a the interdisciplinary nature of the child protection system and the consequent difficulties of allocating responsibility between agencies;
b the delicacy of the authority's task in dealing with children at risk;
c the risk of local authority's adopting a cautious and defensive attitude through fear of liability;
d potential conflict between parents and social workers could generate ill-feeling and litigation;
e the existence of alternative remedies.

Lord Browne-Wilkinson considered that professional standards are likely to suffer in the face of potential litigation. Fear of litigation could lead those fulfilling the duties imposed by the relevant legislation to discharge their obligations in a detrimentally defensive frame of mind; consequently, the local authority might put children at risk by making extended inquiries to obtain concrete facts. Thus, he doubted whether 'a scheme of social welfare for the benefit of the public at large could ever be construed to give rise to an action for breach of statutory duty'.[45]

Their Lordships concluded that a child has no cause of action for harm arising from: (a) an alleged failure of a local authority to comply with its statutory duties under children's welfare legislation; (b) careless performance of a statutory duty by an authority; (c) negligence in respect of alleged failure; and (d) actions or decisions where a common law duty of care might arise, if they came within the ambit of a statutory discretion. In *E (A Minor)* v. *Dorset County Council, Christmas* v. *Hampshire County Council* and *Keating* v. *Bromley London Borough*[46] the same House of Lords applied the same policy concerns to the statutory machinery that regulates the powers and discretions of local education authorities. Thus, the statutory powers and duties under Parts III and IV of the Children Act 1989 are, according to *X* v. *Bedfordshire*, not actionable where a breach occurs. Where local authorities have failed to provide children in need and children at risk of significant harm with the support and services which Chapters 3 and 4 established they were entitled to, and such children's behaviour has deteriorated to the point of delinquency, the local authority will not be held to have been negligent. From these judgments it seems likely that any remedy for improper exercise of local authority's youth crime prevention duties will be a public law action based on judicial review of the local authority's actions.

What about children who have been abused while in care and have gone on to live disruptive lives, and subsequently engage in offending behaviour throughout their youth? Have such children any entitlement to damages? The five policy factors from *X* v. *Bedfordshire County Council* were applied in exactly the same way to negate the imposition of a duty of care in *H* v. *Norfolk County Council*.[47] In *H* the plaintiff was taken into care at the age of 4 and was placed with foster-parents for nine years. Several years after attaining his majority he brought an action in tort against the local authority alleging that his foster-father had abused him and that the local authority had been negligent in failing to monitor and supervise his placement, failing to investigate reports of abuse and in failing to remove him from foster-care. However, in the light of the *Bedfordshire* ruling, his claim was struck out as disclosing no reasonable cause of action.[48]

Barrett v. *Enfield London Borough Council*[49] represents a discernible swing of the pendulum against the restrictive position applying to negligence claims in child protection cases. The plaintiff, by then in his twenties, brought an action in negligence against the local authority claiming for personal injury. He had been made the subject of a care order when he was a baby and had remained in care until his majority. He alleged breaches by the authority of its duty to protect him from physical, emotional, psychiatric and psychological injury, and to promote his development. The pleadings alleged a series of errors over the years he was in care which ultimately resulted in psychological and psychiatric problems, and marriage and employment difficulties. He complained of the authority's failure to arrange his adoption, unsatisfactory placements with foster-parents and in community homes, lack of monitoring, and failure to manage his reintroduction to relatives. If the duties that lay upon the defendants had not been breached, he would not, on the balance of probabilities, have left the care of the local authority as a young man of 18 years with no family or attachments whatsoever and become involved in criminal activities. The House of Lords unanimously held that the *Bedfordshire* case did not in the circumstances prevent a claim of negligence being brought by a child formerly in the local authority's care. The question whether it was fair, just and reasonable to impose a duty of care was not to be decided in the abstract on the basis of assumed hypothetical facts but had to be decided on what was proved. The plaintiff was accordingly entitled to have his claim heard and the facts investigated, and not to have his case summarily dismissed.

The House of Lords in *Barrett*[50] considered the public policy considerations explored in *X v Bedfordshire County Council*. While not disputing the validity of these policy concerns, and thus not overruling this case, their Lordships held that they did not apply with the same force in *Barrett*, as X had involved the sensitive issue of whether or not to take a child into care, whereas in *Barrett* the plaintiff was already in the care of the authority. *Barrett* is concerned with the negligent commission of local authorities' powers and duties once they have assumed care of a child; X related to a local authority's omission to exercise its duties. In reaching this conclusion the House of Lords examined the relevance of each of the policy considerations to Barrett's claim:

1. Regarding the 'interdisciplinary nature of the child protection system', the House of Lords considered that it was wrong to preclude a whole class of actions because of their inherent complexity, as the claimant should not be blamed for the fact that the claim happens to concern intricate facts or issues which occurred some time in the past. In fact, doubts were expressed as to whether the description in *X v. Bedfordshire County Council* of the multidisciplinary process and the role of the local authority was factually accurate.

2. Another policy concern expressed in *X v. Bedfordshire County Council* was 'the delicacy of the authority's task in dealing with children at risk'. It is undeniable that account needs to be taken of the sensitivity of these tasks, and the desirability of allowing those who undertake them a margin of discretion. It is not self-evident, however, that these concerns should be used to exclude liability entirely. Many professionals make sensitive decisions, and do so without the protection afforded by denial of liability. Lord Hutton emphasised that local authorities and social workers are skilled professionals who, in common with health care professionals and teachers, should be subject to a duty of care.[51] Their Lordships were acutely aware that they had to restrain, within reasonable bounds, claims against local authorities exercising statutory powers in the social welfare context. However, the court also stressed the importance of setting reasonable bounds to the immunity such public authorities can assert. In recognition of this conflict of considerations, Lord Slynn stressed that local

authorities can rely on the principle in *Bolam* v. *Friern Hospital Management Committee.*[52] In *Bolam* it was held that

> [a] doctor is not guilty of negligence if he has acted in accordance with a practice accepted as proper by a responsible body of medical men skilled in that particular art. . . . Putting it the other way round, a doctor is not negligent, if he is acting in accordance with such a practice, merely because there is a body of opinion that takes a contrary view.[53]

Applying this ruling to local authorities means that when social workers perform their duties they must do so in accordance with practices accepted at the time by a responsible body of opinion skilled in the particular duties in question. Hence, local authorities will continue to exercise a significant measure of discretion in the course of their child care-related work. They can only be held liable where they have reached a decision that no responsible body of social workers would endorse.

3. 'The risk of local authorities' adopting a cautious and defensive attitude through fear of liability' was one of the policy reasons militating against a duty of care in the *Bedfordshire* case. Empirical evidence is seldom given for this defensive practice phenomenon. It is a matter of impression, expressing a hypothesis rather than any proven conclusion (Stapleton 1995; Wright 1998). It also assumes, perhaps unfairly, that public-sector workers will adopt a rather faint-hearted approach to front-line public service provision when faced with professional negligence standards, in that it presupposes that those persons subject to the legal duty will misread the standard of behaviour that is required of them and react in an overly cautious manner.[54] A robust standard of proof of breach would thwart tendencies towards defensive practice. This approach has been borne out in *Barrett*, as both Lord Hutton and Lord Slynn upheld Evan LJ's contention that

> if the conduct in question is of a kind which can be measured against the standard of the reasonable man, placed as the defendant was, then I do not see why the law in the public interest should not require those standards to be observed.[55]

Moreover, the existence of a duty of care can play an important role in contributing to the maintenance of high standards of public service provision, resulting in fewer children wrongly being taken into care and more children rightly being taken into care. This view is shared by the New Zealand Court of Appeal in *AG* v. *Prince and Gardner,*[56] which explicitly rejected the House of Lords fear in *Bedfordshire* that private law duties would lead to defensive social work. The New Zealand Court of Appeal believed that a private duty of care would reinforce the role of the social worker rather than cut across that role.

4. It has also been held that a duty of care should not arise because of 'the existence of alternative remedies'. The House of Lords in *Barrett* doubted the effectiveness of parallel mechanisms compared to negligence actions and held that these should not exclude a duty of care. It is obviously preferable for expensive litigation to be avoided by resort to alternative dispute mechanisms, but such alternative remedies should not preclude a duty of care.

Lord Slynn in *Barrett* emphasised that the decision as to whether or not to take a child into care was not justiciable; however, the House of Lords concluded that actions or omissions by a local authority, once it was looking after a child, may be actionable depending on the circumstances of the case.[57] *Barrett* established a common law duty to protect and promote the welfare of children in care. Historical barriers against the liability of local authorities in the field of child welfare have been broken down by *Barrett*. As a result of *Barrett*, children who have been in local authority care and suffered harm and, as Chapter 2 found, are at risk of engaging in offending behaviour will be afforded the opportunity to seek to establish that the local authority inflicted reasonably foreseeable harm upon them while in a proximate relationship with them.

Barrett was followed in *S v. Gloucestershire County Council* and *L v. Tower Hamlets London Borough Council*.[58] In both cases the plaintiffs, now adults, had been in the care of their respective local authorities and lived with foster-parents. They both alleged that they had been sexually abused by their respective foster-fathers and brought actions against the local authorities claiming damages for personal injury, including psychiatric damage, suffered as a result of the negligence and breach of duty of care by the local authorities. The whole course of the care of S and L by the defendants, including both acts and omissions, was under scrutiny in this case. S led a deeply disturbed teenage life, engaging in antisocial and offending behaviour. He made a number of court appearances for various offences and was fined on several occasions and sentenced by a youth court to one year's supervision. He was also sentenced to periods of detention in a young offenders' institution. At the time of the hearing he was serving a two-year prison sentence in Belfast for stealing. In court, Dr Friedman, a consultant psychiatrist, gave evidence that S's problems were directly attributable to his abuse by his foster-father. Dr Friedman expressed the opinion that earlier recognition of the abuse would probably have prevented or ameliorated his antisocial behaviour.[59] L had also shown evidence of personality disorder through her teenage years, with truanting, shoplifting, fraud and drug use. Dr Tonks, a consultant psychiatrist who interviewed L, stated that there was a correlation between L's childhood sexual abuse and her disturbed and unstable personality in her teens. May LJ accepted the evidence of the psychiatrists as providing a sufficient case that the negligence alleged did in fact cause the physical and psychological damage, including the offending behaviour. May LJ held that cases that might be labelled as child abuse cases were not bound to fail as a class and that *H v. Norfolk County Council* should not be followed. May LJ determined that there may be circumstances in which a claim in common law negligence might succeed, where an individual claims that he or she has been damaged as a result of the failure of the local authority to look after him or her. It would therefore be unlikely that local authorities could establish a defence that relied upon blanket immunity. *S v. Gloucestershire County Council* is evidence that the courts are more willing to recognise duties of care in the sphere of public authority liability and that local authorities must accept some responsibility for any of their actions or inactions which may contribute to the causes of juvenile offending behaviour.

Barrett v. *Enfield London Borough Council* and *S* v. *Gloucestershire County Council* exemplify a more liberal approach to awarding compensation against public authorities who have placed children in abusive situations, negligently managed their care or failed to prevent harm by others; and, as Chapter 4 demonstrated, harm includes juvenile offending behaviour. On the basis of *Barrett* and *S*, it seems that a child who has been in the care of a local authority and endured hardship and suffering, including engaging in antisocial and offending behaviour, may successfully argue a case of common law negligence. English law has reached the stage where the prospect of a claimant's action being met by a striking-out order has been significantly reduced. The individual factual circumstances in each case will determine whether it is fair, just and reasonable to impose a duty of care on the protection agency. However, the acknowledgement of the inappropriateness of automatic strike-outs should not be equated with a general willingness to impose negligence liability. Thus, although it will be easier to demonstrate the justiciability of any given case, it by no means follows that legal accountability, and damages, will be any easier to obtain. What comfort does this provide to children in need seeking redress for a failure by a local authority to fulfil its obligations under Part III of the Children Act 1989? For children who are not in local authority care, the case of *X v. Bedfordshire County Council* still provides a discouraging obstacle to negligence claims, particularly for alleged carelessness in investigating abuse. From these judgments it seems likely that any remedy for improper exercise of a local authority's youth crime prevention powers and duties will be a public law action based on judicial review of the local authority's actions, or extra-judicial routes such as the complaints procedure or the Ombudsman. The decision as to whether or not to take a child into care therefore appears to be non-justiciable. However, no firm conclusions can be drawn on this latter point until the jurisprudence of the European Court of Human Rights is examined.

European law

Children who have been harmed in care, or children who have suffered as a result of a local authority's failure to prevent their injuries, including those at risk of engaging in offending behaviour, could bring a complaint under the European Convention for the Protection of Human Rights and Fundamental Freedoms. In this section I will examine a number of recent decisions by the European Court of Human Rights which found that the restrictive provisions of tort law in relation to child welfare, as expressed in *X* v. *Bedfordshire County Council*, fell foul of European law.

A relevant case to start with is *Osman* v. *UK*,[60] in which the European Court of Human Rights called into question the approach of the English courts to the liability of public authorities. In this important decision from Strasbourg the European Court of Human Rights considered that the blanket immunity from suit enjoyed by the police for their acts and omissions in respect of their investigation and suppression of crime[61] amounted to a breach of Article 6(1) of the European Convention on Human Rights, the right to a fair hearing.[62] The European Court of Human Rights held that the English Court of Appeal's application of a generalised public interest ground for denying a duty of care[63] amounted to a disproportionate restriction on the plaintiff's right of access to the courts. The English court had failed to demonstrate that it had properly considered the scope and application of any such immunity to the particular facts of the case by seeking out and balancing any competing public interest arguments. *Osman* thus reflects a more liberal view of public authority liability. The effect of this European Court ruling was considered in *Kent* v. *Griffiths*[64] by Lord Browne-Wilkinson, who observed that after *Osman* 'extreme care ... must be taken in striking out claims in this confused and developing area of law.' Similarly, Lord Woolf MR believed that, post-*Osman*, it is much easier for public authorities to be sued for negligence.

Z & Ors v. *UK*[65] is the first case in which the European Convention has been held to impose a positive obligation on the state to take operational measures in order to protect children against abuse and neglect in the family. In *Z & Ors* v. *UK* the applicants in *X* v. *Bedfordshire* complained to the European Court of Human Rights that the local authority failed to protect them from inhuman and degrading treatment in circumstances where the local authority was aware of the serious neglect and abuse that the children suffered at home. They also complained of a lack of procedural safeguards, of a lack of access to court and of a lack of effective remedies in respect of their complaints. The European Court held that Article 3 requires states, and therefore local authorities, to take measures designed to ensure that individuals within their jurisdiction are not subjected to torture or inhuman or degrading treatment, including such ill-treatment administered by private individuals. The court considered that the neglect and abuse suffered by the four child applicants unequivocally reached the threshold of inhuman and degrading treatment. This treatment was brought to the local authority's attention in October 1987; it was under a statutory duty to protect the children and had a range of powers available to it, including removing the children from their home. The children were, however, taken into emergency care only on 30 April 1992. The European Court acknowledged the difficult and sensitive decisions facing social services and the important countervailing principle of respecting and preserving family life. Nonetheless, the facts of the case left no doubt as to the failure of the system to protect these child applicants from serious, long-term neglect and abuse. Accordingly, there had been a violation of Article 3 of the Convention.

The applicants also complained that they had been denied access to court to determine their claims of negligence against the local authority, invoking Article 6 of the Convention. This article gives everyone the right to have a claim relating to his or her civil rights brought before a court or tribunal. The applicants alleged that the House of Lords had unequivocally rejected their claim on the basis that actions against the local authorities for decisions taken in relation to child protection were excluded. However, the European Court found there was no breach of Article 6(1), the court observed that the applicants were not prevented in any practical manner from bringing their claims before the domestic courts. Indeed, the case was litigated with vigour up to the House of Lords, the applicants being provided with legal aid for that purpose. The court held that to bring Article 6(1) into play, it is not enough that the non-existence of a cause of action under domestic law may be described as having the same effect as an immunity, in the sense of not enabling the applicant to sue for a given category of harm. Moreover, the European Court argued that it could not be said that the House of Lords came to its conclusion without a careful balancing of the policy reasons for and against the imposition of liability on the local authority in the circumstances of the applicants' case. The court concluded that the inability of the applicants to sue the local authority flowed not from an immunity but from the applicable principles governing the substantive right of action in domestic law.

Accordingly, the European Court found that there had been no violation of Article 6 of the Convention. Yet the outcome of the domestic proceedings the applicants brought is that they, and any children with complaints such as theirs, cannot sue the local authority in negligence for compensation, however foreseeable and severe the harm suffered and however unreasonable the conduct of the local authority in failing to take steps to prevent that harm. In the European Court's view this is an issue under Article 13, not Article 6(1). Article 13 provides the right to an effective remedy before a national authority where there has been a violation of a Convention right or freedom. In *TP & KM* v. *UK*[66] the European Court of Human Rights interpreted Article 13 of the Convention as guaranteeing a remedy to enforce the substance of the Convention rights and freedoms at the national level in whatever form they might happen to be secured in the domestic legal order. The European Court in *Z* found that the applicants did not have available to them an appropriate means of obtaining a determination of their allegations that the local authority failed to protect them from inhuman and degrading treatment, nor did they have the possibility of obtaining an enforceable award of compensation for the damage suffered thereby. The European Court specified that administrative, or quasi-judicial, remedies such as the Ombudsman or the complaints procedure were ineffective, given the seriousness of the allegations. Thus, while the failure of the law of tort to offer a remedy in damages was not a breach of the right to a fair hearing, under Article 6, the failure to offer any effective remedy for the breach of Convention rights was a breach of Article 13. The European Court held in *Z* that the state failed in its positive duty to protect the applicants against inhuman and degrading treatment. The United Kingdom breached the European Convention because the child welfare system failed to protect the children from long-term neglect and abuse. Thus, it seems that a relationship of care existed within which liability for omission could be imposed.

In *E & Others* v. *UK*[67] four Scottish children complained to the European Court of Human Rights that their local authority failed to carry out its statutory duty to protect them from serious physical and sexual abuse at the hands of their stepfather. The local authority was aware of proven sexual abuse in the past and that this had been continuing for some time. The European Court held that to engage the responsibility of the state there must be a failure by the state authority to take reasonably available measures which could have a real prospect of altering the outcome or mitigating the harm. The pattern of lack of investigation, communication and cooperation by the relevant authorities was regarded as having had a significant influence on the course of events; proper and effective management of the responsibilities of the local authority might have avoided or at least minimised the risk or damage suffered. Thus, there was a breach of Article 3. In cases involving serious child abuse the state authorities will only be held responsible where they were, or should have been, aware of what was going on and taken steps to safeguard the applicants. In *DP & JC* v. *UK*[68] the European Court was not persuaded that the local authority knew of, or had reason to suspect, the sexual abuse. The local authority had complied with its obligations to protect the physical and moral integrity of the applicants and could not be criticised for failing to investigate the possibility of sexual abuse. Therefore, the authority could not be regarded as having failed to take effective steps to protect the children from abuse and there was no breach of Article 3.

In *Osman* v. *UK*, *Z* v. *UK*, *TP and KM* v. *UK*, *E* v. *UK* and *DP & JC* v. *UK* the European Court rejected the *Bedfordshire*-style blanket immunities for public authorities and supported the imposition of liability in the area of child welfare. These European cases require the English courts to completely re-examine this issue and to develop the law to replace those blanket immunities with a much more sophisticated approach. Thus, it may be possible for juveniles who have engaged in offending behaviour to seek redress from a local authority for failure to exercise its child protection duties and discourage them from criminal activity. However, the European decisions examined are quite limited. All the cases concerned children who had suffered inhuman and degrading treatment in the form of serious physical and sexual abuse and neglect. Chapter 2 demonstrated that such children are at high risk of engaging in offending behaviour, but they are only a subset of young people at risk of engaging in antisocial and offending conduct, as identified in Chapter 2. The European case law does not create a right for children in need to receive family support and youth crime prevention services. Also, bringing a successful claim under the European Convention requires the hurdle of administrative discretion to be overcome, as the European Court has frequently held that states parties enjoy a 'margin of appreciation' under the European Convention in the manner in which they implement their child care policies. Therefore, a fair balance must be struck between the competing interests of the individual and the community. For example, in *Johansen* v. *Norway* the European Court of Human Rights stated that:

> the Court's task is not to substitute itself for the domestic authorities in the exercise of their responsibility for the regulation of the public care of children ... but rather to review under the Convention the decision that those authorities have taken in the exercise of their power of appreciation.[69]

Another important drawback is that, while the British government may be forced to change the domestic law and even to compensate the individual if the application is successful, the local authority cannot be forced to change its decision. In such circumstances monetary compensation may be of little value. In any event, bringing a case to Strasbourg is a slow process; by the time the case is determined, it is not very likely to be in the child's welfare to interfere with the original decision. Furthermore, the very delay can be seriously detrimental to the individual child if it impedes implementation of long-term plans.

Nonetheless, the European cases that I have examined will need to be considered by domestic judges because, first of all, the way is now clear for a child to claim that existing legislation is incompatible with the child's rights under the European Convention, and second, and more importantly, because the Human Rights Act 1998 incorporates the European Convention on Human Rights into domestic law. The Human Rights Act 1998 makes it unlawful for any public authority to act incompatibly with the European Convention on Human Rights, and allows for a case to be brought in a UK court or tribunal against the authority if it acts in such an incompatible manner (sections 6 and 7 Human Rights Act 1998). Therefore, local authorities must now ensure that their practices, policies, procedures and service delivery are consistent with Convention rights, and the domestic courts are statutorily obliged to take into account the principles applied by the Strasbourg court (section 8(4) Human Rights Act 1998). The domestic court can grant relief or remedy as it considers appropriate in relation to any local authority action that it considers unlawful (section 8(1) Human Rights Act 1998).

In *W and B (children) and W (children)*[70] the Court of Appeal explored the possibilities of actions being brought against local authorities in public law children cases under the Human Rights Act 1998. Hale LJ noted that individuals whose Convention rights have been breached could bring applications for damages in the family courts; however, only fundamental failure to make good that which has been taken away could be said to involve a breach of the state's positive obligations. Also, ominously, Article 13 of the European Convention is excluded from the list of Convention rights in section 1 of the Human Rights Act 1998, therefore it is questionable whether a court could legitimately use Article 13 to find a cause of action for breach of a statutory duty in the circumstances posited here. Indeed, Selby LJ, sitting as a judge in the European Court, in a case concerning the remedies available to establish responsibility for a prisoner suicide, has indicated that English courts cannot fashion new remedies via the 1998 Act in reliance on Article 13:

> [I]t may be observed that the patriation of the Convention by the Human Rights Act 1998 has not brought the issue [of compliance with Article 13] ... within the processes now available to the national court for securing compliance with the Convention, because Article 13 has not been included in the Convention rights scheduled to the Act[71]

However, when questioned about the omission of Article 13 from the 1998 Act in Parliament during the passage of the Human Rights Bill, the Lord Chancellor stated:

> [The Act] ... gives effect to Article 13 by establishing a scheme under which Convention rights can be raised before our domestic courts ... we believe that section 8 [of the Human Rights Act 1998] provides an exhaustive code of remedies for those Convention rights which have been violated and that nothing further is needed
> (Hansard H.L. vol. 582, col. 475)

The Lord Chancellor thus confirmed that the courts may have regard to Article 13 of the European Convention. This is a view that is also shared by the House of Lords. *W and B (children) and W (children)* was appealed to the House of Lords as *Re S (Minors) (Care Order: Implementation of*

Care Plan); Re W (Minors) (Care Order: Adequacy of Care Plan).[72] Lord Nicholls asserted that the right to a remedy under Article 13 of the European Convention on Human Rights was reflected in sections 7 and 8 of the Human Rights Act, which provide in English law the very remedy Article 13 declares is the entitlement of everyone whose rights are violated.

It is clear from sections 6, 7 and 8 of the Human Rights Act 1998, the parliamentary debates and judicial opinion that the Human Rights Act 1998 was intended to provide the full protection of the European Convention on Human Rights. It would seem, therefore, that the children in *X* v. *Bedfordshire* would have had an action under the Human Rights Act 1998 had it been in force. Although the decisions in *Osman, Z, TP and KM, E* and *DP & JC* do not alter the extent of local authorities' duties towards vulnerable children, the Human Rights Act 1998 renders them justiciable in a new way. These European cases have begun to change how domestic courts interpret the enforcement of local authorities' powers and duties. In *D & Others* v. *East Berkshire Community Health & Others*[73] the Court of Appeal ruled that the Human Rights Act 1998 superseded the House of Lords ruling in *X (A Minor)* v. *Bedfordshire County Council. D & Others* v. *East Berkshire Community Health & Others* concerned three appeals involving accusations of abusing a child made against a parent by the professionals concerned for the welfare of that child. In each case the accusations proved to be unfounded and the parents claimed damages for psychiatric harm caused by the false accusations. Thus, *D & Others* v. *East Berkshire Community Health & Others* relates to a failure by the local authority to investigate alleged instances of child abuse properly, which contrasts with *X* v. *Bedfordshire*, where the local authority failed to investigate at all. In *D & Others* v. *East Berkshire Community Health & Others* the Court of Appeal dismissed the appeals by the parents. However, the child also claimed; the child was 9 years old at the time she was taken into care after a wrongful diagnosis of sexual abuse by her father. The Court of Appeal allowed the appeal by the child and held that *X* v. *Bedfordshire County Council* was contrary to the Human Rights Act 1998 in relation to the position of the child. The court reasoned that where child abuse is suspected, section 1 of the Children Act 1989 requires that the interests of the child are paramount. Local authorities are also obliged to respect a child's European Convention rights by virtue of the Human Rights Act 1998. Lord Phillips MR held that, given these statutory obligations, the recognition of a duty of care to the child should not have a significantly adverse effect on the manner in which local authorities perform their duties. Lord Phillips concluded that it would no longer be legitimate to rule that, as a matter of law, no common law duty of care was owed to a child in relation to the investigation of suspected child abuse and the initiation and pursuit of care proceedings. Whether the imposition of a duty of care was fair, just and reasonable had to be determined on the facts of each case. Whereas *Barrett* and *Phelps* restricted

Bedfordshire to the core proposition that decisions by local authorities whether or not to take a child into care were not reviewable, the Court of Appeal in *D* held that this core proposition could not survive the Human Rights Act 1998. This view was upheld by the House of Lords in *JD (FC)* v. *East Berkshire Community Health NHS Trust and others.*[74]

This case represents a swing away from *X* v. *Bedfordshire* and *Stovin* v. *Wise* towards more traditional negligence principles of foreseeability and proximity. Children are now able to sue when negligence, causation and loss can be established. The public policy considerations that prevented the imposition of liability in *X* v. *Bedfordshire* are no longer applicable. The law in England and Wales now mirrors that in New Zealand since *AG* v. *Prince and Gardner* [1998] 1 NZLR 262 and *B and others* v. *Attorney General of New Zealand* [2003] UKPC 61, [2003] 4 All ER 833, in that child welfare agencies now owe children a duty of care to investigate allegations of abuse with a reasonable degree of care and skill. Child welfare agencies can now be successfully sued if they take a child into care who is not at risk of abuse (for violating Article 8 of the European Convention), or if they fail to take into care a child who is being abused (for violating Article 3 of the European Convention). However, in *D* and *JD* the court held that no duty of care was owed to parents when investigating child abuse. Thus, when considering whether a suspicion of child abuse justifies proceedings for the removal of a child from the parents, a common law duty of care is owed to the child (but not to the parents), therefore providing a legal remedy to children who have been victims of negligence in relation to the investigation of abuse or the initiation of care proceedings. The policy reasons that previously led the House of Lords to hold that no duty of care towards a child exists now cease to apply, and failure to remove a child from the parents could give rise to a valid claim by a child as readily as a decision to remove the child. Thus, the ruling in *X* v. *Bedfordshire* will not stand in the way of a claim by the child against a local authority for negligence in the manner in which it contributed to the child protection investigation.

The Human Rights Act 1998 widens the opportunity to challenge the decisions of local authorities and brings the law into an area of child protection that was previously free from the possibility of liability. Any English court when dealing with a claim in relation to action or inaction on the part of a local authority regarding suspected child abuse must take account of the European Court decisions. The 1998 Act and the judgments in *D* and *JD* enhance the possibility that young people could sue a local authority for failing to discharge their duties under the Children Act 1989 and for failing to take steps to discourage them from engaging in offending behaviour, with the result that local authorities may in the future implement the youth crime prevention provisions of the Children Act 1989 with more vigour and determination than was illustrated in Chapter 5. According to Bailey and Bowman, rather than the application of a blanket immunity for public bodies, we will in future see an '[i]ntense scrutiny of policy arguments for and against imposition of a duty of care in these circumstances' (2000: 131). Indeed, there may be reason to believe that the policy argument that will now have the greatest weight is the most important one of all: 'that wrongs should be righted' (Harris and Harris 2002: 135). However, all the cases examined concerned physical or sexual abuse that was considered sufficiently serious as to fall foul of Article 3 of the European Convention. Where children have suffered harm as a result of a local authority decision, but this harm is not sufficiently serious to violate Article 3 of the Convention, then it appears that judicial review is still the appropriate remedy.

Vicarious liability

Vicarious liability is a form of strict liability under which an employer will be found liable for the torts of an employee where they are committed in the course of employment. There is no requirement of employer fault but there must be a sufficient connection between the employment and the wrong. Could it be argued that the employees of a local authority owe a duty of care in respect of their performance of their statutory powers and duties as social welfare authorities, with the result that the local authority could be vicariously liable for the performance by the employees of those functions? Moreover, could a young person who has become involved in antisocial and offending behaviour hold the local authority vicariously liable for the failure of its employees to discourage him or her from engaging in offending behaviour?

In *F* v. *Wirral Metropolitan BC*[75] Ralph Gibson LJ ruled that a local authority could not be held negligent for the failure of its employee to protect parental rights. He believed that such an action would be 'offensive and inappropriate' and could adversely affect the local authority, and social workers in the employment of the local authority, in the discharge of their duties. Their task is to have regard primarily to the welfare of the child, while taking account of the aims and expectations of the parents. Those social workers, and those who supervise their work, should not be required to consider whether the decisions that they make might be put forward as the basis of claims for damages on the grounds of breaching some duty of care to the parent or the child. In *X* v. *Bedfordshire* Lord Browne-Wilkinson held that local authority employees owed no duty of care to the claimants because they had been employed by the local authority to give it advice and they had not assumed any general professional duty of care to the plaintiff children. This view was also unequivocally expressed in *M* v. *Newham London Borough Council*,[76] in which the House of Lords refused to impose a common law duty of care upon the local authority for the alleged negligence of its servants. These cases mark a decisive rejection of the use of vicarious liability to question a local authority's decision in the child care field.[77]

In *Barrett* v. *Enfield London Borough Council*[78] the House of Lords removed local authorities from the virtually all-encompassing immunity that had been built up around public authorities. Lord Woolf held that social workers, and vicariously a local authority, could be negligent in implementing the local authority's decision, if the necessary causation could be established.[79] In another decision with far-reaching implications for those concerned with the care of children, the House of Lords in *Phelps* v. *Hillingdon London Borough Council*[80] found a local education authority vicariously liable for the failure of an educational psychologist to diagnose a child's dyslexia. The Court of Appeal had previously dismissed the claimant's action in *Phelps*[81] on the grounds that an educational psychologist who assessed a child pursuant to the local authority's statutory obligations under the various Education Acts did not assume responsibility to that child in tort. The Court of Appeal believed that in the absence of such an assumption of personal responsibility, it was not fair, just or reasonable that a duty of care should be imposed, given the difficulties in proving causation in such cases, the inevitable drain on scarce resources that would result from the imposition of such liability, the multidisciplinary nature of the education process and the existence of a detailed statutory appeals system – pretty much the same grounds as outlined by the House of Lords in *X* v. *Bedfordshire County Council*.[82] The House of Lords in *Phelps* disagreed with this view and held that where an educational psychologist is specifically called in to advise in relation to the assessment and future provision for a specific child, and it is clear that the parents acting for the child and the teachers will follow that advice, prima facie a duty of care arises.[83] Lord Nicholls held that the duty to the pupil would march hand in hand with the professional's responsibilities to his or her own employer; the professional should exercise reasonable skill and care when assessing the child and advising the education authority. If the professional fails to do so, the education authority as his or her employer will be vicariously liable to the child for the negligent acts or omissions of the psychologist committed in the course of his or her employment. Lord Nicholls described this type of case as 'an example par excellence of a situation where the law will regard the professional as owing a duty of care to a third party as well as his own employer'.[84]

In reaching this conclusion their Lordships rejected in a robust manner the policy concerns that underlined the Court of Appeal's judgment. For instance, Lord Clyde took the view that the practical problems posed by a multidisciplinary context could not create a legal barrier to claims. Lord Clyde argued that the mere fact that there may be practical difficulties should not thwart otherwise deserving cases, as justice should not be denied on the ground that a claim is of a complex nature. Lords Clyde and Nicholls also asserted their belief that imposing a duty of care could conceivably have the healthy effect of ensuring that high standards are sought and secured. It has long been a fear of the courts that if they recognised new duties of care, a flood of unfounded claims would thereby be unleashed (Fairgrieve 2002). Lord Nicholls rejected this in broad fashion with a phrase that is surely going to be used by a plethora of claimants attempting to break new ground in tort liability: '[D]enial of the existence of a cause of action is seldom, if ever, the appropriate response to fear of its abuse.' The House of Lords reassured that any fear of a flood of claims may be countered by the consideration that in order to get off the ground the claimant must be able to demonstrate that the standard of care fell short of that set by the *Bolam* v. *Friern* test. This deliberately high standard is a recognition of the difficult nature of some decisions that those to whom the test applies are required to make, and accordingly provides room for genuine differences of view on the propriety of one course of action as against another.

The significance of *Phelps* to the children examined in this book cannot be overstated. *Phelps* held that a local authority is vicariously liable for the failure of its employee (the educational psychologist) to identify the needs of a child suffering from dyslexia. Thus, the local authority was vicariously liable for the incompetent acts and omissions of its employee. It was also held that the public policy considerations identified in *X* weigh differently in respect of a claim based on the vicarious liability of a public body than in the context of a direct claim on the basis of the existence of a statutory discretion. Both *Barrett* and *Phelps* are illustrative of broader changes in the sphere of public authority liability. These cases indicate that the court's reluctance to recognise a direct duty of local authorities in the exercise of social welfare powers, and, importantly, discretions, is gradually being whittled away. This process of 'incremental demolition' (Markesinis 2001: 176) is likely to continue; it is hard to believe that the courts in the future will deny a direct duty on public policy grounds alone, as it would be incongruous to reject a direct duty on the basis of public policy concerns that had been comprehensively dismissed in the context of vicarious liability (Fairgrieve 2002: 292). *Barrett* and *Phelps* suggest that a local authority could potentially be held vicariously liable for the negligent performance by its employees of their child care powers and duties. This would imply that a local authority could plausibly be held vicariously liable where its employees have failed to fulfil their powers and duties under the Children Act 1989 to discourage juveniles from engaging in offending behaviour.

Fiduciary duty

Equity may provide an alternative route to reparation, as the classic role of equity has been to ameliorate the harsh rigidity of common law rules. Equity, which derived from the prerogative of the Crown a jurisdiction to act as supreme parent to all children, takes a far broader view of the jurisdiction it exercises over children and parents. The development of the

Chancery jurisdiction on the basis of the welfare of the child has resulted in a gradual judicial realisation of the restrictive nature of the common law court's jurisdiction over children.

Fiduciary obligations are traditionally associated with relationships of trust and confidence in which the fiduciary is afforded a special opportunity to exercise power or discretion to the detriment of another person, who is accordingly vulnerable to abuse by the fiduciary.[85] The essential elements of a fiduciary relationship are that: (1) the fiduciary has scope for the exercise of some discretion or power; (2) the fiduciary can unilaterally exercise that power or discretion so as to affect the beneficiary's legal or practical interest; and (3) the beneficiary is particularly vulnerable to, or at the mercy of, the fiduciary holding discretion or power. Could the relationship between children at risk of engaging in offending behaviour and the local authority be regarded as a fiduciary one? In the United Kingdom, recognised fiduciary relationships include trustee and beneficiary, solicitor and client, principal and agent, partner and co-partner, employer and employee. Notably, all of these retain a distinctly commercial character, and the English judiciary have been reluctant to expand either the concept of undue influence or fiduciary obligation beyond these boundaries. Indeed, when the plaintiff in *Sidaway* v. *Board of Governors of the Bethlem Royal Hospital*[86] argued that a doctor has a fiduciary obligation to disclose medical risks to a patient, her argument was quickly dismissed by both the Court of Appeal and the House of Lords.

In Canada the fiduciary principle has been successfully invoked to remedy instances of sexual abuse within the family. In *K(M)* v. *H(M)*[87] the Canadian Supreme Court held that a father who sexually abused his daughter over a period of nine years was in breach of his fiduciary duty to her. La Forest J observed in *K(M)* v. *H(M)* that 'it is intuitively apparent that the relationship between parent and child is fiduciary in nature'.[88] Similarly, in *C* v. *C*[89] a claim for breach of fiduciary duty in the context of father-daughter incest was upheld, while in *J* v. *J*[90] the fiduciary obligation was extended to the mother, who was held to be in breach for failing to act to protect her daughter from sexual abuse by her father. A fiduciary duty has also been found to exist outside of the biological parent–child relationship to include everyone charged with responsibility for the care of children, including child welfare agencies. In *Justice* v. *Cairnie Estate*[91] Scott CJM authoritatively declared that social workers may be classified as within the scope of the fiduciary relationship. He went on to state that the court should be more ready to find a fiduciary relationship, and to impose a positive obligation to promote and defend the interests of the beneficiary, where the children are incapable of formulating their own course of action and must rely upon the fiduciary's judgement. However, in *A(C)* v. *Critchley*[92] the Canadian Court of Appeal restricted the scope of fiduciary duty in this context. McEachern CJBC declared that recovery based on breach of fiduciary duties should be confined to cases where, in addition to the usual indications such as vulnerability and the exercise of a discretion, the defendant personally takes advantage of a relationship of trust for his or her own direct, or indirect, personal advantage. Here the Crown's employees had acted honestly and in good faith. The evidence did not support the allegation that the Crown employees had enough information about the possibility of sexual abuse for them to be fixed with responsibility in negligence. Ryan JA added that a fiduciary was not a guarantor who breached their duties by failing to obtain the best result for the beneficiary; the duty owed by a fiduciary was merely one of loyalty or fidelity.

It is hoped that the judiciary in England and Wales will adopt a broader approach to the relationship between a local authority and a child at risk of engaging in offending behaviour. Regarding public authorities' duty of care, in *Barrett* v. *Enfield LBC*[93] Lord Hutton observed that it is incumbent on courts in different jurisdictions to learn from each other, because they are all straining to achieve a careful analysis and weighing up of all the relevant considerations. Holding local authorities accountable through equitable principles may possibly deter malpractice and improve the quality of the local authorities youth crime prevention activities.

Should local authorities be held accountable for failing to prevent youth offending?

If local authorities fail in their role to help children who are being raised in a state of severe emotional and physical deprivation, should they share at least some of the blame for any subsequent offending behaviour? To answer this question it is axiomatic first to consider the growing theme of government policy that parents should be held culpable for failing to prevent the antisocial behaviour of their children. For example, section 8 of the Crime and Disorder Act 1998 created the parenting order, which allows courts to order parents of children convicted of an offence to go on corrective courses to learn to exert control and authority over their children, ensure their school attendance and keep them out of trouble. Another example of the growing trend of holding parents responsible for their children's antisocial and offending behaviour is *Bryant* v. *Portsmouth City Council*.[94] This case concerned a grandmother who took in her two grandsons when they were aged 4 and 5 years old and reared them. By the time of the proceedings the boys were two teenagers over whom the grandmother could exercise no control. The boys engaged in a range of antisocial behaviour over a period of ten years, including throwing stones at and spitting at neighbours, assaulting and threatening neighbours, spraying graffiti and damaging property. A suspended possession order under section 84 of the Housing Act 1985 was made against the grandmother on the grounds that she had 'allowed' the boys to engage in antisocial behaviour. The effect of this order was that the grandmother's home of over 30 years could be repossessed. The Court of Appeal took note of the fact that the grandmother could not exercise control over the boys, nor did she encourage or tolerate the boys' behaviour or give them permission to behave in this way. Simon Brown LJ felt it was inappropriate and unnecessary to examine the grandmother's parenting skills and assess whether she could have been more successful in disciplining and controlling the boys.[95] Nonetheless, he held that because she had 'signally failed to prevent' their behaviour, she was in fact 'allowing' them to behave antisocially and therefore had to accept responsibility for their conduct. Sedley LJ outlined that the reason for the power to repossess the grandmother's home is to give legal effect to everyone's fundamental entitlement to live in peace. He added that if those who are responsible for the upbringing of violators wash their hands of their responsibility, the legislative provision is going to be largely frustrated. Given the court's willingness to impose culpability upon the grandmother in this case, I propose that it is reasonable to infer that in failing to ameliorate the conditions that imperil children's well-being and development (as illustrated in Chapter 5) and then crudely denouncing their wrongdoing without any reference to the prevalence of family difficulties, poverty and social exclusion, the state is abrogating its responsibilities under the Children Act 1989 to provide adequate care and protection for children in need and their families and frustrating the youth crime prevention provisions of the Children Act (as analysed in Chapters 3 and 4). In accordance with the Court of Appeal in *Bryant*, the state is effectively 'allowing' young people to engage in antisocial and offending behaviour and should not be permitted to wash its hands of its youth crime prevention responsibilities.

Conclusion

The United Nations Committee on the Rights of the Child has frequently recommended that in England and Wales children should have an effective remedy for violations of their rights (United Nations Committee on the Rights of the Child 2002: 17). This chapter has established that there is no obvious reason why public bodies charged with duties framed in objective terms should be provided with protection from challenge and given immunity from liability which is not afforded to others, including parents and guardians, merely because they are public bodies. Where local authorities have failed to fulfil their duties towards children in their care and such children have engaged in offending behaviour, the local authority should be required to accept responsibility and liability. Liability is not about creating scapegoats but about ensuring accountability. The prospect of liability could encourage local authorities to improve their performance not only in carrying out the legal duties owed to children in need, but also in respect of the overall management of the system (Guthrie 1998; Kelly and Lewis 1994). Introducing liability would require practitioners to show that they took reasonable care and acted with an acceptable level of professional competence,[96] and thus reduce the capricious and defensive practices evidenced in Chapter 5. The courts should seek to ensure that high standards of public service provision are maintained through the imposition of a duty of care. In launching the government's *Respect Action Plan* the Prime Minister, Tony Blair, stated that 'we need to take responsibility for ourselves, our children and our families, support those who want to do the same and challenge those who will not' (Blair 2006: 1). When a local authority fails to follow the law, rules, procedures and standards examined in Chapters 3 and 4 the child should have the right to challenge the authority for this failure.

Summary

Chapters 3 and 4 established that under the Children Act 1989 the kinds of parents discussed in Chapter 2 are entitled to expect the support of the state in meeting their children's needs and fulfilling their parental duties. Similarly, the kinds of children and young people identified in Chapter 2 are legally entitled to expect a reasonable standard of health and development. However, Chapter 5 confirmed that local authorities are not satisfactorily discharging their duties under the Children Act. Accordingly, Chapter 6 has examined the extent to which local authorities can be compelled to use their powers and perform their duties. Chapter 6 has endeavoured to determine whether the youth crime prevention ethos of the book can be legally enforced.

7 Conclusion

Summary

The focus of this book has been on preventing juvenile criminality by reducing the number of children and young people with a disposition to behaving in a criminal manner. The book advocates the preventing of youth offending through the medium of parenting support catering to the families of young people who are not yet seriously engaged in offending and antisocial behaviour, but who might be at risk of developing in that direction. The Children Act 1989 was found to represent a proactive programme for preventing children engaging in offending behaviour. The 1989 Act actively promotes strategies and activities that reduce the impact of risk factors, and enhance the influence of protective factors, in the lives of youth at greatest risk of delinquency. The evidence examined in the book emphasised that the child welfare interventions and family-strengthening policies of the Children Act 1989 are effective as youth crime prevention strategies. The book not only examined the underlying theoretical questions about the prevention of juvenile offending behaviour, but also considered what actually happens in practice. It determined why the Children Act 1989 is not being implemented in full in order to prevent children from becoming involved in offending behaviour, and considered the means available to redress the disparity between legislative policy and its day-to-day operation.

Policies and practices designed to prevent young people from offending have to be based on some explanation of why it is that certain children and young people engage in offending behaviour. While no survey could hope to provide a complete map of cause and effect, Chapter 2 examined the structural shortcomings and the criminogenic forces that characterise young offenders' lives. Chapter 2 identified, within an infinitely complex system of interacting influences, some important features that make a significant contribution to the likelihood of delinquency and juvenile offending behaviour. A significant source of delinquency was found to be 'damaged and damaging' families; effectively, the family problems of young people propel them into deviance and potentially into expanding penal institutions. Chapter 2 concluded that young people are less likely to offend if their physical, emotional, educational and social needs are met throughout childhood, with protection from all forms of neglect, abuse, exploitation or poverty, and if they are provided with the opportunity for the full development of their potential and achievement. The evidence of Chapter 2 connotes that if youth offending is to be prevented there must be an acceptance of policies and programmes that are committed to integration and social inclusion, implying an approach in which all aspects of young people's lives are taken into consideration in order to integrate them or include them in mainstream social, economic and political life. This involves recognition of their social, employment, health, educational, housing and financial needs, among other things, thus necessitating a rethink about the way in which resources for crime prevention are allocated. While there will always be a need for criminal penalties as a last resort, preventing juvenile offending requires a different kind of political exercise from the rhetoric of law and order. The criminal justice system is not designed to improve young people whose deviant attitudes and ways of life have been ingrained from an early age and are continually reinforced by their social situation. Rather, it is concerned with penalising for past offences without necessarily tackling the problems that led the young person to engage in offending behaviour. An effective youth crime prevention philosophy is one that addresses the life experiences of children and in which prevention is promoted through the collaborative and integrated activities of a range of services.

Chapter 3 confirmed that the tools needed for addressing the risk factors which predispose young people to offending behaviour are already in place. Therefore, it is not necessary to legislate in order to ensure that resources of the right kind are made available to young people and their families. In particular, the Children Act 1989 was found to have the overwhelming potential to deter young people from becoming involved in crime, as it compels local authorities to improve the chances for them to lead healthy, productive, crime-free lives by mitigating individual risk factors and reducing economic and social deprivation. The Children Act 1989 allows for the provision of interventions that improve parenting skills and children's physical and mental health, and reduce the risk of child abuse, and consequently reduce the risk of youth offending. The 1989 Act not only requires local authorities to support children in families under stress but also gives them a specific duty to take measures that discourage juvenile involvement in crime. The Children Act also authorises local authorities to request the help of other local authorities, the youth justice system, youth offending teams, the police, youth inclusion panels, housing authorities, education authorities, voluntary organisations and other bodies in seeking to carry out their youth crime prevention duties. Chapter 3 verified that all these initiatives provide sound foundations for developing youth offending preventive interventions, as they pre-date any formal contact with the criminal justice system, improve parenting skills and children's physical and mental health, and reduce risks of child abuse. Chapter 3 provided the empirical evidence that confirmed that improving the family environment could be the most effective and enduring strategy for combating juvenile delinquency and associated behavioural, social and emotional problems. Youth crime prevention policy should therefore focus on the family context in which offenders find themselves, and resources should be diverted from more traditional criminal justice measures and practices. Youth crime prevention strategies that fail to acknowledge the young person's family environment will inevitably fail and will reinforce alienation, marginalisation and exclusion.

The support and services available under the Children Act 1989 which discourage juvenile involvement in crime are not universal services available to all children. To qualify for these services, children must either be 'in need' (section 17 Children Act 1989) or at risk of suffering 'significant harm' (section 31 Children Act 1989). Chapter 4 examined whether those young people whom Chapter 2 identified as at risk of engaging in offending behaviour should be seen as symptomatic of familial problems and consequently as fulfilling the criteria set out in the Children Act 1989. Chapter 4 determined that all children have the right to be discouraged from engaging in offending behaviour, and their families have the right to expect assistance and support in their efforts to cope and care. Juvenile delinquents, and those at risk of delinquency, are victims of deprived and depriving families and should be seen as undersocialised individuals in need of help and assistance, and not as calculating transgressors in need of formal sanctions. Therefore, it is irrefutable that the children analysed in Chapter 2 are at risk of suffering significant harm and in need of the support and services examined in Chapter 3. According to this view, children's physical, emotional, social and intellectual needs must all be met if they are to enjoy life, develop their full potential and grow into participatory contributing adolescents and adults. Similarly, their parents need help to find the support and tools necessary to raise safe, strong and healthy children. Commitment to the realisation of rights as conceived in Chapters 3, 4 and 6 should foster a commitment to social change in the interest of promoting enhanced life opportunities for young people. Only when full recognition of the importance of the treatment of children in troubled circumstances is placed at the centre of practice can a truly preventive philosophy work.

Rationally, society can justifiably punish young offenders for their crimes only to the extent that it has fulfilled its obligations to those young people as members of society. However, as shown in Chapter 2, in England and Wales there is considerable resistance to preventive philosophies in the light of a high degree of commitment to punishment and retribution; a low age, by European standards, of criminal responsibility (10 years of age); an acceptance of 'children's jails' in association with a questioning of the validity of alternative scenarios for dealing with offenders; and a general hardening of the language of delinquency control in its presentation of children and young people as threats to society. As evidenced in Chapter 2, since the 1990s young offenders have been conceptualised as violent predators warranting retribution, rather than as wayward children in need of a guiding hand. Present policy tends to focus primarily on retaliatory responses to youth crime. Consequently, the youth justice system in England and Wales has developed into a formal and rigid system which draws younger children into contact with the youth justice system that escalates them up the sentencing ladder and into custody. This tough approach to youth justice contrasts with the other youth justice systems examined in Chapter 4 which emphasise a 'welfare' approach. The 'welfare' proponents argue that young offenders require welfare-oriented and, often, long-term resources. The welfare model treats young offenders in accordance with a perception of their need for help and pursuit of their best interests. This book abandons this traditional 'welfare versus justice' dichotomy and instead outlines a new synthesis that focuses on the rights and needs of young people in troubled circumstances and their families. This approach recognises the right of young people in trouble to the development and delivery of preventive services. By shifting the debate from the nature of the offence to the offender, my intention is to shift justifiable intervention from the penal system to the child and family welfare system. The needs of troubled and troublesome young people should be met through mainstream social welfare provision. This route avoids early involvement in the formal criminal justice system, which is likely to be damaging to young people.

The child and family welfare system does not give children in need and children suffering significant harm unlimited rights of receipt; the claims of such children are described as 'an eligibility' rather than a right or entitlement. Local authorities enjoy almost complete autonomy in deciding to what degree the youth crime prevention powers and duties of the Children Act 1989 will be discharged. Accordingly, Chapter 5 examined how local authorities interpret their child welfare and youth crime prevention powers and duties under the Children Act 1989 and evaluated whether in practice local authorities were acting in accordance with the preventive analysis of Chapters 3 and 4. The findings from Chapter 5 were contentious, as the evidence suggests that local authorities are failing to fulfil the youth crime prevention role envisaged for them in the Children Act 1989. In general, local authorities have an inconsistent understanding of 'reasonable standard of health and development' and 'significant impairment'; they do not understand that both sections 17 and 47 can be used as gateways to gain access to the services specified in the 1989 Act. Social workers lack the skills or training to undertake direct work with families and young people as a form of support; and resources are wasted by unnecessary investigations under section 47 of the Act. Chapter 5 highlighted that there exist pockets of effective and innovative practice in local areas. However, that chapter also underlined the fact that the resourcing of preventive efforts simply does not match the scale of the problem. At a macro level, policy trends have served to promote rather than reduce criminality. Youth work has found itself vulnerable to cuts in local authority spending. Increases in family breakdown and child poverty have coincided with reductions in the ability of local authorities to undertake preventive social work. Thus, over-burdened local authorities are reluctant to take on the youth crime preven-tion responsibilities of the Children Act. The Children Act 1989 offers a means of providing a proactive programme of support for children at risk of engaging in offending behaviour and their families, but where the legal system fails is in the application, operation and interpretation of legislative provisions.

If the youth crime prevention goals of the Children Act 1989 are to be achieved, local authorities must devote far more attention to prioritising resources in the direction of preventive services. The broad intentions of the Children Act and the broad definition of need in section 17 must not be distorted by the minimalist reading of the Act and its *Guidance* and Regulations evident throughout Chapter 5. If local authorities are to offer a truly preventive service and discourage juvenile offending, then a more discriminatory use of the formal child protection system could free up resources to support children at an earlier stage of need. Risks must be taken in order to achieve a more successful outcome for the child by keeping various avenues of family support firmly in mind when child pro-tection inquiries are under way. There could be a profound difference in outcome if local authorities could coordinate and humanise their services and if awareness of the legal rights of parents and the best interest of chil-dren, as expressed in Chapters 3 and 4, were coupled with sensitivity to the unique needs of each family and child in trouble. To achieve this result there needs to be a rebalancing of child protection work so that there is a greater concentration on children in need and, by implication, 'parenting style', and investigations should be reframed as 'inquiries' and carried out with a lighter touch.

If local authorities are not implementing the legislation fully, can dissat-isfied children and families complain that local authorities have failed them on the basis that part, if not all, of the responsibility for juvenile offending lies in the failure of the state to instil the sense of responsibility that pre-cludes criminal behaviour? Chapter 6 endeavoured to answer this question by examining the means of redress available to a person who suffers harm as a result of a failure by a local authority to use any of its powers or perform its duties. This final main chapter addressed the extent to which those children at risk of engaging in offending behaviour can enforce their right to local authority services. Chapter 6 concluded that those possessing professional skills should not expect any favours from the court in terms of the determination of whether a duty of care is owed merely because they work in difficult and sensitive areas and work for a public authority. This is important, as the prospect of liability for negligence in relation to their duty to discourage young people from involvement in crime may well encourage local authorities to improve their performance in carrying out their duties with regard to preventing youth offending. Chapter 6 proved that the legal right to the receipt of the youth crime prevention support and services of the Children Act (established in Chapters 3 and 4) enjoyed by young people at risk of engaging in offending behaviour (as identified in Chapter 2) is a legally enforceable right.

Recommendations

The integrated youth crime prevention programme advocated in this book demands the juggling of the needs of young people, the punitive clamour of the media, the capacity of the available workforce, the legitimate concerns of the magistracy and judiciary, and the incessantly changing demands and priorities of politicians. Protecting children and improving parenting techniques is not merely an academic exercise designed to advance knowledge about explaining and preventing offending behaviour. It is an intensely practical exercise designed to reduce offending and to improve young people's lives. Family investment in children sets in motion a process whereby protection against crime deepens. The family is consequently transformed from a static and passive socialising unit to being actively engaged in steering youth away from criminogenic risks. If there is to be a shift towards a truly preventive youth crime strategy based on the need to recognise the social and familial context in which children and young people find themselves, there are a number of implications for those responsible for developing law and policy.

A change in political vision has to be made from short-term and supposed immediate gains to one in which long-term investment in the lives of children is accepted. Preventing juvenile antisocial and offending behaviour requires resources to be allocated to intervene positively in young people's lives to prevent them engaging in offending behaviour, before offending has become so ingrained that neither support nor punishment is an effective response. However, Chapter 5 demonstrated that politicians tend to have short time horizons particularly when it comes to the resourcing of youth crime prevention schemes. This myopia impedes planning youth crime prevention initiatives that are likely to take ten to twenty years to bear fruit. One way of making this argument more compelling is to compare the wide-ranging costs and benefits of prevention strategies. For example, in evaluating the Perry Preschool Program in Michigan it was found that for every $1 invested in the programme, there was a long-term saving of over $7 in real terms. Likewise, the Audit Commission (2004) stressed that if effective early intervention had been provided for just one in ten young offenders in custody, annual savings in excess of

£100 million could have been achieved. This kind of analysis could demonstrate to policy-makers how investment in an apparently expensive developmental programme can be cost-effective in the long term. This is essential if investment in long-term prevention programmes is to compete with the pressures to deliver improved outcomes in the short term.

Identifying children at risk of offending requires there to be efficient and effective sharing of critical information and the coordination of assessments that have been made by different professionals. The government's Green Paper *Every Child Matters* (Chief Secretary to the Treasury 2003) sets out a comprehensive framework in which universal services such as schools, health services, family support and child care should provide help and information to families, especially at key transition points in their children's lives. Among the many objectives of the Green Paper was that of reducing the number of children engaged in offending or antisocial behaviour. *Every Child Matters* proposed the strengthening of preventive services for children by focusing on four key themes: (a) supporting families and carers; (b) ensuring necessary intervention before children reach crisis point and protecting children from falling through the net; (c) addressing underlying problems such as weak accountability and poor service integration; and (d) ensuring that people working with children are trained, valued and rewarded. In November 2004 the Children Act 2004 became law. Underpinning this Act and *Every Child Matters* is the proposal for a common assessment framework to identify children's needs as early as possible and to avoid duplication between agencies. A lead professional will develop a relationship with each child and ensure clear accountability for each case. The expectation is that children and young people will receive effective help as soon as they need it in a more coherent way. However, *Every Child Matters* and the Children Act are cost-neutral proposals. Merely restructuring services will not recruit a single extra social worker. As the Green Paper documented, vacancies in children's services are up to four times as high as in any other public service. Chapter 5 graphically illustrated that chronic shortages have hit even the most crucial specialist teams dealing with children at risk and have undermined the youth crime prevention provisions of the Children Act. The goals of *Every Child Matters* and the Children Act need to be developed in accordance with the recommendations and conclusions of this book with targets that reflect the preventive philosophy of this book and with the resources to match. Fundamentally, what is most needed is recognition that we all have a personal stake in finding the solution to youth crime and recognition that all Britain's citizens stand to profit from or pay for what becomes of British children. Without this realisation we are doomed to repeat flawed juvenile justice policies time and again while ignoring promising opportunities for the next generation.

Much of what is recommended as good practice in this book may seem idealistic to practitioners who every day struggle to maintain services in the face of pressure to make cuts. The approach I have advocated can lead to young people and their families making demands on, or resisting the actions of, local authorities. Yet local authorities come into contact with the most serious casualties of society and they have a responsibility to work towards a future in which juvenile offending is prevented. Utopian as this may seem in the current political, economical and ideological climate, it is essential that we retain a vision of how things should be done. In searching out the moral grounds for the prevention of juvenile offending we must believe that this fight will be strengthened and that, ultimately, the condition of childhood will be ameliorated, with the ensuing result that juvenile offending behaviour will be prevented. Without such an agenda all that is left is a series of *ad hoc*, short-term and financially low-cost initiatives that may provide some temporary relief for a few, but leave the majority of marginalised youth untouched, unsupported and vulnerable to criminalisation.

Notes

1 Introduction

1 The criminological research referred to will be examined in depth in Chapter 2.
2 Children looked after by local authorities refers to children who are in the care of the local authority or provided with accommodation by the local authority (section 2(1) Children Act 1989).
3 For example, section 8 of the Crime and Disorder Act 1998 created the parenting order, which allows courts to order parents of children convicted of an offence to go on corrective courses to learn to exert control and authority over their children, ensure their school attendance and keep them out of trouble.

2 Family life and youth offending

1 Now repealed and re-enacted in the Powers of Criminal Courts Act 2000, sections 90–92.
2 A child is 'looked after' by a local authority for the purposes of the Children Act 1989 if he is in their care by virtue of a care order, or is provided with accommodation by them (for a continuous period of more than 24 hours) under a voluntary arrangement (Sections 22(1) and 105(4) Children Act 1989).
3 Three or more offences admitted in the last 12 months, and/or at least one serious offence.
4 Senator Scott, *Senate Debates* 1907–08, p. 1044.
5 Ironically, based on the recommendation of the Moloney Committee, section 44 of the Children and Young Persons Act 1933 required only that the court should have regard to the welfare of the child, as opposed to considering the child's welfare the paramount concern.
6 This section was repealed by section 90(1)(2) Children Act 1989.
7 John Major, from an interview with the editor of the *Mail on Sunday*, Jonathan Holbrow, 21 February 1993, p. 8.
8 Respectively repealed section 1(2)(f) and section 7(7) Children and Young Persons Act 1969.
9 Under section 53(2) Children and Young Persons Act 1933, now repealed and re-enacted in the Powers of Criminal Courts Act 2000, sections 90–92.

3 Role of the local authority in preventing youth crime

1 *Guidance* does not carry the same legal force as the Statute or the Regulations. Nonetheless, *Guidance* is issued under section 7 of the 1970 Local Government (Social Services) Act and local authorities are required to act in accordance

with such guidance. *Guidance* does not determine the meaning of the Act but it does give some insight into the way in which the Act was intended to operate.

2 'Supervised activities' are those which are supervised by a responsible person (section 18(7)).

3 A child is 'in need' if: (a) he is unlikely to achieve or maintain, or to have the opportunity of achieving or maintaining a reasonable standard of health or development without the provision of services by a local authority, or (b) his health or development is likely to be significantly, or further, impaired without the provision for him of such services, (c) or if he is disabled (section 17(10)).

4 *Mitchell* v. *Wright* (1905) 7 F 568; *Watson* v. *Nikolaisen* [1955] QB 286, [1955] 2 All ER 427.

5 [1993] AC 509.

6 [2003] UKHL 57.

7 Schedule 2, paragraph 7(a)(ii) provides that every local authority shall take reasonable steps designed to reduce the need to bring criminal proceedings against such children, and paragraph 7(b) requires local authorities to encourage children within their area not to commit criminal offences.

8 Ten is the age of criminal responsibility in England and Wales – that is, the minimum age at which a person can be prosecuted in criminal proceedings.

9 In these circumstances the threshold criteria do not have to be satisfied (section 12(7) Crime and Disorder Act 1998).

10 [2001] 1 WLR 358.

11 [1994] 2 AC 402, [1994] 3 All ER 313.

12 [2002] 1 FLR 217, para. 30.

13 A child has a learning difficulty if he experiences significantly greater difficulty in learning than the majority of children of his age or if he has a disability that prevents or hinders him from making use of the educational facilities which are generally provided for school children of his age (section 312(2) Education Act 1996).

14 Section 37(1) Crime and Disorder Act 1998: 'It shall be the principal aim of the youth justice system to prevent offending by children and young people.' Section 37(2): 'In addition to any other duty to which they are subject, it shall be the duty of all persons and bodies carrying out functions in relation to the youth justice system to have regard to that aim.'

15 *Re V (Care or Supervision Order)* [1996] 2 FCR 555, [1996] 1 FLR 776, CA.

16 *Re T (A Minor) (Care or Supervision Order)* [1994] 1 FLR 103, 106, CA.

17 [1994] 2 FLR 892, 898.

18 [1996] 2 FLR 693, 698.

19 [2000] Fam Law 600.

20 Also *Re C and B (Care Order: Future Harm)* [2001] 1 FLR 811.

21 *Re O (Care or Supervision Order)* [1996] 2 FLR 755, 763.

22 *Re S(J) (A Minor) (Care or Supervision Order)* [1993] 2 FLR 919, 939.

23 *Oxfordshire County Council* v. *L (Care or Supervision Order)* [1998] 1 FLR 70, 76. Also *Re B (Care or Supervision Order)* [1996] 2 FLR 693.

24 *Re S(J) (A Minor) (Care or Supervision Order)* [1993] 2 FLR 919; *Re S (Care or Supervision Order)* [1996] 1 FLR 753.

25 *Re T (A Minor) (Care or Supervision Order)* [1994] 1 FLR 103.

26 [1998] 1 FLR 70, 74.

27 The threshold criteria are that: (a) the child concerned is suffering significant harm, or is likely to suffer significant harm; and (b) the harm or likelihood of harm is attributable to – (i) the care given to the child, or likely to be given to him if the order were not made, not being what it would be reasonable to expect a parent to give to him; or (ii) the child being beyond parental control.

28 [1993] 1 FLR 811, [1993] Fam Law 456.

29 [1997] AC 489, [1996] 4 All ER 871.
30 The same penalty applies to convictions for failure to comply with a school attendance order.
31 *Bath & North East Somerset District Council* v. *Warman* [1999] ELR 81; *Jarman* v. *Mid-Glamorgan Education Authority* [1985] LS Gaz R 1249.
32 'Walking distance' is defined in section 444(5) of the Education Act 1996.
33 See Chapter 2.
34 Defined as accommodation for a continuous period of more than 24 hours (Section 22(2)).
35 A child is 'looked after' by a local authority for the purposes of the Children Act 1989 if he is in their care by virtue of a care order, or is provided with accommodation by them (for a continuous period of more than 24 hours) under a voluntary arrangement (Sections 22(1) and 105(4) Children Act 1989).
36 [2001] 1 FCR 629.
37 [2001] 2 All ER 719, [2001] 1 FLR 526.
38 Children (Secure Accommodation) Regulations 1991 (SI 1991 No. 1505) Reg. 10.
39 Children (Secure Accommodation) Regulations 1991, Reg. 11.
40 *R* v. *Oxfordshire County Council (Secure Accommodation Order)* [1992] Fam 150 Butler-Sloss LJ.
41 [1986] SLT 683.
42 The UN Rules on the Administration of Juvenile Justice ('Beijing Rules') 1985. The 'Beijing Rules' have been approved by each of the members of the United Nations. In 1985 the Beijing Rules were adopted by the Committee of Ministers of the Council of Europe.
43 Adopted by the Committee of Ministers on 17 September 1987 at the 410th meeting of the Ministers' Deputies.
44 Parliamentary Assembly of Europe, Recommendation 1286, 1996.

4 Young people at risk of offending: children at need of protection

1 [1997] 2 WLR 459 at p. 463.
2 Section 2(1) of the Chronically Sick and Disabled Persons Act 1970 requires local authorities to (i) assess the needs of the chronically sick and disabled and (ii) to provide services to meet those needs in circumstances where intervention on the part of local authorities is deemed to be necessary.
3 *F* v. *Suffolk County Council* [1981] 125 SJ 307.
4 (1860) 2 F&F 202.
5 [1998] 27 EHRR 611.
6 Article 3 states that 'No one shall be subjected to torture or to inhuman or degrading treatment or punishment.'
7 [2001] EWCA Crim 1024, [2001] 2 FLR 431, CA.
8 No definition of persistent offenders was included in the survey as it was hoped that this approach would provide for a flexible definition or set of criteria for identifying the appropriate group of young people as a starting point for the project.
9 Section 90(1) Children Act 1989 repealed section 1(2)(f) Children and Young Persons Act 1969, section 90(2) Children Act 1989 repealed section 7(7) Children and Young Persons Act 1969.
10 Article 8 states: '1. That everyone has the right to respect for his private and family life, his home and his correspondence. 2. There shall be no interference by a public authority with the exercise of this right except such as is in accordance with the law and is necessary in a democratic society in the interests of

national security, public safety or the economic well-being of the country, for the prevention of disorder or crime, for the protection of health or morals, or for the protection of the rights and freedom of others.'

11 The inclusion of emotional abuse gives statutory effect to the decision in *F v. Suffolk County Council* (1981) 2 FLR 208.

12 [1999] 2 FLR 359.

13 [2000] 2 FLR 865, 874.

14 Also *Re L (Contact: Domestic Violence); Re V (Contact: Domestic Violence); Re M (Contact: Domestic Violence); Re H (Contact: Domestic Violence)* [2000] 2 FLR 334, 339.

15 [1992] 4 All ER 905, [1992] 2 FLR 7.

16 *Re M (Secure Accommodation Order)* [1995] 1 FLR 418.

17 [1993] 1 FLR 832, Waite, J.

18 [1995] 2 FLR 867.

19 This was cited by Sir Stephen Brown P at p. 873 and approved by the Court of Appeal p. 878.

20 [2001] 2 FLR 1111.

21 (1998) 158 DLR (4th) 539 LEXIS 362 Ontario Court (General Division).

22 At p. 546. See also *Catholic Children's Aid Society of Metro Toronto v. M(C)* (1994) 113 DLR (4th) 321, Supreme Court of Canada.

23 [1999] 3 WLR 79, 106.

24 [1993] 1 FLR 257. This judgment was followed in *In the Matter of T & P (Care Order, Residence Order, Sexual Abuse; Standard of Proof)* 5 April 2002 The High Court, Family Division.

25 Per Prowse JA. *S(B) v. BC CCF and C Services* (1998) 160 DLR (4th) 264, 297 British Columbia Court of Appeal.

26 [1994] 3 All ER 298.

27 [1994] 3 All ER 298, 305 per Lord Mackay. Also *Re G (Children) (Care Order: Evidence)* [2001] EWCA Civ. 968; *Southwark London Borough Council v. B* [1998] 2 FLR 1095, [1999] 1 FCR 550.

28 [1993] 1 FLR 554.

29 At p.557. Both *Re M (A Minor) (Care Order: Threshold Conditions)* and *Northamptonshire County Council v. S* were cited with approval by Hollis J in *Re SH (Care Order: Orphan)* [1995] 1 FLR 746, 748.

30 *Newham London Borough Council v. AG* [1993] 1 FLR 281.

31 [1996] 1 FLR 80, See also *Re G (Secure Accommodation Order)* [2001] 1 FLR 884; *Newham London Borough Council v. AG* [1993] 1 FLR 281; *Re H & Ors (Minors) (Sexual Abuse: Standard of Proof)* [1996] AC 563 sub nom *H & R (Child Sexual Abuse: Standard of Proof)* [1996] 1 FLR 80.

32 [1996] 1 All ER 1, 21, per Lord Nicholls.

33 [1996] 1 All ER 1, 21–22, per Lord Nicholls.

34 [1993] 2 FLR 541, [1993] Fam Law 205.

35 [1996] 1 All ER 1. Also see *Re M (A Minor)* [1994] 3 All ER 298.

36 [1996] 1 All ER 1.

37 [1996] 1 All ER 1, 20.

38 [1999] 2 FLR 833.

39 [1997] EWCA Civ 1268.

40 *Re M (a child) (secure accommodation)* [2001] EWCA Civ. 458, [2001] 1 FCR 692.

41 *Re F (Contact: Child in Care)* [1995] 1 FLR 510, [1994] 2 FCR 1354.

42 *Re L (a minor)* [1997] EWCA Civ 1268.

43 *Re R (A Minor) (Recovery Order)* [1998] 3 FCR 321, FD; *M v. Birmingham City Council* [1995] 1 FCR 50, *South Glamorgan County Council v. W and B* [1993] 1 FLR 574.

44 [1994] 2 FLR 141, 147.
45 Per Lord Mackay in *Dawson* v. *Wearmouth* [1999] 2 AC 308, 321, [1999] 1 FLR 1167, 1173.
46 [2002] EWHC 1379 (Fam); [2002] 2 FLR 730.
47 [2000] 2 FLR 254.
48 [2000] 1 FLR 612, para. 11.
49 Adopted by Goddard LCJ in *Lee* v. *Nursery Furnishings Ltd* [1945] 1 All ER 387, 389.
50 Adopted by Parker J in *Adsett* v. *K & L Steelfounders and Engineers Ltd* [1953] 1 All ER 97, 98.
51 [1996] 1 FLR 424. See also *Jordan* v. *Norfolk County Council* [1994] 4 All ER 218 (DC).
52 [1996] 1 FLR 425.
53 At p. 426.
54 [1995] 2 FLR 203.
55 [1995] 2 All ER 124.
56 At p. 137.
57 [1997] 2 WLR 459; [1997] AC 548.
58 [1997] 2 WLR 469.
59 [1997] WLR 469; [1997] AC 604.
60 [1997] 4 All ER 532, CA.
61 Per Lord Woolf MR at p. 543.
62 [1998] 2 FLR 1082.
63 [2002] UKHL 10, para 27.
64 (1998) 29 EHRR 245, para. 91.
65 (1998) 29 EHRR 245, para. 116.
66 [2001] EWCA Civ 757.
67 [1998] 2 All ER 769, [1998] 2 WLR 834.
68 [1998] 3 All ER 788, [1998] 2 WLR 834, 891–892.
69 Now section 19 of the Education Act 1996.
70 Unreported 12 June 1998.
71 *Barry* was distinguished on the basis that the needs were 'real needs' and by reference to the statutory area.
72 [1993] 1 FLR 860, [1992] 2 FLR 394.
73 [1993] 2 WLR 475, [1993] 1 FLR 569.
74 Section 38(6) provides that 'Where the court makes an interim care order, or interim supervision order, it may give such directions (if any) as it considers appropriate with regard to the medical or psychiatric examination or other assessment of the child; but if the child is of sufficient understanding to make an informed decision he may refuse to submit to the examination or other assessment.'
75 [1997] AC 489 Similar ruling in *R* v. *London Borough of Barnet, ex parte B* [1994] 1 FLR 592.
76 (1998) 1 CCL Rep 315. Also per Henry J in *R* v. *Avon CC ex p M* [1994] 2 FCR 259, 263.
77 (1998) 1 CCL Rep 581.
78 At 597.
79 [2002] 1 FLR 217.
80 Amended by law no. 85-1407 of 30 December 1985.
81 The Law of 23rd December 1958 entrusted the juvenile court judge with the additional role of protecting children. The Law of 18 February 1975 extends the role of the *juge des enfants* to protecting young people aged 18–21 years.

5 Local authorities' interpretation of their youth crime prevention duties

1 See Chapter 4 for a discussion of what was envisaged by the drafters of the Children Act 1989.
2 The Local Government (Wales) Act 1994 established 22 unitary local authorities which from April 1996 replaced the eight county councils and 37 district councils in Wales.
3 Of the 1,368, 925 were investigated.
4 Per Parliamentary Under-Secretary of State for the Home Department, Bob Ainsworth, Hansard, 8 May 2003, col. 102.
5 For a discussion of these duties, see Chapter 3.
6 Section 17(5) Children Act 1989 provides that every local authority (a) shall facilitate the provision by others (including in particular voluntary organisations) of services which the authority have power to provide by virtue of this section, or section 18, 20, 23 or 24; and (b) may make such arrangements as they see fit for any person to act on their behalf in the provision of any such service.

6 Enforcing the role of local authorities in preventing youth crime

1 [1998] 2 FLR 1082.
2 [1994] 2 FCR 996, [1994] 1 FLR 203, CA.
3 *R* v. *Commissioner for Local Administration, ex p Eastleigh BC* [1988] QB 855; *R* v. *Commissioner for Local Administration, ex p Croydon LBC* [1989] 1 All ER 1033.
4 Per Peter Gibson LJ in *R* v. *London Borough of Brent, ex parte S* [1994] 1 FLR 203, 211.
5 (1992) 11 BMLR 141, cited by Peter Gibson LJ in *R* v. *London Borough of Brent, ex parte S* [1994] 1 FLR 203, 213.
6 [1994] 1 FCR 232, [1994] 1 FLR 798.
7 [1948] 112 KB 223.
8 Per Wall J, *Re T (Judicial Review: Local Authority Decisions Concerning Children in Need* [2003] EWHC 2515 (Admin), [2004] 1 FLR 601 QBD.
9 *Chief Constable of the North Wales Police* v. *Evans* [1982] 1 WLR 1155, per Hailsham LC at 1160.
10 *R* v. *Barnet London Borough Council, ex p B* [1994] 2 FCR 781, [1994] 1 FLR 592.
11 *R* v. *Birmingham City Council, ex parte A* [1997] 2 FCR 357.
12 [1994] 1 FLR 203, CA.
13 Per Gibson LJ at p. 211. See also *R* v. *Secretary of State for the Home Department, ex parte Swati* [1986] 1 WLR 477, per Donaldson MR at 485.
14 [1994] 1 FCR 232, [1994] 1 FLR 798.
15 [1990] Fam 133, [1990] 1 FLR 79.
16 At p. 150.
17 [1993] 3 All ER 815.
18 [2003] UKHL 57.
19 Other judicial observations which favour the view that section 17 creates only a 'target' duty include *R* v. *London Borough of Barnet, ex parte B* [1994] 1 FLR 592; *X* v. *Bedfordshire County Council* [1995] 2 AC 633; *R* v. *London Borough of Bexley, ex parte B* (2000) 3 CCL Rep 15; *Queen on the application of G* v. *Barnet London Borough Council* [2001] EWCA Admin 5; *Queen on the Application of A* v. *Lambeth London Borough Council* [2001] EXCA Civ 1624, [2002] 1 FLR 353.

20 Per Lord Hope, para. 85.
21 [2002] EWCA Civ 613, [2002] 2 FLR 327.
22 (1990) *The Times*, 21 February (1990) 2 Admin LR 822, 828.
23 [1994] 1 FLR 592.
24 At pp. 611–612.
25 [1995] 1 FLR 669.
26 [1999] 4 All ER 161, 174.
27 [2001] EWCA Civ 1624, [2002] 1 FLR 353.
28 At p.378. Other cases that recognise section 17 as imposing an enforceable duty owed to a child in need include *R* v. *Tower Hamlets London Borough Council, ex parte Bradford* (1998) 1 CCL Rep 294; *R* v. *Wigan Metropolitan Borough Council, ex parte Tammadge* (1998) 1 CCL Rep 581; *R* v. *Lambeth London Borough Council, ex parte K* (2000) 3 CCL Rep 141; *Mayor and Burgesses of London Borough of Lambeth, ex parte K* (2000) 3 CCL Rep 141; *R* v. *Ealing London Borough Council, ex parte C* (2000) 3 CCL Rep 122.
29 [2003] UKHL 57.
30 [1995] FCR 517, [1995] 1 FLR 159.
31 [1994] 2 FCR 259, [1994] 2 FLR 1006. Also *R* v. *Solihull Metropolitan Borough Council, ex p C* [1984] FLR 363.
32 [1990] 2 QB 71, [1990] 2 All ER 129.
33 *R* v. *Derbyshire County Council, ex p T* [1990] 1 FLR 237 (CA); *R* v. *Secretary of State for Home Department, ex p Brassey* [1989] 2 FLR 486.
34 *R* v. *East Sussex County Council, ex parte Tandy* [1998] ELR 251.
35 *R* v. *Bedfordshire County Council, ex p C* [1987] 1 FLR 239; *R* v. *Herefordshire County Council, ex p B* [1987] 1 FLR 239. Also *R* v. *Royal Borough of Kingston-upon-Thames, ex p T* [1994] 1 FLR 798 and *R* v. *E Sussex County Council ex p W* [1998] 2 FLR 1082.
36 [1997] ELR 66. Also *A* v. *London Borough of Lambeth* [2001] 2 FLR 1201.
37 [2001] EWHC Admin 709, [2002] 1 FLR 469, [2002] Fam Law 180, [2001] All ER (D) 08.
38 [1990] 1 All ER 568, 627. Lord Oliver of Aylmerton emphasised the same point in *Murphy* v. *Brentwood District Council* [1991] AC 398, 486.
39 [1995] 2 AC 633, [1995] 3 All ER 353 (HL).
40 [1995] 2 AC 633, 771.
41 [1996] 3 All ER 801, 828, [1996] AC 923, 953.
42 This case concerned an appeal by a highway authority against the imposition of a duty of care regarding its failure to improve safety at a road junction.
43 (1985) 157 CLR 424, 464.
44 [1996] AC 923, 953–955.
45 [1995] 3 All ER 353, 378–379.
46 [1995] 3 All ER 353, [1995] 2 AC 633, [1995] ELR 404, HL.
47 [1997] 1 FLR 384.
48 In *S* v. *Gloucestershire County Council* [2000] 1 FLR 828, [2001] Fam 313 CA; [2001] 2 WLR 909 the court ruled that *H* v. *Norfolk County Council* should not be followed.
49 [1999] 2 FLR 426, [1998] QB 367, [1997] 3 All ER 171.
50 [1999] 3 All ER 193, 207, 227.
51 Further support for the general application of the *Barrett* approach can be derived from the High Court of Australia decision in *Pyrenees Shire Council* v. *Day* (1998) 192 CLR 330.
52 [1957] 2 All ER 118, [1957] 1 WLR 582.
53 Per McNair J at [1957] 2 All ER 118, 122.
54 Cases in other jurisdictions have cast doubt upon this concern, for example in New Zealand *AG* v. *Prince and Gardner* [1998] 1 NZLR 262, 284; in France

this concern has been dealt with by means of requiring proof of grave fault (Chapus, R. *Droit administratif général*, 12th edn, Paris, 1998).

55 [1999] 3 All ER 193, 208, 228.
56 [1998] 1 NZLR 262.
57 In *Palmer* v. *Tees Health Authority* [1999] Lloyd's Rep Med 351, *The Times*, 6 July 1999, 45 BMLR 88 the Court of Appeal read *Barrett* as authority for the proposition that a case should not be struck out on the ground that it was not fair, just and reasonable to impose a duty of care. See also *Gower* v. *London Borough of Bromley* [1999] ELR 356 Court of Appeal.
58 [2000] 1 FLR 828, [2001] Fam 313 CA.
59 [2000] 1 FLR 828, 829.
60 [2000] 29 EHRR 245, [1999] 1 FLR 193, ECHR.
61 Following the decision in *Hill* v. *West Yorkshire Constabulary* [1988] 2 All ER 238, [1989] AC 53.
62 Article 6(1) provides: 'In the determination of his civil rights and obligations or of any criminal charge against him, everyone is entitled to a fair and public hearing within a reasonable time by an independent and impartial tribunal established by law.'
63 *Osman* v. *Ferguson* [1993] 4 All ER 344.
64 [2001] QB 36, 50.
65 [2002] 34 EHRR 30, [2001] 2 FLR 612 ECHR.
66 [2002] 34 EHRR 2, [2001] 2 FLR 549 ECHR.
67 [2003] 1 FLR 348 ECHR.
68 [2003] 1 FLR 50 ECHR.
69 (1997) 23 EHRR 33, para 64.
70 [2001] EWCA Civ. 757, [2001] All ER (D) 285.
71 *Keenan* v. *UK* (2001) 33 EHRR 38.
72 [2002] UKHL 10, para 62.
73 [2003] EWCA Civ 1151; [2003] All ER (D) 547 (Jul).
74 [2005] UKHL 23.
75 [1991] 2 All ER 648.
76 [1995] 2 AC 633, [1995] 3 All ER 353, HL.
77 *M* v. *Newham LBC* was quoted extensively and approved by the Supreme Court of South Australia in *Hillman* v. *Black* [1996] 67 SASR 490, 494–502 per Matheson J. A local authority's vicarious liability was also contemplated in *Surtees* v. *Kingston-upon-Thames Borough Council* [1991] 2 FLR 559. However, on the facts the injuries were not deliberately inflicted, and Stocker LJ's comments regarding vicarious liability were merely *obiter*.
78 [1997] 3 All ER 171.
79 At p. 636. This decision was approved by Auld LJ in *Gower* v. *London Borough of Bromley* [1999] ELR 356 Court of Appeal.
80 [2000] All ER (D) 1076.
81 [1999] 1 All ER 421.
82 [1995] 2 AC 633, [1995] 3 All ER 353 (HL).
83 The House of Lords were following *E (A Minor)* v. *Dorset County Council*, *Christmas* v. *Hampshire County Council*, *Keating* v. *Bromley London Borough* [1995] 3 All ER 353, [1995] 2 AC 633, [1995] ELR 404, HL; *Christmas* v. *Hampshire County Council* [1998] ELR 1.
84 At [2001] 2 AC 619, 666.
85 Hospital Products Ltd. v US Surgical Corporation (1984) 156 CLR 41 per Mason J at p. 97.
86 [1984] 1 QB 493, [1985] 1 AC 871.
87 (1992) 96 DLR 4th 289.
88 At p. 323.

89 (1994) 114 DLR 4th 151.
90 (1993) 102 DLR 4th 177.
91 (1993) 105 DLR 4th Manitoba Court of Appeal.
92 (1999) 166 DLR 4th 475 British Columbia Court of Appeal.
93 [1999] 3 WLR 79, 106.
94 (2000) 32 HLR 906.
95 See also *West Kent Housing Association Ltd.* v. *Davies* (1998) 31 HLR 415.
96 See comments of Evans LJ in *Barrett* v. *Enfield LBC* [1997] 3 All ER 171, 181.

References

Akers, R.L. (1997) *Criminological Theories: Introduction and Evaluation*, 2nd edn, Los Angeles: Roxbury.

Aldgate, J., Statham, J. (2001) *The Children Act Now: Messages from Research*, London: The Stationery Office.

Aldgate, J., Tunstill, J. (1995a) *Making Sense of Section 17: Implementing Services for Children in Need within the 1989 Children Act*, London: HMSO.

—— (1995b) *Implementing Section 17 of the Children Act: The First 18 Months*, Leicester: Leicester University Press/Department of Health.

Allen, N. (1992) *Making Sense of the Children Act*, 2nd edn, Chichester: Wiley.

Andry, R.G. (1957) 'Faulty parental and maternal-child relationships, affection and discipline', *British Journal of Delinquency*, 8: 34–48.

Aristotle (1941) 'Ethica Nicomachea', Bk II Ch. 3: 11048, translated by W.D. Ross, in R. McKeon (ed.) *The Basic Works of Aristotle*, New York: Random House.

Arnold, J., Jordan, B. (1998) 'Poverty', in S. Merrington (ed.) *A Guide to Setting Up and Evaluating Programmes for Young Offenders*, Winchester: Waterside Press.

Arthur, R. (1999) 'The European Court of Human Rights and the abolition of corporal punishment in Ireland', *Irish Journal of Family Law* 4: 7–13.

—— (2002) 'Tackling youth crime: supporting families in crisis', *Child and Family Law Quarterly*, 14(4): 401–426.

—— (2004a) 'Corporal punishment', *Journal of Commonwealth Law and Legal Education*, 3(1): 53–65.

—— (2004b) 'Young offenders: children in need of protection', *Law and Policy*, 26(3/4): 309–327.

—— (2005a) 'Punishing parents for the crimes of their children', *Howard Journal of Criminal Justice*, 44(3): 233–253.

—— (2005b) 'Ending corporal punishment of Irish children: complying with Ireland's international law obligations', *Irish Journal of Family Law*, 4: 8–11.

—— (2005c) 'The youth justice system in England and Wales: complying with international human rights law', *International Family Law*, September, 157–160.

Audit Commission (1994) *Seen but Not Heard: Coordinating Community Child Health and Social Services for Children in Need*, London: HMSO.

—— (1996) *Misspent Youth: Young People and Crime*, London: Audit Commission.

—— (1998) *Misspent Youth '98: The Challenge for Youth Justice*, London, Audit Commission.

—— (1999a) *Children in Mind: Child and Adolescent Mental Health Services*, London, Audit Commission.

—— (1999b) *Getting the Best from Children's Services: Findings from Joint Reviews of Social Services, 1998/9*, London: Audit Commission.

—— (2004) *A Review of the Reformed Youth Justice System*, London, Audit Commission.

Bailey, S, Bowman, M. (2000) 'Public authority negligence revisited', *Cambridge Law Journal*, 59: 85–132.

Bainham, A. (1990) *Children: The New Law*, Bristol: Family Law.

—— (1998) *Children: The Modern Law*, Bristol: Family Law.

Baker, R.L., Mednick, B.R. (1984) *Influences on Human Development*, Boston: Kluwer-Nijhoff.

Ball, C. (1996). *Law for Social Workers*, 3rd edn, Aldershot: Arena.

Ball, C., Connolly, J. (2000) 'Educationally disaffected young offenders: youth court and agency response to truancy and school exclusion', *British Journal of Criminology*, 40: 594–616.

Bandalli, S. (1998a) 'Abolition of the presumption of *doli incapax* and the criminalisation of children', *Howard Journal of Criminal Justice*, 37: 114–123.

—— (1998b) 'Juvenile justice in England and Wales and the United Nations Convention on the Rights of the Child: a problem with principles', *Youth Justice Matters*, September: 20–23.

Bangard, V.L. (1997) 'Childhood maltreatment and the mental health of low income women', *American Journal of Orthopsychiatry*, 69: 161–191.

Bartol, C.R., Bartol, A.M. (1998) *Delinquency and Justice: A Psychological Approach*, Englewood Cliffs, NJ: Prentice Hall.

Bates, J., Pugh, R., Thompson, N. (eds) (1997) *Protecting Children: Challenges and Change*, Aldershot: Arena.

Bazelon, D. (1976) 'The morality of the criminal law', *Southern California Law Review*, 49: 385–405.

Bennett, T. (1998) *Drugs and Crime: The Results of Research on Drug Testing and Interviewing Arrestees*, London: Home Office.

—— (2000) *Drugs and Crime: The Results of the Second Developmental Stage of the NEW-ADAM Programme*, London: Home Office.

Bensley, L.S., Van Eenwyk, J., Simmons, K.W. (2000) 'Self-reported childhood sexual and physical abuse and adult HIV-risk behaviours and heavy drinking', *American Journal of Preventive Medicine*, 18: 151–158.

Berlino, M., Wansell, G. (1974) *Caught in the Act*, Harmondsworth: Penguin.

Biehal, N., Clayden, J., Stein, M., Wade, J. (1995) *Moving On: Young People and Leaving Care Schemes*, London: HMSO.

Blair, T. (1997) *New Labour Because Britain Deserves Better*, London: Labour Party.

—— (2006) 'Give respect Get respect', in Respect Task Force, *Respect Action Plan*, London, Home Office.

Blatier, C. (1998) 'The specialised jurisdiction in France: a better chance for minors', *International Journal of Law, Policy and the Family*, 12(2): 146–160.

—— (1999a) 'Juvenile justice in France: the evolution of sentencing for children and minor delinquents', *British Journal of Criminology*, 39(2): 240–252.

—— (1999b) 'Towards a constructive response to young offenders: reparation at the levels of justice and individual psychology', *Journal of Social Work Practice*, 13(1): 211–220.

—— (2000) 'Locus of control, causal attributions and self-esteem: a comparison between prisoners', *International Journal of Offender Therapy and Comparative Criminology*, 44(1): 97–110.

Blatier, C. (2002) *La Délinquance des mineurs: l'enfant, le psychologue, le droit*, 2nd edn, Grenoble: Presses Universitaires de Grenoble.

Blatier, C., Corrado, R. (2001) 'Government agencies response to high risk families', in R. Corrado, R. Roesch, S.D. Hart (eds) *Multi-problem Violent Youth: A Foundation for Comparative Research on Needs, Interventions, and Outcomes*, Amsterdam: IPS Press.

Blatier, C., Robin, M. (2001) *La Délinquance des mineurs en Europe*, Grenoble: Presses Universitaires de Grenoble.

Boswell, G. (1995) *Violent Victims: The Prevalence of Abuse and Loss in the Lives of Section 53 Offenders*. London: The Prince's Trust.

Bottoms, A. (1974) 'On the decriminalisation of the English juvenile court', in R. Hood (ed.) *Crime, Criminology and Public Policy*, London: Heinemann.

—— (1995) *Intensive Community Supervision of Young Offenders: Outcomes, Process and Cost*, Cambridge: University of Cambridge Institute of Criminology.

Bowman, M., Bailey, S. (2000) 'Public authority negligence revisited', *Cambridge Law Journal*, 59: 85–132.

Boys, L, Warburton, F., Sampson, D. (2001) *Crime and Disorder Act 1998 – Section 17: A Briefing for Local Authorities on the Implementation of Section 17 of the Crime and Disorder Act 1998*, London: NACRO, LGA.

Brandon, M. (1995) 'Children and violence: report of the Commission on Children and Violence convened by the Gulbenkian Foundation', *ChildRIGHT*, 125: 10.

Brandon, M., Lewis, A. (1996) 'Significant harm and children's experience of domestic violence', *Child and Family Social Work*, 1: 33–42.

Brandon, M., Thoburn, J., Lewis, A., Way, A. (1999) *Safeguarding Children with the Children Act 1989*, London: The Stationery Office.

Bridge, G. (2001) 'An independent person in action under the Children Act 1989 Complaints Procedure', *Children and Society*, 15: 219–230.

Bridge, J., Bridge, S., Luke, S. (1990) *Blackstone's Guide to the Children Act 1989*, London: Blackstone.

Bright, J. (1998) 'Preventing youth crime', *Criminal Justice Matters*, 33: 15–17.

Broad, B. (1998) *Young People Leaving Care: Life after the Children Act 1989*, London: Jessica Kingsley.

Broadbent, B. (1997) *Child Abuse and Neglect in Australia 1995–96*, Sydney: Australian Institute of Health and Welfare.

Brody, S. (1996) *The Children Act and Homeless 16 and 17 year olds*, London: CHAR.

Brown, S. (1998) *Understanding Youth and Crime: Listening to Youth*, Buckingham: Open University Press.

Buehler, C., Anthony, C., Krishnakumar, A., Stone, G., Gerard, J., Pemberton, S. (1997) 'Interparental conflict and youth problem behaviours: a meta-analysis', *Journal of Child and Family Studies*, 6: 233–247.

Campbell, S. (2002a) *Implementing Anti-social Behaviour Orders: Messages from Practitioners*, London: HMSO.

—— (2002b) *A Review of Anti-social Behaviour*, London: HMSO.

Campbell, S., Harrington, V. (2000) *Youth Crime: Findings from the 1998/99 Youth Lifestyles Survey*, London: Home Office.

Candappe, M., Bull, J., Cameron, C., Moss, P., Owen, C. (1996) *Policy into Practice: Day Care Services for Children under Eight*, London: Thomas Coram Research Unit, Institute of Education.

Cannan, C. (1992) *Changing Families, Changing Welfare: Family Centres and the Welfare State*, Hemel Hempstead: Harvester Wheatsheaf.

Cap Gemini Ernst & Young (2003) *Splash 2002*, London: Youth Justice Board.

Capaldi, D.M., Patterson, G.R. (1991) 'Relation of parental transition to boys' adjustment problems: (i) a linear hypothesis. (ii) Mothers at risk for transitions and unskilled parenting', *Developmental Psychology*, 27(3): 489–504.

Carlen, P. (1996) *Jigsaw: A Political Criminology of Youth Homelessness*, Buckingham: Open University Press.

Catalano, R.F., Hawkin, J.D. (1996) 'The Social Developmental Model: A Theory of Antisocial Behaviour', in J.D. Hawkins (ed.) *Delinquency and Crime: Current Theories*, New York: Cambridge University Press.

Catrano, C.E. (2000) 'Social support principles for strengthening families: messages from the USA', in J. Canavan, P. Dolan, J. Pinkerton (eds) *Family Support. Direction from Diversity*, Jessica Kingsley, London, 2000.

Cavadino, M., Dignan, J. (1992) *The Penal System: An Introduction*, London: Sage.

Cernkovich, S.A., Giordano, P.C. (1987) 'Family relationships and delinquency', *Criminology*, 16: 259–319.

Chesney-Lind, M., Shelden, R.G. (1992) *Girls, Delinquency and Juvenile Justice*, Pacific Grove, CA: Brooks/Cole.

—— (1998) *Girls, Delinquency and Juvenile Justice*, 2nd edn, Belmont, CA: West/Wadsworth.

Chief Inspector of Prisons (1997) *Young Prisoners: A Thematic Review*, London: HMSO.

Chief Secretary to the Treasury (2003) *Every Child Matters*, London: HMSO.

Claussen, A.H., Crittenden, P.M. (1991) 'Physical and psychological maltreatment: relations among types of maltreatment', *Child Abuse and Neglect*, 15: 5–18.

Cleaver, H., Unell, I., Aldgate, J. (1999) *Children's Needs – Parenting Capacity: The Impact of Parental Mental Illness, Problem Alcohol and Drug Use, and Domestic Violence on Children's Development*, London: The Stationery Office.

Cohen, P., Brook, J.S. (1994) 'The reciprocal influence of punishment and child disorder', in J. McCord (ed.) *Coercion and Punishment in Long-Term Perspectives*, New York: Cambridge University Press, 1994.

Coleman, R., Cassell, D. (1995) 'Parents who misuse drugs and alcohol', in P. Reder, C. Lucey (eds) *Assessments of Parenting Psychiatric and Psychological Conditions*, London: Routledge.

Collins, D.M. (2001) 'Anti-social behavioural orders: a new false dawn', *New Law Journal*, 15 June 876–877.

Collinson, M. (1994a) 'Drugs and delinquency: a non-treatment paradigm', *Probation Journal*, 41(4); 203–207.

—— (1994b) 'Drug offenders and criminal justice: careers, compulsion, commitment and penalty', *Crime, Law and Social Change*, 21: 49–71.

—— (1996) 'In search of the high life: drugs, crime, masculinity and consumption', *British Journal of Criminology*, 36(3): 428–443.

Colton, M., Drury, C., Williams, M. (1995a) *Staying Together: Supporting Families under the Children Act*, Aldershot: Arena.
—— (1995b) 'Children in need: definition, identification and support', *British Journal of Social Work*, 25: 711–728.
—— (1995c) 'Factors which influence the educational attainment of children in foster family care', *Community Alternatives*, 7(1): 15–38.
—— (1995d) *Children in Need*, Aldershot: Avebury.
Committee for Investigating the Causes of the Alarming Increase of Juvenile Delinquency in the Metropolis (1816) *Report of the Committee for Investigating the Causes of the Alarming Increase of Juvenile Delinquency in the Metropolis*, London: J.F. Dove.
Committee on the Judiciary (1974) *Report on the Juvenile Justice and Delinquency Prevention Act 1974*, Washington DC: Government Printing Office.
Conger, R.D. (1992) 'A family process model of economic hardship and adjustment of early adolescent boys', *Child Development*, 63: 526–541.
Conseur, A., Rivara, F.O., Barnowski, R., Emmanuel, I. (1997) 'Maternal and perinatal risk factors for later delinquency', *Pediatrics*, 99: 785–790.
Consortium for Longitudinal Studies (1995) *As the Twig Is Bent … Lasting Effects of Pre-school Programs*, Hillsdale, NJ: Erlbaum.
Cooper, P. (2002) *Delivering Quality Children's Services: Inspection of Children's Services*, London: Department of Health, London.
Coupet, S.M. (2000) 'What to do with the sheep in wolf's clothing: the role of rhetoric and reality about youth offenders in the constructive dismantling of the juvenile justice system', *University of Pennsylvania Law Review*, 148: 1303–1346.
Craig, E., Barry, D., Young, L. (1990) 'An investigation into the nature of registered emotional abuse in New South Wales Dept. of Family and Community Services Child Abuse and Neglect', Paper given at Australian Child Protection Conference, Sydney.
Crime and Criminal Justice Unit (2000) *Criminal Statistics England & Wales 1999*, London: Home Office.
—— (2001) *Criminal Statistics England & Wales 2000*, London: Home Office.
—— (2002) *Criminal Statistics England & Wales 2001*, London: Home Office.
Curran, D.J., Cook, S. (1993) 'Growing fears, rising crime: juveniles and China's justice system', *Crime and Delinquency*, 39(3): 296–315.
Curtis, S. (1999) *Children who Break the Law, or Everybody Does It*, Winchester: Waterside Press.
Daly, C. (2000) 'How can I complain? Making a complaint to the Social Services Department', *ChildRIGHT*, no. 163 Jan/Feb: 11–14.
Daniel, B. (1999) 'Beliefs in child care: social work consensus and lack of consensus on issues of parenting and decision-making', *Children and Society*, 13: 179–191.
Dartington Social Research Unit (1995) *Matching Needs and Services: The Audit and Planning of Provision for Children Looked After by Local Authorities*, Totnes: Dartington Social Research Unit.
Davenport, Y.B., Zahn-Waxler, C., Adland, M.C., Mayfield, A. (1989) 'Early child-rearing practices in families with a manic depressive parent', *American Journal of Psychiatry*, 141: 230–235.
Davidson, H. (1995) 'No consequences: re-examining parental responsibility laws', *Stanford Law and Policy Review*, 7: 23–30.

Dembo, R., Ramirez-Garnica, G., Rollie, M., Schmeidler, J., Livingstone, S., Harts-field, A. (2000) 'Youth recidivism twelve months after a family empowerment intervention: final report', *Journal of Offender Rehabilitation*, 31(3/4): 29–65.

Deng, F., Vaughan, M.S., Huang, F. (1994) 'Correlates of crime in Taiwan', *Crime, Law and Social Change*, 21: 267–285.

Dennis, N., Erdos, G. (1992) *Families without Fatherhood*, London: London Institute of Economic Affairs.

Department for Education and Employment (1996) *Code of Practice on the Identification and Assessment of Special Educational Needs*, London: HMSO.

Department of Health (1988) *Protecting Children: A Guide for Social Workers Undertaking a Comprehensive Assessment*, London: HMSO.

—— (1991a) *Children Act 1989 Guidance and Regulations*, vol. 1: *Court Orders*, London, HMSO.

—— (1991b) *The Children Act 1989 Guidance and Regulations*, vol. 2: *Family Support, Day Care and Educational Provision for Young Children*, London: HMSO.

—— (1991c) *Children Act 1989 Guidance and Regulations*, vol. 4: *Residential Care*, London: HMSO.

—— (1991d) *Children Act 1989 Guidance and Regulations*, vol. 7: *Guardians ad Litem and Other Court Related Issues*, London: HMSO.

—— (1991e) *Working Together under the Children Act 1989: A Guide to Inter-agency Co-operation for the Protection of Children from Abuse*, London: HMSO.

—— (1991f) *Children Act 1989 Guidance and Regulations*, vol. 3: *Family Placements*, London: HMSO.

—— (1994) *The Children Act Report 1993*, London: HMSO.

—— (1995a) *The Children Act Report 1994*, London: HMSO.

—— (1995b) *Child Protection: Messages from Research*, London: HMSO.

—— (1996) *Focus on Teenagers*, London: HMSO.

—— (1997) *Me, Survive, Out There?* London: The Stationery Office.

—— (1998) *Someone Else's Children*, London: The Stationery Office.

—— (1999) *Me, Survive Out There? New Arrangements for Young People Living in and Leaving Care*, London: The Stationery Office.

—— (2000a) *Framework for the Assessment of Children in Need and Their Families*, London: The Stationery Office.

—— (2000b) *Protecting Children, Supporting Parents: A Consultation Document on the Physical Punishment of Children*, London: The Stationery Office.

—— (2001a) *Studies Informing the Framework for the Assessment of Children in Need and Their Families*, London: The Stationery Office.

—— (2001b) *The Children Act Report 2000*, London: The Stationery Office.

—— (2002) *The Children Act Report 2001*, London: The Stationery Office.

Department of Health and Social Services (1985) *Review of Child Care Law: Report to Ministers of an Interdepartmental Working Party*, London: HMSO.

Department of Health, Home Office, Department for Education and Employment (1999) *Working Together to Safeguard Children: A Guide to Inter-agency Working to Safeguard and Promote the Welfare of Children*, London: The Stationery Office.

—— (2003) *Victoria Climbié Inquiry: Report of an Inquiry by Lord Laming*, London: The Stationery Office.

Devaney, J. (1999) 'An evaluation of the criteria used in decision making in child protection referrals', *Child Care in Practice*, 5(2): 151–160.

DiFonzo, J.H. (2001) 'Parental responsibility for juvenile crime', *Oregon Law Review*, 80(1): 1–108.

Dillon, J., Statham, J. (1998) 'Private and voluntary day care facilities for children in need', *Child and Family Social Work*, 3: 113–123.

Dimigen, G., Del Priore, C., Butler, S., Evans, S., Fergusson, L., Swan, M. (1999) 'The need for a mental health service for children at commencement of being looked after and accommodated by the local authority: questionnaire survey', *British Medical Journal*, 319: 675.

Dolgin, J.L. (1999) 'The age of autonomy: legal reconceptualizations of childhood', *Quinnipiac Law Review*, 18: 421–450.

Eamon, M.K. (2001) 'Antecedents and socioemotional consequences of physical punishment on children in two-parent families', *Child Abuse and Neglect*, 6: 787–802.

Edleson, J. (1999) 'Children's witnessing of adult domestic violence', *Journal of Interpersonal Violence*, 14: 839–870.

Elliott, D.S., Huizinga, D., Ageton, S.S. (1985) *Explaining Delinquency and Drug Use*, London: Sage.

Ely, P. (1990) 'Child crime: the Dunkirk spirit', *New Law Journal*, 140: 731.

Erel, O., Burman, B. (1995) 'Interrelatedness of marital relations and parent–child relations: a meta-analytic review', *Psychological Bulletin*, 118: 108–132.

Everall, M. (1991) 'Judicial review of local authorities after the Children Act 1989', *Family Law*, June: 212, 213.

Fairgrieve, D. (2002) 'Pushing back the boundaries of public authority liability: tort law enters the classroom', *Public Law*, 288–308.

Farmer, E., Owen, M. (1995) *Child Protection Practice: Private Risks and Public Remedies: A Study of Decision-Making, Intervention and Outcome in Child Protection Work*, London: HMSO.

Farrington, D.P. (1983) *Further Analysis of a Longitudinal Survey of Crime and Delinquency*, Washington, DC: National Institute of Justice.

—— (1992) 'Juvenile delinquency', in J.C. Coleman (ed.) *The School Years*, 2nd edn, London: Routledge.

—— (1994) 'Early developmental prevention of juvenile delinquency', *Criminal Behaviour and Mental Health*, 4: 209–227.

—— (1996) *Understanding and Preventing Youth Crime*, York: Joseph Rowntree Foundation.

—— (1997) 'Human Development and Criminal Careers', in M. Maguire, R. Morgan, R. Reiner (eds) *The Oxford Handbook of Criminology*, Oxford: Oxford University Press.

Farrington, D.P., Loeber, R. (1999) 'Transatlantic replicability of risk factors in the development of delinquency', in P. Cohen, C. Slomkowski, L.N. Robins (eds) *Historical and Geographical Influences on Psychopathology*, Mahwah, NJ: Lawrence Erlbaum.

Farrington, D.P., West, D.J. (1993) 'Criminal, penal and life histories of chronic offenders: risk and protective factors and early identification', *Criminal Behaviour and Mental Health*, 3: 492–523.

Farrington, D., Barnes, G., Lambert, S. (1996a) 'The concentration of offending in families', *Legal and Criminal Psychology*, 1: 47–63.

Farrington, D.P., Loeber, R., Van Kammen, W.,(1996b) 'Long-term criminal outcomes of hyperactivity-impulsivity-attention deficit and conduct disorder in childhood', in L. Robins, I. Holloway (eds) *Straight and Devious Pathways from Childhood to Adulthood*, Cambridge: Cambridge University Press.

Farrington, D.P., Jolliffe, D., Loeber, R., Stouthamer-Loeber, M., Kalb, L.M. (2001) 'The concentration of offenders in families and family criminality in the prediction of boy's delinquency', *Journal of Adolescence*, 24: 579–596.

Feld, B.C. (1991) 'The Transformation of the Juvenile Court', *Minnesota State Law Review*, 75: 691–725.

—— (1998) 'The juvenile court meets the principle of offense: punishment, treatment, and the difference it makes', *Boston University Law Review*, 68: 821–915.

Feldman, L. (1992) *Child Protection Law*, London: Longman.

Feldman, L., Mitchels, B. (1990) *The Children Act 1989: A Practical Guide*, London: Longman.

Felitti, V.J., Anda, R.F., Nordenberg, D., Williamson, D.F., Spitz, A.M., Edwars, V., Koss, M.P., Marks, J.S. (1998) 'Relationship of childhood abuse and household dysfunction to many of the leading causes of death in adults', *American Journal of Preventive Medicine*, 14: 245–258.

Fergusson, D.M., Harwood, L.J. (1998) 'Exposure to interparental violence in childhood and psychological adjustment in young adulthood', *Child Abuse and Neglect*, 22: 339–357.

Fergusson, D.M., Lynskey, M.T. (1997) 'Physical punishment/maltreatment during childhood and adjustment in young adulthood', *Child Abuse and Neglect*, 21(7): 617–630.

Fischer, T., Bingley-Miller, L., Sinclair, I. (1995) 'Which children are registered at case conferences?', *British Journal of Social Work*, 25: 191–207.

Fleming, J. (1998) 'Childhood sexual abuse: an update', *Current Opinions in Obstetrics and Gynecology*, 10: 383–386.

Flood-Page, C., Campbell, S., Harrington, V., Miller, J. (2000) *Youth Crime: Findings from the 1998/99 Youth Lifestyles Survey*, London: Home Office.

Fox, S.J. (1996) 'The early history of the court', *The Future of Children*, 31: 29–39.

France, A., Wiles, P. (1996) *The Youth Action Scheme: A Report of the National Evaluation*, London: Department for Education and Employment.

France, A., Hine, J., Armstrong, D., Canina, M. (2004) *The On Track Early Intervention and Prevention Programme: From Theory to Action.* London: Home Office.

Frensch, K., Cameron, G. (2002) 'Treatment of choice or a last resort? A review of residential mental health placements for children and youth', *Child and Youth Care Forum*, 31(5): 307–339.

Gallagher, P. (1998) 'Care orders and the state's responsibilities', *New Law Journal*, 87: 670–672.

Garapon, A. (1995) *Carnet du Palais: regards sur le Palais de Justice de Paris*, Paris: Albin Michel.

Gardner, R. (1992) 'Developing family support in local authorities', in J. Gibbons (ed.) *The Children Act 1989 and Family Support: Principles into Practice*, London: HMSO.

Gelsthorpe, L., Morris, A. (1999) 'Much ado about nothing: a critical comment on key provisions relating to children in the Crime and Disorder Act 1998', *Child and Family Law Quarterly*, 11(3): 209–221.

Ghate, D., Ramella, M. (2002) *Positive Parenting: The National Evaluation of the Youth Justice Board's Parenting programme*, London: Youth Justice Board.

Gibbons, J., Thorpe, S., Wilkinson, P. (1990) *Family Support and Prevention: Studies in Local Areas*, London: HMSO.

Gibbons, J., Conroy, S., Bell, C. (1995) *Operating the Child Protection System*, London: HMSO.

Giller, H. (1993) *Children in Need Definition, Management and Monitoring*, Manchester: Social Information Services.

Gilligan, R. (2000) 'Family support: issues and prospects', in J. Canavan, P. Dolan, J. Pinkerton (eds) *Family Support: Direction from Diversity*, London: Jessica Kingsley.

Gladstone, F. (1978) 'Vandalism among adolescent boys', in R.V.G. Clarke (ed.) *Tackling Vandalism*, London: HMSO.

Glueck, S., Glueck, E. (1950) *Unraveling Juvenile Delinquency*, Cambridge, MA: Harvard University Press.

—— (1962) *Family Environment and Delinquency*, London: Routledge.

—— (1974) *Of Delinquency and Crime: A Panorama of Years of Search and Research*, Springfield, IL: Charles C. Thomas.

Goldson, B. (1999) 'Punishing times for children in trouble: recent developments and the Crime and Disorder Act 1998', *Representing Children*, 11(4): 274–288.

Goldstein, J., Freud, A., Solnit, A.J. (1979) *Before the Best Interests of the Child*, New York: Free Press.

Gorman-Smith, D., Tolan, P.H., Huesmann, L.R., Zelli, A. (1996) 'The relation of family functioning to violence among inner-city minority youth', *Journal of Family Psychology*, 10: 115–129.

Gottfredson, M., Hirschi, T. (1989) *A General Theory of Crime*, Stanford, CA: Stanford University Press.

Goulden, C., Sondhi, A. (2001) *At the Margins: Drug Use by Vulnerable Young People in the 1998/99 Youth Lifestyle Survey*, London: Home Office, 2001.

Graham, J., Bowling, B. (1995) *Young People and Crime*, London: Home Office.

Graham, P. (1986) 'Behavioural and intellectual development in childhood epidemiology', *British Medical Bulletin*, 42: 155–162.

Gray, P. (1997) 'Deconstructing the delinquent as a subject of class and cultural power', *Journal of Law and Society*, 24(4): 526–531.

Greco-Vigorito, C., Drucker, P.M., Moore-Russell, M., Avaltroni, J. (1996) 'Affective symptoms in young children of substance abusers correlate with parental distress', *Psychological Reports*, 79(2): 547–552.

Gronger, J. (1997) 'Estimating the incarceration-related costs of early childbearing', in R. Maynard (ed.) *Kids Having Kids*, Washington, DC: Urban Institute Press.

Guerra, N.G., Huesmann, L.R., Tolan, P.H., Van Acker, R., Eron, L.D. (1995) 'Stressful events and individual beliefs as correlates of economic disadvantage and aggression among urban children', *Journal of Consulting and Clinical Psychology*, 63: 518–528.

Gunn, J. Maden, A., Swinton, M. (1991) 'Treatment needs of prisoners with psychiatric disorders', *British Medical Journal*, 303: 338–341.

Guthrie, T. (1998) 'Legal liability and accountability for child-care decisions', *British Journal of Social Work*, 28: 403–422.

Hagan, J., Parker, P. (1999) 'Rebellion beyond the classroom: a life-course capitalization theory of the intergenerational causes of delinquency', *Theoretical Criminology*, 3(3): 259–285.

Hagell, A., Newburn, T. (1994) *Persistent Young Offenders*, London: Policy Studies Institute.

Haines, K., Drakeford, M. (1999) *Young People and Youth Justice*, London: Macmillan.

Hammersley, R., Marsland, L., Reid, M. (2003) *Substance Use by Young Offenders: The Impact of the Normalisation of Drug Use in the Early Years of the 21st Century*, London: Home Office.

Hammond, W.R., Yung, B.R. (1994) 'African Americans', in L.D. Eron, J.H. Gentry, P. Schlegel (eds) *Reason to Hope: A Psychosocial Perspective on Violence and Youth*, Washington, DC: American Psychosocial Association.

Hardiker, P. (1996) 'The legal and social construction of significant harm', in M. Hill, J. Aldgate (eds) *Child Welfare Services: Developments in Law, Policy, Practice and Research*, London: Jessica Kingsley.

Harker, R.M., Dobel-Ober, D., Lawrence, J., Berridge, D., Sinclair, R. (2003) 'Who takes care of education? Looked after children's perception of support for educational progress', *Child and Family Social Work*, 8: 89–120.

Harris, R., Harris, M. (2002) 'Local authorities and child protection: the mosaic of accountability', *Child and Family Law Quarterly*, 14(2): 117–136.

Harris, R., Timms, N. (1993) *Secure Accommodation in Child Care*, London: Routledge.

Harrist, A.W., Ainslie, R.C. (1998) 'Marital discord and child behavior problems: parent–child relationship quality and child interpersonal awareness as mediators', *Journal of Family Issues*, 19: 140–163.

Hartless, J.M., Ditton, J., Nair, G., Phillips, S. (1995) 'More sinned against than sinning: a study of young teenagers' experience of crime', *British Journal of Criminology*, 35(1): 114–133.

Haskell, M. and Yablonsky, L. (1982) *Juvenile Delinquency*, 3rd edn, Boston: Houghton Mifflin.

Hawkins, J.D. (1996) *Delinquency and Crime: Current Theories*, Cambridge: Cambridge University Press.

Hawkins, J.D., Catalano, R.F. (1992) *Communities That Care*, San Francisco: Jossey-Bass.

—— (1993) *Risk-Focused Prevention Using the Social Developmental Strategy*, Seattle, WA: Developmental Research and Programs.

Hawkins, J.D., Catalano, R.F., Miller, J.Y. (1992) 'Risk and protective factors for alcohol and other drug problems in adolescence and early adulthood: implications for substance abuse prevention', *Psychological Bulletin*, 112: 64–105.

Hawkins, J.D., Catalano, R.F., Brewer, D.D. (1995) 'Effective strategies from conception to age 6', in J.C. Howell, B. Krisberg, J.D. Hawkins, J. Wilson (eds) *A Sourcebook: Serious, Violent and Chronic Juvenile Offenders*, London: Sage.

Hawthorne Kirk, R. (1995) 'Social support and early years centres' in M. Hill, R. Hawthorne Kirk, D. Part (eds) *Supporting Families*, Edinburgh: HMSO.

Hayes, M. (1999) 'Offending behaviour and children under 10', *Family Law*, May: 317–321.

Hayes, M., Williams, C. (1999) *Family Law: Principles, Policy and Practice*, 2nd edn, London: Butterworths.

Henricson, C., Coleman, J., Roker, D. (2000) 'Parenting in the youth justice context', *Howard Journal of Criminal Justice*, 39(4): 325–338.

Henricson, C., Katz, I., Mesie, J., Sandison, M., Tunstill, J. (2001) *National*

Mapping of Family Services in England and Wales: A Consultation Document, London: National Family and Parenting Institute.

Herrenkohl, E.C., Herrenkohl, R.C., Egolf, B. (1994) 'Resilient early school-age children from maltreating homes: outcomes in late adolescence', *American Journal of Orthopsychiatry*, 64: 301–309.

Herrera, V.M., McCloskey, L.A. (2001) 'Gender differences in the risk for delinquency among youth exposed to family violence', *Child Abuse and Neglect*, 25: 1037–1051.

Hester, M., Pearson, C. (1998) *From Periphery to Centre: Domestic Violence in Work with Abused Children*, Bristol: Policy Press.

Hill, M., Hawthorne Kirk, R., Part, D. (1995) 'Support to families: dilemma, changes and challenges', in M. Hill, R. Hawthorne Kirk, D. Part (eds) *Supporting Families*, Edinburgh: HMSO.

Hindelang, M.J. (1971) 'Age, sex and the versatility of delinquency involvement', *Social Problems*, 18: 522–535.

Hirschi, T. (1983) 'Crime and family policy', *Journal of Contemporary Studies*, 6: 3–16.

Hogg, K. (1999) *Youth Crime in Scotland*, Edinburgh: Scottish Executive Policy Unit.

Hoggett, B. (1993) *Parents and Children*, 4th edn, London: Sweet & Maxwell.

Holdaway, S., Davidson, N., Dignan, J., Hammersley, R., Hine, J., Marsh, P. (2001) *New Strategies to Address Youth Offending: The National Evaluation of the Pilot Youth Offending Teams*, London: RDS Occasional Paper No. 69.

Holman, B. (1988) *Putting Families First: Prevention and Child Care*, London: Macmillan.

Home Affairs Committee (1993) *Sixth Report: Juvenile Offenders Sessions 1992–93*, London: HMSO.

Home Office (1927) *Report of the Departmental Committee on the Treatment of Young Offenders*, London: HMSO.

—— (1946) *The Care of Children*, London: HMSO.

—— (1960) *Report on the Committee on Children and Young Persons*, London: HMSO.

—— (1991) *National Prison Survey*, London: Research and Statistics Department.

—— (1997) *No More Excuses: A New Approach to Tackle the Roots of Juvenile Crime in England and Wales*, London: The Stationery Office.

—— (1998) *Youth Justice: Preventing Offending*, London: The Stationery Office.

—— (2000) *Crime and Disorder Act 1998: Guidance Document*, London: The Stationery Office.

—— (2001) *Local Child Curfew: Guidance Documents: Working Draft*, London: The Stationery Office.

—— (2002) *Justice for All*, London: The Stationery Office.

—— (2003a) *Respect and Responsibility: Taking a Stand against Anti-social Behaviour*, London: Home Office.

—— (2003b) *Youth Justice: The Next Steps*, London: Home Office.

—— (2004) *Confident Communities in a Secure Britain: The Home Office Strategic Plan 2004–2008*, London: Home Office.

Home Office, Department of Health, Department of Education and Science, Welsh Office (1991) *Working together under the Children Act 1989*, London: HMSO.

Home Office, Department of Health, Welsh Office, Department for Education and

Employment (1998) *Inter-departmental Circular on Establishing Youth Offending Teams*, London: Home Office.

Horwath, J. (2002) 'Maintaining a focus on the child: first impressions of the framework for the assessment of children in need and their families in cases of child neglect', *Child Abuse Review*, 11: 195–213.

House of Commons Research Paper (2001) *The Criminal Justice and Police Bill: Bill 31 of 2000–2001*, London: House of Commons.

Howard, J., Zibert, E. (1990) 'Curious, bored and wanting to feel good: the drug use of detained young offenders', *Drug and Alcohol Review*, 9: 225–231.

Howard League (1996) *The Trouble-shooter Project*, York: Howard League for Penal Reform.

Huizinga, D., Loeber, R., Thornberry, T. (1994) *Urban Delinquency and Substance Abuse*, Washington, DC: Office of Juvenile Justice and Delinquency Prevention, US Department of Justice.

Humphreys, C., Mullender, A., Lowe, P., Hague, G., Abrahams, H., Hester, M. (2001) 'Domestic violence and child abuse: developing sensitive policies and guidance', *Child Abuse Review*, 10: 183–197.

Hunt, J. (1998) 'A moving target: care proceedings as a dynamic process', *Child and Family Law Quarterly*, 10(3): 281–289.

Hutton, S., Liddiard, M. (1994) *Youth Homelessness: The Constructions of a Social Issue*, London: Macmillan.

Inciardi, J., Pottieger, A. (1991) 'Kids, crack and crime', *Journal of Drug Issues*, 21: 257–270.

Ireland, T.O., Smith, C.A., Thornberry, T.P. (2002) 'Developmental issues in the impact of child maltreatment on later delinquency and drug use', *Criminology*, 40(2): 359–400.

James, O. (1995) *Juvenile Violence in a Winner–Loser Culture*, London: Free Association Books.

Johnson, B.D., Wish, E.D., Schmeidler, H., Huizinga, D. (1991) 'Concentration of delinquent offending: serious drug involvement and high delinquency rates', *Journal of Drug Issues*, 21: 205–229.

Johnson, T., Parker, V. (1996) *Is a Persistent Young Offender a 'Child in Need'? A Survey of London Local Authorities*, London: Rainer.

Joint Committee on Human Rights (2003) *Anti-social Behaviour Bill: Thirteenth Report of Session 2002–03*, London: The Stationery Office.

Jones, M.B., Offord, D.R. (1989) 'Reduction of antisocial behaviour in poor children by nonschool skill-development', *Journal of Child Psychology and Psychiatry*, 30: 737–750.

Kazdin, A.F., Siegel, T.C., Bass, D. (1992) 'Cognitive problem-solving skills training and parent management training in the treatment of antisocial behaviour in children', *Journal of Consulting and Clinical Psychology*, 60: 733–747.

Kelly, A. (1996). *Introduction to the Scottish Children's Panel*, Winchester: Waterside Press.

Kelly, M., Lewis, R. (1994) 'Child abuse in residential homes', *New Law Journal*, March 11: 367.

Kendziora, K.T., O'Leary, S.G. (1993) 'Dysfunctional parenting as a focus for prevention and treatment of child behavior problems', in H. Ollendick, R.J. Prinz (eds) *Advances in Clinical Child Psychology*, vol. 15, New York: Plenum Press.

Kiernan, K. (1992) 'The impact of family disruption in childhood on transitions made in young adult life', *Population Studies*, 46: 213–234.

—— (1995) *Transition to Parenthood: Young Mother, Young Fathers: Associated Factors and Later Life Experiences*, London: London School of Economics.

Kilbrandon, Lord (1964) *Report of the Committee on Children and Young Persons*, Edinburgh: HMSO.

Kilpatrick, D.G., Acierno, R., Saunders, B., Resnick, H.S., Best, C.L., Schnur, P.P. (2000) 'Risk factors for adolescent substance abuse and dependence: data from a national sample', *Journal of Consulting and Clinical Psychology*, 68: 19–30.

King, M. (1997) *A Better World for Children: Explorations in Morality and Authority*, London: Routledge.

Kolvin, I., Miller, F.J.W., Scott, D.M., Gatzanis, S.R.M., Fleeting, M. (1990) *Continuities of Deprivation? The Newcastle 1000 Family Study*, Avebury: Aldershot.

Kumpfer, K., Alvarado, R.J. (2000) 'Strengthening American's families', *Juvenile Justice Journal*, 7(3): 8–18.

Kurtz, Z., Thornes, R., Wolkind, S. (1994) *Services for the Mental Health of Children and Young People in England: A National Review*, London: Department of Health.

Lauritsen, J.L. (1993) 'Sibling resemblance in juvenile delinquency: findings from the National Youth Survey', *Criminology*, 31: 387–409.

Layborn, A. (1986) 'Traditional working class parenting: an undervalued system', *British Journal of Social Work*, 16: 625–644.

Learmouth, J. (1995) *More Willingly to School? An Independent Evaluation of the Truancy and Disaffected Pupils GEST Programme*, London: Department for Education and Skills.

Lewis, N., Birkinshaw, P. (1993) *When Citizens Complain: Reforming Justice and Administration*, Milton Keynes: Open University Press.

Lloyd, C. (1998) 'Risk factors for problem drug abuse: identifying vulnerable groups', *Drugs Education Prevention and Policy*, 5(3): 217–232.

Lloyd, S. (1995) 'Social work and domestic violence', in P. Kingston, B. Penhale (eds) *Family Violence and the Caring Professions*, Basingstoke: Macmillan.

Loeber, R., Farrington, D.P. (eds) (1998) *Serious and Violent Juvenile Offenders: Risk Factors and Successful Interventions*, Thousand Oaks, CA: Sage.

Loeber, R., LeBlanc, M. (1991) 'Toward a developmental criminology', in M. Tonry, N. Morris (eds) *Crime and Justice*, vol. 12, Chicago: University of Chicago Press.

Loeber, R., Stouthamer-Loeber, M. (1986) 'Family factors as correlates and predictors of juvenile conduct problems and delinquency', in M. Tonry, N. Morris (eds) *Crime and Justice: An Annual Review of Research*, vol. 7, Chicago: University of Chicago Press.

Loeber, R., Stouthamer-Loeber, M., Van Kammen, W., Farrington, D.P. (1991) 'Initiation, escalation and desistance in juvenile offending and their correlates: Pittsburgh Youth Study', *Journal of Criminal Law and Criminology*, 82(1): 36–82.

Loeber, R., Farrington, D.P., Stouthamer-Loeber, M., Van Kammen, W. (1998) *Antisocial Behavior and Mental Health Problems: Explanatory Factors in Childhood and Adolescence*, Mahwah, NJ: Erlbaum.

McCarthy, B., Hagan, J. (1991) 'Homelessness: a criminogenic situation?', *British Journal of Criminology*, 31(4): 393–410.

McCluskey, J. (1993) *Reassessing Priorities: The Children Act 1989 – A New Agenda for Homeless Young People?* London: CHAR.

McCord, J. (1982) 'A longitudinal view of the relationship between parental absence and crime', in J. Gunn, D.P. Farrington (eds) *Abnormal Offenders, Delinquency and the Criminal Justice System*, New York: Wiley.

—— (1991) 'The cycle of crime and socialization practices', *Journal of Criminal Law and Criminology*, 82: 211–228.

McCord, W., McCord, J. (1959) *Origins of Crime*, New York: Columbia University Press.

McGuigan, W.M., Pratt, C.C (2001) 'The predictive impact of domestic violence on three types of maltreatment', *Child Abuse and Neglect*, 25: 869–883.

Mack, J.W. (1909) 'The juvenile court', *Harvard Law Review*, 23: 104–122.

McKay, M.M. (1994) 'The link between domestic violence and child abuse: assessment and treatment considerations', *Child Welfare*, 73: 29–39.

Mackie, A., Burrows, J., Hubbard, R. (2003) *Evaluation of the Youth Inclusion Programme*, London: Youth Justice Board.

McLanahan, S., Sandefar, G.D. (1994) *Growing Up with a Single Parent*, Cambridge, MA: Harvard University Press.

Maguire, M. (1997) 'Crime Statistics, Patterns and Trends: Changing perceptions and their Implication', in M. Maguire, R. Morgan, R. Reiner (eds) *The Oxford Handbook of Criminology*, Oxford: Oxford University Press.

Markesinis, B. (2001) 'Plaintiff's tort law or defendant's tort law? Is the House of Lords moving towards a synthesis?', *Torts Law Journal*, 9: 168–176.

Marsh, P., Peel, M. (1999) *Leaving Care in Partnership: Family Involvement with Care Leavers*, London: The Stationery Office.

Maxwell, G., Robertson, J. (1995) *Child Offenders: A Report to the Minister of Justice, Police and Social Welfare*, Wellington, New Zealand: Office of the Commissioner for Children.

Miller, F., Court, S., Knox, E., Brandon, S. (1974) *The School Years in Newcastle upon Tyne*, London: Oxford University Press.

Milner, J. (1993) 'A disappearing act: the differing career paths of fathers and mothers in child protection investigations', *Critical Social Policy*, 13: 48–661.

Minnis, H., Del Priore, C. (2001) 'Mental health services for looked after children: implications from two studies', *Adoption and Fostering*, 25: 27–38.

Minnis, H., Pelosi, A., Knapp, M., Dunn, J. (2001) 'Mental health and foster carer training', *Archives of Disease in Childhood*, 84: 302–306.

Minty, B., Pattinson, G. (1994) 'The nature of child neglect', *British Journal of Social Work*, 24: 733–747.

Mitchell, G. (1991) 'The child assessment order: a breach of principle?', *Liverpool Law Review*, 13(1): 53–62.

Mitchell, J.J. (2000) 'Working together to safeguard children: child protection and assessment', *Family Law*, 30: 501–505.

Moffitt, T.E. (1994) 'Natural histories of delinquency', in E.G.M. Weitekamp, H.-J. Kerner (eds) *Cross-national Longitudinal Research on Human Development and Criminal Behavior*, Amsterdam: Kluwer.

Moffitt, T.E., Silva, P.A. (1988) 'I.Q. and delinquency: a direct test of the differential detection hypothesis', *Journal of Abnormal Psychology*, 97: 330–333.

Morash, M., Rucker, L. (1989) 'An exploratory study of the connection of mother's age at childbearing to her children's delinquency in four data sets', *Crime and Delinquency*, 35: 45–93.

Morgan, R. (2005) 'The value of targeted prevention programmes', *Youth Justice Board News* 26: 11.

Munro, E. (1996) 'Avoidable and unavoidable mistakes in child protection', *British Journal of Social Work*, 26: 793–808.

Nagin, D.S, Farrington, D.P., Pogarsky, G. (1997) 'Adolescent mothers and the criminal behavior of their children', *Law and Society Review*, 31(1): 137–162.

National Commission of Inquiry into the Prevention of Child Abuse (1996) *Childhood Matters*, vol. 1: *The Report*, London, The Stationery Office.

New South Wales Bureau of Crime Statistics and Research (1997) *Social and Economic Stress, Child Neglect and Juvenile Delinquency*, Sydney: NSW Bureau of Crime Statistics and Research.

New South Wales Department of Community Services (1993) *Domestic Violence Guidelines*, Ashfield, NSW: Department of Community Services.

Newburn, T. (1997) 'Youth, crime and justice', in M. Maguire, R. Morgan, R. Reiner (eds) *The Oxford Handbook of Criminology*, 2nd edn, Oxford: Oxford University Press.

—— (1999) 'Drug prevention and youth justice: issues of philosophy, politics and practice', *British Journal of Criminology*, 39(4): 609–624.

Newson, J., Newson, E. (1989) *The Extent of Parental Physical Punishment in the UK*, London: Approach.

Nugent, M., Labram, A., McLoughlin, L. (1998) 'The effects of child sexual abuse on school life', *Educational and Child Psychology*, 15 (4): 68–78.

Office for National Statistics (2000) *Mental Health of Children and Adolescents in Great Britain*, London: The Stationery Office.

O'Hagan, K. (1993) *Emotional and Psychological Abuse of Children*, Buckingham: Open University Press.

O'Hara, M. (1995) 'Child deaths in the context of domestic violence', *ChildRIGHT*, 115: 15–18.

O'Keefe, M. (1995) 'Predictors of child abuse in mutually violent families', *Journal of Interpersonal Violence*, 10: 3–25.

Olds, D.L., Eckenrode, J., Henderson, C.R. Jr, Kitzman, H., Powers, J., Cole, R., Sidora, K., Morris, P., Pettitt, L.M., Luckey, D. (1997) 'Long-term effects of home visitation on maternal life course and child abuse and neglect: fifteen-year follow-up of a randomized trial', *Journal of the American Medical Association*, 278: 637–643.

Osborn, A.F. (1984) *The Social Life of Britain's Five-Year-Olds: A Report of the Child Health and Education Study*, London: Routledge & Kegan Paul.

Osborn, S.G., West, D.J. (1984) 'Conviction records of fathers and sons compared', *British Journal of Criminology*, 19: 254–256.

Osofsky, J.D., Fenichel, E. (1994) 'Caring for infants and toddlers in violent environments: hurting, healing and hope', *Zero to Three*, 14: 1–48.

Ousten, J. (1984) 'Delinquency, family background and educational attainment', *British Journal of Criminology*, 24: 2–26.

Packman, J., Hall, C. (1998) *From Care to Accommodation: Support, Protection and Control in Child Care Services*, London: The Stationery Office.

Parker, H., Measham, F., Aldridge, J. (1995) *Drugs Futures: Changing Patterns of Drug Use amongst English Youth*, London: Institute for the Study of Drug Dependence.

Parkinson, P., Humphries, C. (1998) 'Children who witness domestic violence: the implications for child protection', *Child and Family Law Quarterly*, 10: 147–159.

Passino, A.W., Whitman, T.L., Borkowski, J.G., Schellenbach, S.E.M., Keogh, D., Rellinger, E. (1993) 'Personal adjustment during pregnancy and adolescent parenting', *Adolescence*, 28: 97–122.

Patterson, G.R. (1986) 'Performance models for antisocial boys', *American Psychologist*, 41: 432–444.

Peacock, M. (1999) 'Taking care to the extreme: juvenile crime', *Children First Journal*, 3: 9–11.

Phelan, J. (1983) *Family Centres: A Study*, London: The Children's Society.

Pinkerton, J., Stein, M. (1995) 'Responding to the needs of young people leaving state care: law practice and policy in England and Northern Ireland', *Children and Youth Services Review*, 17(5/6): 683–695.

Pitthouse, A., Lindsell, S., Cheung, M. (1998) *Family Support and Family Centre Services*, Aldershot: Ashgate.

Pösö, T. (1991) 'Welfare for girls, justice for boys? Treatment of troublesome youth in the Finnish residential child welfare system', in A. Snare (ed.) *Youth, Crime and Justice*, Scandinavian Studies in Criminology vol. 12, Oslo: Norwegian University Press.

Province of Ontario (1891) *Report of the Commission Appointed to Enquire into the Prison and Reformatory System of Ontario*, Toronto: Warwick.

Pugh, G. (1994) *Study of Three Early Childhood Centres in Hampshire*, London: National Children's Bureau.

Pulkkinen, L. (1988) 'Delinquent development: theoretical and empirical considerations', in M. Rutter (ed.) *Studies of Psychological Risk*, Cambridge: Cambridge University Press.

Quinn, K., Epstein, M.H. (1998) 'Characteristics of children, youth and families served by local interagency systems of care', in M.H. Epstein, K. Kutash, A.J. Duchnowski (eds) *Outcomes for Children and Youth with Emotional and Behavioral Disorders and their Families*, Austin, TX; Pro-Ed.

Respect Task Force (2006) *Respect Action Plan*, London: Home Office.

Rickel, A.U., Becker-Larsen, E. (1995) 'Intergenerational influence on child outcomes: implications for prevention and intervention', in B.A. Ryan, G.R. Adams, T.P. Gullottu, R.P. Weissberg, R.L. Hampton (eds) *The Family–School Connection: Theory, Research and Practice*, Thousand Oaks, CA: Sage.

Riley, D., Shaw, M. (1985) *Parental Supervision and Juvenile Delinquency*, London: HMSO.

Robbins, D. (2000) *Tracking Progress in Children's Services: An Evaluation of Local Responses to the Quality Protect Programme*, London: Department of Health.

Rodgers, M.E., Sparrow, P. (1999) 'The Crime and Disorder Act 1998: issues for child care and sentencing', *Nottingham Law Journal*, 8(1): 23–33.

Rutherford, A. (1998) 'A bill to be tough on crime', *New Law Journal*, 9 June: 13.

Ruttenberg, H. (1994) 'The limited promise of public health: methodologies to prevent youth violence', *Yale Law Journal*, 103: 1885–1900.

Rutter, M. (ed.) (1990) *Straight and Devious Pathways from Childhood to Adulthood*, Cambridge: Cambridge University Press.

Rutter, M., Giller, H. (1983) *Juvenile Delinquency: Trends and Perspectives*, London: Penguin.

Rutter, M., Smith, D.J. (eds) (1995) *Psychosocial Disorders in Young People: Time, Trends and Their Causes*, London: Wiley.

Rutter, M., Giller, H., Hagell, A. (1998) *Antisocial Behavior by Young People*, New York: Cambridge University Press.

Ruxton, S. (1996) *Children in Europe*, London: NCH Action for Children.

Ryan, M. (1999) *The Children Act 1989: Putting It into Practice*, 2nd edn, Aldershot: Ashgate.

Sampson, R.B., Laub, J.J. (1993) *Crime in the Making: Pathways and Turning Points through life*, Cambridge, MA: Harvard University Press.

Sarnecki, J. (1991) 'Reaction to crimes committed by young people', in A. Snare (ed.) *Youth, Crime and Justice*, Scandinavian Studies in Criminology vol. 12, Oslo: Norwegian University Press.

Schweie, K. (1994) 'Labour market, welfare state and family institutions: the links to mothers' poverty risks', *Journal of European Social Policy*, 4(3): 201–224.

Schweinhart, L.J., Barnes, H.V., Weikart, D.P. (1993) *Significant Benefits: The High/Scope Perry Preschool Study through Age 27*, Ypsilanti, MI: High/Scope Press.

Scott, S., Spender, Q., Doolan, M., Aspland, H. (2001) 'Multi-centre controlled trial of parenting groups for childhood antisocial behaviour in clinical practice', *British Medical Journal*, 323: 194–196.

Scottish Office (1992) *Child Protection in Scotland: Management Information*, Edinburgh: Scottish Office.

—— (1993) *Scotland's Children: Proposals for Child Care Policy and Law*, Edinburgh: HMSO.

Segal, L., Pelo, J., Rampa, P. (1999) 'Asicamtheni magents – let's talk magents: youth attitudes towards crime', *Crime and Conflict*, 15: 23–27.

Seydlitx, R., Jenkins, P. (1998) 'The influence of families, friends, schools and community in delinquent development', in T.P. Gullotta, G.R. Adams, R. Montemayor (eds) *Delinquent Violent Youth Theory and Interventions*, Thousand Oaks, CA: Sage.

Sheridan, M.J. (1995) 'A proposed model of substance abuse, family functioning and abuse/neglect', *Child Abuse and Neglect*, 119: 519–530.

Sherman, L.W. (1997) 'Family-based crime prevention', in Sherman, L.W. *Preventing Crime: What Works, What Doesn't, What's Promising* Washington, DC: US Department of Justice.

Shiner, M., Young, T., Newburn, T., Groeben, S. (2004) *Mentoring Disaffected Young People: An Evaluation of Mentoring Plus*, York: Joseph Rowntree.

Shoemaker, D.J. (1995) *Theories of Delinquency: An Explanation of Delinquent Behavior*, 3rd edn, New York: Oxford University Press.

Simon, J. (1995) 'Power without parents: juvenile justice in a postmodern society', *Cardozo Law Review*, 16: 1363–1426.

Simons, R.L., Johnson, C., Conger, R.D., Elder, G. (1998) 'A test of latent trait versus life-course perspectives on the stability of adolescent anti-social behaviour', *Criminology*, 36: 217–244.

Simons, R.L., Wu, C., Lin, K., Gordon, L., Conger, R.D. (2000) 'A cross-cultural examination of the link between corporal punishment and adolescent antisocial behavior', *Criminology*, 38(1): 47–79.

Sinclair, R. (2001) 'The language of need: Social workers describing the needs of children', in Department of Health *Studies Informing the Framework for Assessment of Children in Need and Their Families*, London: HMSO.

Sinclair, R., Carr-Hill, R. (1995) *The Categorisation of Children in Need*, York: Centre for Health Economics, University of York.

Smith, C.A., Stern, S.B. (1997) 'Delinquency and antisocial behaviour: a review of family processes and intervention research', *Social Services Review*, September, 382–420.

Smith, C.A., Thornberry, T.P. (1995) 'The relationship between childhood maltreatment and adolescent involvement in delinquency', *Criminology*, 33(4): 451–481.

Smith, C.A., Lizotte, A.J., Thornberry, T.P., Krohn, M.D. (1995) 'Resilient youth: identifying factors that prevent high-risk youth from engaging in delinquency and drug-use', in J. Hagan (ed.) *Delinquency in the Life Course*, Greenwich, CT: JAI Press.

Smith, M., Bee, P., Heverin, A., Nobes, G. (1995) *Parental Control within the Family: The Nature and Extent of Parental Violence to Children*, London: Thomas Coram Research Unit.

Smith, V. (1991) 'Children Act 1989 care proceedings: a journey through the new procedures', *Family Law*, 21: 407–409.

Snyder, J., Patterson, G.R. (1987) 'Family interaction and delinquent behavior', in H.C. Quay (ed.) *Handbook of Juvenile Delinquency*, New York: Wiley.

Social Exclusion Unit (1999) *Teenage Pregnancy*, London: The Stationery Office.

Social Services Inspectorate (1991) *The Right to Complain: Practice Guidance on Complaints Procedure*, London: HMSO.

—— (1996) *Children in Need*, London: The Stationery Office.

—— (1997) *Responding to Families in Need: Inspection of Assessment, Planning and Decision-Making in Family Support Services*, London: The Stationery Office.

—— (1998) *Someone Else's Children: Inspections of Planning and Decision Making for Children Looked After and the Safety of Children Looked After*, London: The Stationery Office.

—— (1999a) *Getting Family Support Right: Inspection of the Delivery of Family Support Services*, London: The Stationery Office.

—— (1999b) *Planning to Deliver: Inspection of Children's Services Planning*, London: The Stationery Office.

—— (2002) *Safeguarding Children: A Joint Chief Inspectors' Report on Arrangements to Safeguard Children*, London: Department of Health.

—— (2005) *Safeguarding Children: The Second Joint Chief Inspectors' Report on Arrangements to Safeguard Children*, London: Department of Health.

Social Services Inspectorate, Office for Standards in Education (1995) *The Education of Children Who Are Looked After by Local Authorities*, London, HMSO.

Socialstyrelsen (2000) *Social Services in Sweden 1999: Needs–Interventions–Development*, Stockholm: National Board of Health and Welfare.

Sparks, C., Spencer, S. (2002) *Them and Us? The Public, Offenders and the Criminal Justice System*, London: Institute for Public Policy Research.

Stapleton, F. (1995) 'Duty of care: peripheral parties and alternative opportunities for deterrence', *Law Quarterly Review*, 11: 301–345.

Statham, J., Dillon, J., Moss, P. (2001) *Placed and Paid For: Supporting Families through Sponsored Day Care*, London: The Stationery Office.

Statistical Bulletin (2001) *Children Looked After in England 2000*, London: The Stationery Office.

Stattin, H., Klackenberg-Larsson, I. (1993) 'Early language and intelligence development and their relationship to future criminal behaviour', *Journal of Abnormal Psychology*, 162: 369–388.

Stattin, H., Magnusson, D. (1995) 'Onset of official delinquency: its co-occurrence in time with educational, behavioural and interpersonal problems', *British Journal of Criminology*, 35(3): 417.

—— (1996) 'Antisocial development: a holistic approach', *Development and Psychopathology*, 8: 617–645.

Stattin, H., Romelsjo, A., Stenbacka, M. (1997) 'Personal resources as modifiers of the risk for future criminality: an analysis of protective factors in relation to 18 year old boys', *British Journal of Criminology*, 37(2): 198–223.

Steele, L. (2000) 'A day fostering scheme for children in need and their parents', *Child and Family Social Work*, 5: 317–325.

Stein, J.A., Leslie, M.B., Nyamathi, A. (2002) 'Relative contributions of parent substance use and childhood maltreatment to chronic homelessness, depression and substance abuse problems among homeless women: mediating roles of self-esteem and abuse in adulthood', *Child Abuse and Neglect*, 26: 1011–1027.

Stein, M. (1990) *Living Out of Care*, Ilford: Barnardos.

Steinberg, L. (1990) 'Autonomy, conflict and harmony in the family relationship', in J. Feldman, G. Elliot (eds) *At the Threshold: The Developing Adolescent*, Cambridge, MA: Harvard University Press.

Stephenson, T. (1995) 'Child protection: the paediatrician's contribution', *Child and Family Law Quarterly*, 7(3): 95–103.

Straus, M.A. (1991) 'Discipline and deviance: physical punishment of children and violence and other crime in adulthood', *Social Problems*, 38: 133–154.

Straus, M.A., Donnelly, D.A. (1995) *Beating the Devil out of Them: Corporal Punishment in American Families*, New York: Lexington Books.

Straus, M.A., Sugarman, D.B., Giles-Sims, J. (1996) 'Spanking by Parents and Subsequent Antisocial Behavior of Children', *Archives of Pediatrics and Adolescent Medicine*, 151: 761–767.

Svensson, B. (1995) *Criminal Justice Systems in Sweden*, Stockholm: National Council for Crime Prevention.

Sylva, K. (1994) 'The impact of early learning on children's later development', in C. Ball (ed.) *Start Right: The Importance of Early Learning*, London: Regional Studies Association.

Tarling, R. (1993) *Analysing Offending Data, Models and Interpretations*, London: HMSO.

Thoburn, J., Wilding, J., Watson, J. (1997) 'Family support plans for neglected children referred to social service departments', *Family Support Network Newsletter*, 10: 3–5.

—— (2000) *Family Support in Cases of Emotional Maltreatment and Neglect*, London: The Stationery Office.

Thornberry, T.P. (1996) 'Empirical support for interactional theory: a review of the literature', in J.D. Hawkins (ed.) *Delinquency and Crime: Current Theories*, New York: Cambridge University Press.

Thornberry, T.P., Lizotte, A.J., Krohn, M.D., Farnworth, M., Joon Jang, S. (1991) 'Testing interactional theory: an examination of reciprocal causal relationships among family, school and delinquency: Rochester Youth Delinquent Study', *Journal of Criminal Law and Criminology*, 82(1): 3–35.

Tolstoy, L.N. (1899) *Resurrection*, authorised English translation by Louise Maude London: Brotherton Publishing.

Tracy, P.E., Wolfgang, M.E., Figlio, R.M. (1990) *Delinquency Careers in Two Birth Cohorts*, New York: Plenum Press.

Tremblay, R.E., Vitro, F., Bertrand, L., LeBlanc, M., Beauchesne, H., Boileau, H., David, L. (1992) 'Parent and child training to prevent early onset of delinquency: the Montreal longitudinal-experimental study', in J. McCord, R.E. Tremblay (eds) *Preventing Antisocial Behaviour: Interventions from Birth through Adolescence*, New York: Guilford.

Tremblay, R.E., McCord, J., Boileau, H., Charlebois, P., Gagnon, C., LeBlanc, M., Larivee, S. (1999) 'Can disruptive boys be helped to become competent?', *Psychiatry*, 54: 148–161.

Tunstill, J. (1997) 'Implementing the family support clauses of the 1989 Children Act: legislative, professional and organisational obstacles', in N. Parton (ed.) *Child Protection and Family Support: Tensions, Contradiction and Possibilities*, London: Routledge.

Tunstill, J., Aldgate, J. (2000) *Services for Children in Need: From Policy to Practice*, London: The Stationery Office.

Tunstill, J., Allnock, D., Meadows, P., McLeod, A. (2002) *Early Experiences of Implementing Sure Start*, Nottingham: Department for Education and Skills.

Turner, I., Finklehor, D. (1996) 'Corporal punishment as a stressor among youth', *Journal of Marriage and the Family*, 58: 155–166.

UNICEF (2000) *A League Table of Child Poverty in Rich Nations*, Florence: Innocenti Research Centre.

United Nations Committee on the Rights of the Child (2002) *Consideration of Reports Submitted by State Parties under Article 44 of the Convention. Concluding observations: United Kingdom of Great Britain and Northern Ireland* CRC/C/15/Add.188 Geneva: Committee on the Rights of the Child.

United States Government (1967) *President's Commission on Law Enforcement and Administration of Justice: Task Force Report*, Washington, DC: US Government Printing Office.

University of Leicester, Department of Health (1991) *Children in Need and Their Families, A New Approach: A Manual for Managers on Part III of the Children Act 1989*, London: Department of Health.

Utting, D. (1995) *Family and Parenthood: Supporting Family Preventing Breakdown*, York: Joseph Rowntree Foundation.

—— (1996) *Reducing Criminality Among Young People: A Sample of Relevant Programmes in the United Kingdom*, London: Home Office.

—— (1997) *People Like Us: The Report of the Review of the Safeguards for Children Living Away from Home*, London: Home Office.

Utting, D., Bright, J., Henricson, C. (1993) *Crime and the Family: Improving Child-Rearing and Preventing Delinquency*, London: Family Policy Studies Centre.

Van Beuren, G. (1992) 'Child oriented justice – an international challenge to Europe', *International Journal of Law and the Family*, 6(3): 381–399.

Vaughan, B. (2000) 'The government of youth: disorder and dependence', *Social and Legal Studies*, 9(3): 347.

Velerman, R. (1996) 'Alcohol and drug problems in parents: an overview of the impact on children and the implications for practice', in M. Gopfert, J. Webster,

M.V. Seeman (eds) *Parental Psychiatric Disorder: Distressed Parents and Their Families*, Cambridge: Cambridge University Press.

Vestergaard, J. (1991) 'Juvenile contracting in Denmark: paternalism revisited', in A. Snare (ed.) *Youth, Crime and Justice*, Scandinavian Studies in Criminology vol. 12, Oslo: Norwegian University Press.

Wadsworth, M.E.J. (1979) *Roots of Delinquency*, London: Martin Robertson.

Walsh, C. (2002) 'Curfews: no more hanging around', *Youth Justice*, 2(2): 70–81.

Walters, I. (2002) *Evaluation of the National Roll-Out of Curfew Orders*, London: Home Office.

Ward, J., Henderson, Z., Pearson, G. (2003) *One Problem among Many: Drug Use among Care Leavers In Transition to Independent Living*, London: Home Office.

Warner, N. (2002) 'Preventing youth crime now and in the future', *ACPO Youth Justice Conference*, Bristol: Thistle Bristol.

Waterhouse, L. (1997) 'Child abuse', in M. Davies (ed.) *The Blackwell Companion to Social Work*, London: Blackwell.

Watson, S. (1973) 'The children's department and the 1963 Act', in J. Stroud (ed.) *Services for Children and Their Families*, Oxford: Pergamon.

Webster-Stratton, C., Hollinsworth, T., Kolpacoff, M. (1989) 'The long-term effectiveness and clinical significance of three cost-effective training programs for families with conduct-problem children', *Journal of Consulting and Clinical Psychology*, 57(4): 550–553.

Wedge, P., Boswell, G., Dissel, A. (2000) 'Violent victims in South Africa: key factors in the backgrounds of young offenders', *Acta Criminologica*, 13(1): 16–38.

Weiss, B., Dodge, K.A., Bates, J.E., Pettit, G.S. (1992) 'Some consequences of early harsh discipline: child aggression and a maladaptive social information processing style', *Child Development*, 63: 1321–1335.

Wells, K., Whittington, D. (1993) 'Characteristics of youths referred to residential treatment: implications for program design', *Children and Youth Services Review*, 15(3): 195–271.

Welsh, B.C., Farrington, D.P., Sherman, L.W. (2001) *Costs and Benefits of Preventing Crime*, Boulder, CO: Westview Press.

Werner, E.E., Smith, R.S. (1992) *Overcoming the Odds: High Risk Children from Birth to Adulthood*, Ithaca, NY: Cornell University Press.

West, D.J. (1969) *Present Conduct and Future Delinquency: First Report of the Cambridge Study in Delinquent Development*, London: Heinemann.

—— (1973) *Who Becomes Delinquent? Second Report of the Cambridge Study in Delinquent Development*, London: Heinemann.

—— (1982) *Delinquency: Its Roots, Careers and Prospects*, London: Heinemann.

West, D.J., Farrington, D.P. (1977) *The Delinquent Way of Life: Third Report of the Cambridge Study in Delinquent Development*, London: Heinemann.

White, J.L. (1990) 'How early can we tell? Predictors of childhood conduct disorder and adolescent delinquency', *Criminology*, 28(4): 507–533.

White, R., Liell, P. (1992) 'Enforcement of duties under the Children Act 1989', *New Law Journal*, 142: 497.

Whyte, B. (2003) 'Young and persistent: recent developments in youth justice policy and practice in Scotland', *Youth Justice*, 3: 74–85.

Widom, C.S. (1989a) 'Child abuse, neglect and violent criminal behavior', *Criminology*, 27(2): 251.

—— (1989b) 'Does violence beget violence? A critical examination of the literature', *Psychological Bulletin*, 106: 3–28.

—— (1991) 'Childhood victimization: risk factor for delinquency', in M.C. Colton, S. Gore (eds) *Adolescent Stress: Causes and Consequences*, New York: Aldine de Gruyter.

Widom, C.S., Maxfield, M.G. (1996) 'The cycle of violence: revisited 6 years later', *Archives of Pediatrics and Adolescent Medicine*, 150: 390–395.

Wiebush, R.G., Baird, C., Krisberg, B., Onek, D. (1995) 'Risk assessment and classifications for serious violent and chronic juvenile offenders', in J.C. Howell, B. Krisberg, J.D. Hawkins, J. Wilson (eds) *A Sourcebook: Serious, Violent and Chronic Juvenile Offenders*, London: Sage.

Wiles, P., Holdaway, S., Marsh, R., Hammersley, R., Dignan, J., Davidson, N., Hine, J. (1999) *Interim Evaluation of Youth Offending Teams*, Sheffield and Hull: Sheffield University and Hull University.

Williamson, S., Griffiths, P., Noble, A., Bacchus, L., Strang, J., Gossop, M. (1996) *Patterns of Drug Use amongst a Sample of Young Offenders*, Report to Bexley and Greenwich Drug Action Team and Greenwich Safer Cities.

Wilson, H. (1980) 'Parental supervision: a neglected aspect of delinquency', *British Journal of Criminology*, 20: 203–235.

—— (1987) 'Parental supervision re-examined', *British Journal of Criminology*, 27(3): 275–301.

Wincup, E., Buckland, G., Bayliss, R. (2003) *Youth Homelessness and Substance Use: Report to the Drugs and Alcohol Research Unit*, London: Home Office Research, Development and Statistics Directorate.

Wright, J. (1998) 'Local authorities, the duty of care and the European Convention on Human Rights', *Oxford Journal of Legal Studies*, 18: 1–18.

Wright, K.N., Wright, K.E. (1994) *Family Life, Delinquency and Crime: A Policymaker's Guide*, Washington, DC: Office of Juvenile Justice and Delinquency Prevention.

Yokoyama, M. (1992) 'Guarantee of human rights in juvenile justice system in Japan', *Kokugakuin Journal of Law and Politics*, 30(2): 1–30.

—— (1996) 'The relationship between criminal and social welfare policies in Japan', in L. Sebba (ed.) *Social Control and Justice: Inside and Outside the Law?* Jerusalem: Magnes Press.

—— (1997) 'Juvenile justice: an overview of Japan', in J.A. Winterdyk (ed.) *Juvenile Justice Systems: International Perspectives*, Toronto: Canadian Scholars Press, Toronto.

Yoshikawa, H. (1994) 'Prevention as cumulative protection: effects of early family support and education on chronic delinquency and its risks', *Psychological Bulletin*, 115: 28–54.

Youth Justice Board (2001) *The Preliminary Report on the Operation of the New Youth Justice System*, London: Youth Justice Board.

—— (2002a) *Youth Justice Board Review 2001/02: Building on Success*, London: Youth Justice Board.

—— (2002b) *Corporate Plan 2002–03 to 2004–05 and Business Plan 2002–03*, London: Youth Justice Board.

—— (2005a) *Youth Justice: Annual Statistics 2003/04*, London: Youth Justice Board.

—— (2005b) *Corporate Plan 2005–06 to 2007–08*, London: Youth Justice Board.

Zahn-Waxler, C., Iannotti, R.J., Cummings, E.M., Denham, S. (1990) 'Antecedents of problem behaviors in children of depressed mothers', *Development and Psychopathology*, 2: 271–291.

Zhang, L., Messner, S.F. (1994) 'Family deviance and delinquency in China', *Criminology*, 33(3): 359–387.

Zingraff, M.T., Leiter, J., Myers, K.A., Johnson, M.C.M. (1993) 'Child maltreatment and youthful problem behavior', *Criminology*, 31(2): 173–202.

Zingraff, M.T., Leiter, J., Johnson, M.C.M., Myers, K.A. (1994) 'The mediating effect of good school performance on the maltreatment–delinquency relation

Index